INTERGOVERNMENTAL FISCAL RELATIONS

RECENT ECONOMIC THOUGHT SERIES

Editors:

Warren J. Samuels
Michigan State University
East Lansing, Michigan, USA

William Darity, Jr.
University of North Carolina
Chapel Hill, North Carolina, USA

Other books in the series:

INTERGOVERNMENTAL FISCAL RELATIONS

edited by

Ronald C. Fisher
Michigan State University

Kluwer Academic Publishers
Boston/Dordrecht/London

Distributors for North America:
Kluwer Academic Publishers
101 Philip Drive
Assinippi Park
Norwell, Massachusetts 02061 USA

Distributors for all other countries:
Kluwer Academic Publishers Group
Distribution Centre
Post Office Box 322
3300 AH Dordrecht, THE NETHERLANDS

Library of Congress Cataloging-in-Publication Data
Intergovernmental fiscal relations / edited by Ronald C. Fisher.
    p.   cm. -- (Recent economic thought series ; 56)
  Includes bibliographical references and index.
  ISBN 0-7923-9918-8 (alk. paper)
  1. Intergovernmental fiscal relations.   I. Fisher, Ronald C.
II. Series.
HJ197.I569   1997
336.1'85--dc21   97-9290
                                                                    CIP

To Cathy,
for her support and encouragement.

CONTENTS

LIST OF FIGURES

LIST OF TABLES

LIST OF CONTRIBUTORS

William N. Evans is associate professor of economics at the University of Maryland. A specialist in applied microeconomics, he works on topics concerning public finance, industrial organization, and health economics. His many publications in major professional journals include work on incorporating health status into utility functions, peer-group effects in education, and the US airline industry. His current research centers on the relative efficiency of private and public high school education and the impact of education finance reform.

Ronald C. Fisher is professor of economics and Director of the Honors College at Michigan State University. He is the author of *State and Local Public Finance* (Irwin, 1996 and Scott Foresman, 1989) in addition to numerous public finance articles and reports. He has served as Deputy Treasurer (Taxation and Economic Policy) for the State of Michigan, as a research economist with the US Advisory Commission on Intergovernmental Relations, and as Visiting Fellow at the Australian National University.

William F. Fox is professor of economics and Director of the Center for Business and Economic Research at the University of Tennessee. He is Vice-President of the National Tax Association and will serve as President for 1997-98. His particular research interests include taxation, especially sales taxation, and economic development. He is the editor of *Sales Taxation: Critical Issues in Policy and Administration* (Praeger, 1992) among many other books and articles.

Daphne Kenyon is associate professor of economics at Simmons College, Boston. She served previously as senior economist with the Urban Institute, on the staff of the Office of Tax Analysis at the US Department of the Treasury, and with the US Advisory Commission on Intergovernmental Relations. In addition to a number of articles, she has published two books: *Competition among States and Local Governments* (The Urban Institute, 1991, with J. Kincaid) and *Coping with Mandates* (The Urban Institute, 1990, with M. Fix).

David King is Senior Lecturer in economics at the University of Stirling, Scotland. Author of *Fiscal Tiers, The Economics of Multi-Level Government* (George Allen & Unwin, 1984) among other books and numerous articles, he has also worked on secondment for the government of the United Kingdom in various capacities, served extensively as a consultant for the OECD, most recently concerning fiscal reform in Eastern Europe, and held the post of Visiting Fellow at the Australian National University.

Therese J. McGuire is associate professor of economics and public affairs in the Institute of Government and Public Affairs and the College of Urban Planning and Public Affairs at the University of Illinois at Chicago. She also serves as Associate Director of the Institute. A specialist in state and local public finance and regional economic development, she has worked with several state governments on tax reform commissions and published a number of research articles in the leading public finance journals.

Matthew N. Murray is associate professor of economics and Associate Director of the Center for Business and Economic research at the University of Tennessee. A specialist on tax policy and state and local economic development, he is responsible for the Tennessee Econometric Model and prepares regular economic forecasts for the state and region. He also has worked internationally as a consultant on tax policy in such countries as Poland, Romania, and Egypt, among others.

Sheila E. Murray is assistant professor of economics in the Martin School of Public Policy and Administration and the Department of Economics at the University of Kentucky. A specialist on education finance reform, her Ph.D. dissertation completed at the University of Maryland won the 1996 dissertation awards from both the National Tax Association and the American Education Finance Association. In addition to her continuing work on court-ordered education reform, she also written on financing long-term health care for the elderly.

Dick Netzer is professor of economics and public administration in the Robert F. Wagner Graduate School of Public Service at New York University. Professor Netzer served as Dean of the Wagner School from 1969 to 1982. Perhaps best known for his work on the institutional structure and economic effects of property and land taxation, including his seminal book *Economics of the Property Tax* (Brookings, 1966), his broader research interests concern urban public finance, particularly in the US and Latin America.

Jeffrey Petchey is Senior Fellow in the School of Economics and Commerce at Murdoch University in Western Australia and Director of the Centre for Federal and Regional Studies. Since receiving his Ph.D. in 1993 from the Australian National University, he has written and published about the distribution of spending and taxation responsibilities and about tax competition and interstate transfers and is currently working on a book concerning international cooperation and federation (with Perry Shapiro).

Robert M. Schwab is professor of economics at the University of Maryland, where he also serves as Director of Graduate Studies for the Department of Economics. A former Gilbert White Fellow at Resources for the Future, he has published numerous articles in the leading economics journals on such topics as infrastructure and economic development, land taxation, life-cycle tax incidence, local public goods, and tax amnesties. His most recent research focuses on education finance reform and the distribution of education resources and the comparative effectiveness of public and private schools.

Perry Shapiro is professor of economics at the University of California, Santa Barbara, where he previously chaired the Department. Well known for his work on state taxation, public education, and issues of property rights, his current research (with Jeffrey Petchey) focuses on the political economy of federalism. A recent paper with Petchey concerning the Australian Constitutional prohibition of state excise taxes was selected for the best paper award of the *Economic Record* for 1995. Having substantial international experience, he has held appointments at The London School of Economics and as a Fulbright Scholar at the Australian National University.

Cliff Walsh is Executive Director of the Centre for South Australian Economic Studies, a joint venture of Adelaide and Flinders Universities in Adelaide, Australia. He served previously as Director of the Federalism Research Centre at the Australian National University and is the author of numerous books and articles concerning federalism in Australia.

ACKNOWLEDGMENTS

Production of this volume would not have been possible without the careful, consistent, and high quality work of Marneta Griffin, who prepared the manuscript for publication. I also very much appreciate the research assistance and organizational efforts of Jeffrey Guilfoyle.

1 INTERGOVERNMENTAL FISCAL RELATIONS: POLICY DEVELOPMENTS AND RESEARCH PROSPECTS

Ronald C. Fisher

Intergovernmental fiscal relations traditionally has occupied a respectable but small niche in the field of public finance. The major standards or traditional studies from an economic point of view include Maxwell (1965), Musgrave (1965), Break (1967), and Oates (1972). More recent general surveys include those by King (1984), Rubinfeld (1987), and Fisher (1988, 1996). But now a number of recent and very significant policy developments are refocusing attention on intergovernmental fiscal relations and will require, and no doubt induce, substantial new research about the topic. Suddenly, it seems, intergovernmental fiscal relations is at the forefront of public finance policy, both in the United States and other areas of the world.

These policy developments are in most cases now quite familiar. The creation of the new Russian Federation provides a laboratory both to test and to apply old theories and expectations. In a number of emerging and developing nations -- Poland, South Africa, and Korea are prominent examples -- the governmental and fiscal structure is being rethought. The gradual development of the European Union is creating new intergovernmental fiscal issues for the established nations of that region. And many of the older, existing federations also are undergoing substantial change. Canadians continue to wrestle with the appropriate relationship between the federal government and Quebec. In Australia, the states (and territories) continue to press for more fiscal and economic autonomy. And in the United States, state governments are being forced by the courts to take more responsibility for education and are requesting increased responsibility from the federal government for social welfare programs.

These policy developments make it an especially opportune time to restate the important theories and evidence resulting from economic analysis of intergovernmental fiscal issues, especially those recent developments or discoveries of the past 20 years. Thus one important objective of the papers in this volume is to present surveys (and bibliographies) of that literature, or as I put it to the authors: *"What do we know?"*

Even more importantly, these significant policy changes will require a new research effort, both to guide the creation of new fiscal institutions and to test their effectiveness. And even better, the variety of changes in different nations and states will provide the data to allow that research. Thus, the most crucial role for the papers in this book is to attempt to establish at least a preliminary agenda for that new research effort. The authors of these papers, as established scholars on the topic of intergovernmental fiscal relations, are in an excellent position to identify gaps in our knowledge, uncertainties in the empirical literature, or missing theoretical structures. My second charge to the authors, then, was to discuss information important to know for intergovernmental fiscal policy purposes that is currently not known, not addressed, or unresolved. That is, *"What should we know, and don't?"*

The organization of the book and papers naturally falls into two sections. In the first, the core body of intergovernmental fiscal relations and main general topics are covered. These include i) the organization of government, including the optimal sizes (and thus number) of jurisdictions and the appropriate assignment of public sector functions among those jurisdictions, ii) the formation and execution of tax policy in a multi-jurisdictional setting, and iii) the appropriate structure and use of intergovernmental transfers. In the second main section, this core knowledge is applied to major specific policy areas. The four policy areas covered here, and in my judgment the four most important policy areas based on current policy actions, are i) education, ii) welfare, iii) economic development, and iv) intergovernmental fiscal interaction in urban areas.

WHAT DO WE KNOW (OR THINK WE KNOW)?

Governmental Structure and Fiscal Assignment

David King provides in Chapter 2 a careful and comprehensive review of the now standard or conventional theory of optimal government size and its implications for intergovernmental fiscal relations. In its most basic form, the optimal size government for providing any given public service derives from a tradeoff of economies of scale and internalization of externalities on the one hand and the importance of differences in demand for government services on the other. Once these optimal governments are determined, various services may be grouped together to conserve on administration and compliance costs, creating several possible tiers of government. This is the familiar structure of most federations.

King argues that this conventional perspective understates the value of service provision by subcentral governments, as other advantages include greater opportunity for policy experimentation, managerial gains from specialization in providing only selected services, and a better opportunity for voters to convey their preferences to politicians through frequent elections concerned with a relatively narrow range of issues.

He also shows that one assumption commonly believed crucial to the case for decentralized provision of services may not be necessary. If there is a large variation in tastes for government services *and* individuals with similar tastes are located together, then the standard result favors decentralized provision, all else equal. But King argues that *even if the distribution of tastes for public services does not vary geographically,* there still may be substantial welfare gains from decentralized as opposed to centralized provision. Essentially, he argues that if the disagreement in preferences among individuals rises as jurisdiction size is increased, then there may be a net welfare loss. In such a case it would be better to maintain decentralized provision.

King also believes, consistent with the view of Rivlin (1992) and others, that it is essential in the application of this theory of optimal government structure that the primary responsibility for provision of each service lay clearly with one tier of government. Such a "sorting out" of functions does not deny the importance of vertical fiscal interactions, especially intergovernmental transfers, but in King's view is required if the possible advantages of decentralized (or centralized) provision are to be achieved.

But King also notes that the power of this conventional economic theory should not be oversold. Subnational governments have not always originated for reasons consistent with this conventional theory, and perhaps for no theoretical reason at all. Still, once a multi-tier governmental structure is in place, for whatever reason, the question of the appropriate role for those subcentral governments becomes crucial.

If the functional responsibilities of the various tiers of government are determined, the next logical issue is how those responsibilities can be met financially; that is, what revenues are available to finance services. In Chapter 3, Daphne Kenyon examines both vertical and horizontal tax policy issues, using the tax structures and policy issues in the federations of Australia, Canada, Germany and the United States to illustrate key trends and policy responses.

Concerning tax policy among the various tiers (vertical policy), she considers how tax authority should be balanced against the service responsibility discussed previously, what influences the appropriate mix of taxes available to each tier, and whether it is desirable to allow the various levels of government to utilize the same tax sources (or whether tax exclusivity for each level is appropriate and required). Kenyon is not persuaded by arguments that specific taxes should become the sole (or primary) domain of specific tiers of government, arguing instead that the equity and efficiency properties of each tax *given the circumstances of each jurisdiction* determine the appropriate tax structure for that jurisdiction. Restricting broad-based income taxes to the federal government, as is done in Australia for instance, prevents some states and localities from using that tax even if it would be the most economically efficient revenue source for that jurisdiction. For example, state or local income taxes might be sensible due to the distribution of benefits of the service provided by that jurisdiction (i.e., education) or because of a substantial flow of service benefits to nonresident workers in the jurisdiction.

It should be noted that the issue of tax exclusivity is separate from that of fiscal balance. Although some have argued that assigning specific taxes to specific levels would contribute to greater fiscal accountability, accountability seems more related to the *level* of taxation compared to expenditures, the balance issue, rather then the sources of tax revenue. Even if all jurisdictions at a given level, states for instance, were limited to a single tax, revenue still could be much less than spending, requiring intergovernmental transfers. Alternatively, if states were required to generate all of their revenue, even from a variety of taxes, then state officials would be accountable for funding all budget decisions (although this would create other problems).

If governments at each tier are to have access to a variety of taxes, then a number of issues related to the choice of revenue structure by those jurisdictions become important. Among these horizontal issues, Kenyon considers competition among governments on tax level and mix, the possibility of exporting tax burdens, and the question of variety in detail or administration of the selected taxes. It is in this arena where Kenyon argues that additional uniformity may be appropriate. Increased administration and compliance cost arises if jurisdictions in a given tier have very different structures within each tax that they select. For instance, in Kenyon's view, if half the states selected sales taxes and half income taxes, the administration and compliance cost problems need not be severe if all of the sales taxes were structurally similar to each other, with the income taxes structured similarly to each other as well. The important component of tax uniformity or diversity, then, is the structure within each tax rather than the mix of taxes selected.

It is partly for this reason that Kenyon argues against any substitution of consumption taxes for income taxes by the US federal government. From her perspective, there is little concern about the federal government "invading" a tax source ceded to the states. But if the federal government were to abandon the income tax, the concern is that states would find it more difficult to administer state income taxes, if the states desired to retain them, and a force for similarity or uniformity of state income taxes would be lost.

Given an assignment of service responsibility and tax options among the levels of government and the actual choice of tax structure by the various jurisdictions, there may be a need or opportunity for fiscal transfers among

6

those governments, either vertically or horizontally. In Chapter 4, Jeffrey Petchey, Perry Shapiro, and Cliff Walsh explore both the efficiency and equity roles for intergovernmental transfers in federal systems. In addition to providing a survey, explanation, and critique of the traditional arguments and rationale for transfers on both counts, they also present a different perspective that evaluates transfers in the context of the formation and operation of the federal system of government itself.

Petchey, Shapiro, and Walsh note that the traditional arguments for both matching and equalizing intergovernmental transfers rest on concerns about economic efficiency. First, if subnational governments make fiscal decisions in the presence of externalities, then those decisions may be inefficient from a social viewpoint. A federal government that is aware of those externalities and can measure their magnitudes may be able to use a set of specific matching grants to alter the prices faced by subnational government and thus move their fiscal decisions toward Pareto efficiency. In essence, the federal government assists subnational governments in achieving socially-efficient outcomes. One concern with this perspective is that the federal government may not be in the position to acquire the information necessary to set optimal transfers any more than the subnational governments were in a position to make efficient decisions. In addition, if externalities lead states to make inefficient fiscal decisions, then there is a possibility for states to cooperate for their mutual benefit to correct that inefficiency without federal government action, as suggested by Coase and others.

Petchey, Shapiro, and Walsh further argue that if a federal government does not have the information to implement optimal matching grants or if it does not desire to do so, it may still use that rationale for grants to justify a set of transfers intended to expand federal government influence beyond that justified by any externalities. Also, the externality justification for matching grants may be used to develop grants that in actuality are intended for equalization or other redistributive purposes.

Second, equalization grants may be used to correct for inefficiencies that result from excessive mobility due to an unequal distribution of resources or differences in costs of providing public services. Although such grants have an explicit equalization function, the objective is to prevent economic inefficiency.

In contrast to these traditional arguments, Petchey, Shapiro, and Walsh propose and concentrate on an entirely different rationale for equalization transfers. According to this view, there may be several potential gains from federation, including economies of scale, risk pooling, freer trade among the jurisdictions in the federation, and a stronger bargaining position with other nations or federations. Against these gains, there may be potential costs from federation, including loss of autonomy. Certain states or jurisdictions may have larger net gains from federation than others, but these gains can be attained only by cooperation of all the states. If those jurisdictions that gain most from federation are willing to compensate those that gain less (or even lose), then more of these possible welfare-enhancing unions might occur. Put another way, equalization transfers are a way of creating or maintaining federation stability.

Indeed, this possible role for transfers is related to one crucial issue about growth and stabilization policy, discussed in Chapter 8. A federal government may limit economic or fiscal competition for national reasons even though that action limits potential gains by poorer regions. Or a national government may impose restrictions that reduce economic development opportunities for certain jurisdictions (such as environmental preservation regulations or ownership of federal land). In these types of cases, equalization transfers may be called for to preserve the federation and the overall social benefits.

The review of the theoretical and empirical literature, at least as interpreted by this group of authors, in this first section of the book suggests a fiscal structure with the following characteristics: i) different levels or tiers of government would be assigned *primary* responsibility for the various service responsibilities; ii) jurisdictions at each level or tier might have access to all revenue sources, although within each revenue source there would be substantial structural, definitional, and administrative uniformity, and iii) national or federal equalization grants would be prominent to reduce disparities or compensate those jurisdictions that benefit least from the association. Of course, as the discussion in all three of these chapters makes clear, the degree to which actual fiscal arrangements approach this structure varies greatly among the major federal nations.

8

Specific Policy Areas

The theme in the first section of this book is the overall intergovernmental structure suggested by theoretical and empirical economic analysis. The theme in the second section, which includes papers examining specific policy areas, is that much of the conventional economic thinking about intergovernmental fiscal institutions and problems for these specific services is misplaced or based on faulty or incomplete evidence. Obvious research needs then follow from this perspective.

The primary issue examined in Chapter 5 by William Evans, Sheila Murray, and Robert Schwab is whether centralizing responsibility for providing public education is appropriate. Although there has been a 30-year trend of increasing state responsibility for financing primary and secondary education in the US, the actual effects of that centralization were uncertain. But these authors suggest that the theoretical concerns and evidence from California suggesting that centralization might reduce education spending may not be generally applicable. In contrast, there seems to be substantial evidence from other states that at least *court-ordered* school finance reform involving centralization in most cases *increases* the overall level of education spending and reduces spending inequality. In their view, such reforms have been driven by concerns about the intrastate distribution of school spending, and thus court action is targeted toward reducing those differences. Importantly, the reduction in disparities in these cases is accomplished by increasing spending among low-spending districts.

Evans, Murray, and Schwab also note research results suggesting that increased educational spending may increase education a attainment, contrary to the prevalent view in the literature that educational results have not improved with additional spending. The key issue, not surprisingly, is how one measures educational improvement. They argue that increased spending increases the percentage of students staying in school longer, which actually has the effect of reducing average test scores. If centralization does indeed raise spending and that increased educational spending leads to improved outcomes, these authors then question whether the concerns about differences in school spending within states should be expanded to include differences in education spending and services among states, which are substantial.

In contrast to the case of education, Therese McGuire notes in Chapter 6 that despite substantial remaining differences in the level of social welfare expenditures among states in the US with important federal government intervention, the policy focus has been on *decentralizing* responsibility for that service. And in contrast to other federal nations where there generally is more redistributive spending, US residents seem to have less of a taste for that type of service and think of income redistribution more as a local public good. The result is an interesting dichotomy: more centralization in response to less tolerance for educational service differences, but decentralization and apparently more tolerance for differences in social welfare services.

Focusing on intergovernmental issues in urban areas, Dick Netzer's analysis in Chapter 7 leads to a view that is strikingly similar to that of Petchey, Shapiro, and Walsh's about intergovernmental transfers: although traditional economic analysis has been concerned about inefficiency due to externalities and scale economies, he argues that such inefficiency in practice is minor and that the substantial urban policy issue concerns distributional differences and the need for equalization. And consistent with the national equalization perspective, Netzer argues that these urban economic and fiscal differences also require intervention by higher-level governments - whether states or a federal government.

Finally, in Chapter 8 William Fox and Matthew Murray challenge the conventional wisdom about subnational governments and macroeconomic policy in at least three ways. They report evidence that subnational government tax policy is destabilizing for national macroeconomic policy, they argue that there are a number of reasons why subnational government stabilization and growth policies are appropriate and even necessary, and they report evidence showing that such subnational growth policies are in many cases quite effective.

POLICY TRENDS

The discussion throughout the book, especially in the specific policy chapters, identifies two particularly apparent and important policy trends. One is the relative increase in fiscal importance of states (or the equivalent middle tier) in federations, which in some circumstances already has occurred and in others is the focus of policy proposals. The other striking trend is the relative importance of distributional issues, both in terms of what policy questions are receiving attention and in terms of the criteria for determining the desired policy structure. Both of these trends stand in contrast to the traditional main

10

or core focus of public finance research, which remains on efficiency issues and the behavior of national governments.

The increasing importance of states is clear, as noted in the introduction to this paper. In the US, over the past 20 years the courts have transferred, implicitly or explicitly, substantial responsibility for primary and secondary education from local government to the states. This certainly applies to financing responsibility, and as the states took on an added role in financing, many also insisted on additional responsibility for the provision of education as well. Also in the US, over the past decade states have been given increasing autonomy to develop and operate social welfare programs that differ from the standard federal form. Now the centerpiece of the sweeping reform to the federal structure adopted in 1996 essentially is devolution of the overall responsibility to the states, providing opportunity to experiment with new social welfare objectives and programs.

The circumstances in other nations are different, but the trend is similar. In Australia, the states have long been concerned about the so-called "imbalance" between their service responsibilities and tax authority. In addition, with the reduction in federal government control of the Australian economy, that is "microeconomic reforms" that allow a greater role for the private market in the overall economy, there is an additional force for an increased state role to both monitor and regulate these markets. In Canada, several forces have combined to raise the policy profile of states. The most obvious is the continuing issue of the relationship between Quebec and the other federation states, with its attendant instability. In addition, however, the continuing budget deficit of the federal government has limited its ability to maintain its influence and increased the attractiveness of a greater independent role for states.

It is somewhat ironic, however, that these federal systems have turned, consciously or by accident, toward state action to resolve long-standing policy problems even though individuals have been uncertain as to the effectiveness of states as a tier of government. A series of surveys by the US Advisory Commission on Intergovernmental Relations (1994) in which people have been asked from which level of government they get "the most for their money" showed for many years that individuals perceived states as the least cost effective government tier. That has changed. In the most recent survey, individuals reported that they got the least for their money from the federal government, with states and local government rated about equally at a higher level of satisfaction.

The central role currently being played by distributional issues arises in the context of each specific policy area. Evans, Murray, and Schwab state explicitly that the motivating factor behind reform of education finance in the US, especially through court action, has been concern about differences in the quality of educational service in different jurisdictions and the fact that the quality seems related to individuals' wealth or income. In contrast, economists concerns about the inefficiency that might result from the external social benefits associated with education seem to have been less important for policy.

With regard to social welfare policy in the US, the connection arises in two ways. First and most obviously, this whole policy matter concerns income distribution. Second, the motivation for changing the delivery system of social welfare programs seems to have been driven more by concern about the *level* of support that is to be provided rather than the efficiency of the delivery system. Admittedly, some who have been unhappy with federal provision of this service point to concerns about implementation: rules made in Washington do not take account of local circumstances, certain structural features create undesirable incentives, etc. But the bulk of the argument about reassigning primary responsibility for social welfare programs to the states has concerned the appropriate level of benefits: Should the benefits be an entitlement? Should there be a limited time period? Should service in exchange for benefits be required? Should benefits be extended to particular groups of citizens or individuals with particular circumstances? Is the level of benefit too high or growing too fast?

Similarly, one can argue that much of the current policy debate about subnational government attempts to stimulate economic growth and the problems of intergovernmental interaction in urban areas are largely distributive. As noted by Fox and Murray, a theme that runs throughout the empirical literature concerning economic development incentives is that a large part of their effect is simply moving economic activity from one location to another. Moreover, if the federal government restricts subnational government stabilization and growth policy on the grounds of some national objective, then specific regions or jurisdictions may have to forego potential welfare gains for the national welfare. By restricting subnational economic development policy the federal government engages in redistributive actions. In the urban context, Netzer argues that while inefficiencies in urban areas due to public sector externalities are small (with the exception of transportation), the equity problems are severe. In his view, the existence of many, small income-segregated jurisdictions that stand in contrast to the central city in most urban areas is a fundamental barrier to effective redistribution through the local public sector. Thus, distribution issues substantially influence the governmental structure in urban areas, which limits distribution in turn.

WHAT SHOULD WE KNOW, AND DON'T?
RESEARCH PROSPECTS

As one main objective for this book is to identify some fundamental questions for a new research agenda about intergovernmental fiscal relations, it seems appropriate at least to state the main ones here. Of course, appreciation of the depth and importance of these ideas may come only after reading the individual chapters, in which the knowledge gaps that create these needs are identified and elaborated upon. But it should not be surprising to learn that many of the research suggestions advanced by the authors of these papers overlap and intertwine; consequently, a unified research theme nearly emerges.

Several authors call for more current and authoritative estimates of fiscal incidence. Kenyon sees a need for new estimates of interstate tax exporting, while Netzer suggests providing estimates of tax exporting in urban areas based on the actual operation and administration of local tax systems. Such estimates would allow a re-examination of the efficiency and equity implications of tax choices by subcentral governments. Netzer also argues for measures of expenditure incidence, which, together with the tax exporting measures, would allow estimates of overall fiscal incidence or distribution. Although these are largely horizontal issues, such basic information about fiscal incidence seems crucial so that policy evaluation about governmental structure and the optimal size of jurisdictions within tiers can proceed.

Indeed, re-examination of the appropriate subcentral governmental structure is another common theme. Petchey and colleagues call for more fundamental research about the federation process - both the objectives and operational dynamics of federation. In short, what do jurisdictions (or groups of individuals) hope to gain by joining together and how might the barriers to formation of those federations be lowered? Toward application of these principles, Netzer suggests additional research about the fiscal effects of governmental consolidation in urban areas. If those fiscal effects can be estimated accurately and then well understood, policies may be devised or institutions created to allow the benefits of consolidation (junior federation, if you will) without creating major new redistributions and welfare losers.

In the area of education, at least, the state role already has increased in the US and already was substantial in some other federations. Thus, Evans, Murray, and Schwab suggest three potential consequences of increased state finance of education for additional research. First, in the US, the increased state responsibility for education has occurred simultaneously with increasing state responsibility for social welfare programs and increasing demand for state public safety actions, especially in corrections. This raises the issue of competition among programs within a jurisdiction's budget. Second, as states provide additional funds for education, it is also important to examine the resulting changes in how those funds are spent - that is, how the production of education changes as a result of centralization.[1] Third, if increased centralization is accompanied by equalization in public school spending, there are possible incentives for increased private school enrollment. That is, the private school alternative may be a mechanism for some to avoid the redistribution or equalization intended by the public sector.

Finally, there are a number of research suggestions concerning transfers, both among governments and among individuals. Petchey, Shapiro, and Walsh argue that the traditional efficiency arguments for intergovernmental grants should be re-examined in models that allow for imperfect information on the part of both recipient and granting governments and with constraints on the instruments to be used. They also suggest that the opportunity to use tax sharing arrangements or revenue sharing grants to improve the efficiency of revenue collection should be explored further by devising and estimating better measures of the relative tax efficiency by level of government.

Concerning individual transfers through government, McGuire notes the importance of two empirical issues: the mobility of high income people to avoid income redistributive taxation and individual attitudes about the local poor compared to low-income people on a national scale. She suggests that additional empirical evidence concerning these key questions is called for, perhaps based upon local experiments or new surveys. The question of whether income redistribution is perceived to be a national or local public good seems particularly interesting, given the major differences among the federal nations in their tolerance for geographic income differences. The absence of major equalization grants in the US seems consistent with the view of income redistribution as a local public good.

Perhaps partly because of wide regional economic differences and the absence of federal equalizing aid programs, fiscal competition for economic gains has been a prominent feature in the US. And such competition seems to have been increasing recently in Australia partly as a result of less federal government control of the private economy (Australian Industry Commission, 1996). Fox and Murray suggest, therefore, that new evidence about the long run, general equilibrium effects of interjurisdictional competition and fiscal incentives is called for. While there is substantial evidence, reviewed by Fox and Murray, about the partial equilibrium effects of incentives on specific outcomes - new investment or overall employment or new business start-ups - there is much less evidence and understanding of the effects of these incentives on economic welfare, more broadly defined. For instance, what are the long run effects of incentives on factor shares, who receives the jobs if employment rises, and how much time does it take before these effects of incentives are felt?

This is an ambitious research agenda, and achieving progress could occupy public finance scholars for a number of years. But I would make two additions, still. First, it seems clear that traditionally public finance research has focused more on tax and revenue policy than on either the choice or the effects of expenditure policy. Thus, we know much more about the effects of relatively obscure or minor capital tax treatments than we do about the incidence or effects on long-run economic growth of public investment (such as interstate highways) or education. And these types of expenditure programs are very intergovernmental in character.

Second, I would argue that there needs to be additional research about the establishment of fiscal institutions and *choice* of fiscal policies rather than the traditional focus on the *effects* of those institutions and policies. This has been done to some extent for tax structures, with analysis of how and why states select particular tax mixes or tax incentives. But it needs to be extended to examine why and how jurisdictions adopt certain intergovernmental arrangements, especially different state roles in funding education, different types of intergovernmental transfer programs, and different levels of social welfare support.

The contributors in this volume hope that you find their descriptions and explanations about intergovernmental fiscal relations informative, and even more we hope our suggestions for a research agenda stimulate your interest and action.

NOTES

1. For instance, one possibility is that in a centralized system there would be more focus on the breadth or distribution of outcomes rather than the average level. Thus, local schools might want to maximize average test scores for a smaller group of students while states might want to maximize the probability that students complete school.

REFERENCES

Advisory Commission on Intergovernmental Relations. "Public Attitudes on Governments and Taxes 1994." *Intergovernmental Perspective* 20 (Summer/Fall 1994): 29.

Australian Industry Commission. *State, Territory, and Local Government Assistance to Industry.* Melbourne: 1996.

Break, George F. *Intergovernmental Fiscal Relations in the United States.* Washington, DC: The Brookings Institution, 1967.

Evans, William N., Sheila E. Murray, and Robert M. Schwab. "Toward Increased Centralization In Public School Finance." In *Intergovernmental Fiscal Relations*, edited by Ronald C. Fisher. Boston: Kluwer Academic Publishers, 1997.

Fisher, Ronald C. *State and Local Public Finance.* Chicago: Richard D. Irwin, Inc., 1996. (First edition published by Scott Foresman and Co., 1988.)

Fox, William F. and Matthew H. Murray. "Intergovernmental Aspects of Growth and Stabilization Policy." In *Intergovernmental Fiscal Relations*, edited by Ronald C. Fisher. Boston: Kluwer Academic Publishers, 1997.

Kenyon, Daphne A. "Tax Policy In An Intergovernmental Setting: Is It Time for the U.S. to Change?" In *Intergovernmental Fiscal Relations*, edited by Ronald C. Fisher. Boston: Kluwer Academic Publishers, 1997.

King, David. "Intergovernmental Fiscal Relations: Concepts and Models." In *Intergovernmental Fiscal Relations*, edited by Ronald C. Fisher. Boston: Kluwer Academic Publishers, 1997.

King, David. *Fiscal Tiers.* London: George Allen & Unwin, 1984.

Maxwell, James A. *Financing State and Local Governments.* Washington, DC: The Brookings Institution, 1965.

McGuire, Therese J. "Intergovernmental Fiscal Relations and Social Welfare Policy." In *Intergovernmental Fiscal Relations*, edited by Ronald C. Fisher. Boston: Kluwer Academic Publishers, 1997.

Musgrave, Richard N., ed. *Essays in Fiscal Federalism.* Washington, DC: The Brookings Institution, 1965.

Netzer, Dick. "Metropolitan-Area Fiscal Issues." In *Intergovernmental Fiscal Relations*, edited by Ronald C. Fisher. Boston: Kluwer Academic Publishers, 1997.

Oates, Wallace. *Fiscal Federalism.* New York: Harcourt Brace Jovanovich, 1972.

Petchey, Jeffrey, Perry Shapiro, and Cliff Walsh. "Transfers In Federal Systems: A Critical Survey." In *Intergovernmental Fiscal Relations*, edited by Ronald C. Fisher. Boston: Kluwer Academic Publishers, 1997.

Rivlin, Alice. *Reviving the American Dream: the Economy, the States, and the Federal Government.* Washington, DC: The Brookings Institution, 1992.
Rubinfeld, Daniel L. "The Economics of the Local Public Sector." In *Handbook of Public Economics*, edited by A.J. Auerbach and M. Feldstein. New York: Elsevier Science Publishers B.V., 1987.

2 INTERGOVERNMENTAL FISCAL RELATIONS: CONCEPTS AND MODELS

David King

INTRODUCTION

This chapter sets the scene for the later chapters in this volume. It begins by considering the rationale for having more than one tier of government authorities to perform the various functions that are entrusted to the government sector. It then considers the issue of the optimum size of authority for each of these functions and the appropriate number of tiers of authorities to have. Finally, it examines the issues of vertical and horizontal fiscal relations, both of which arise in the context of multi-level government.

THE RATIONALE FOR MULTI-LEVEL GOVERNMENT

Perhaps the most fundamental question in fiscal federalism is why countries have more than tier of government. Why might a country choose to have a central government plus one or more lower tiers of decentralized government rather than entrusting all government functions to the central government? The following sections consider some of the advantages and also some of the problems that arise when countries opt for some decentralization by having systems of multi-level government.

Allowing for Varied Service Provision

Fiscal federalism has tended to focus on one particular, and certainly important, argument for decentralization. This is that decentralization can improve the efficiency of public service provision by allowing the provision of government services to vary from area to area in accordance with local wishes. Certainly this advantage can be expected to appeal to economists for, as Oates (1972, 11-12) stated, "if all the individuals who make up a society are compelled to consume the same level of output of a good when variations in consumption among different subsets of the population are possible, an inefficient allocation of resources is the likely result."

In fact, this advantage of multi-level government is even greater than it may at first appear. For not only does a system of multi-level government enable service provision to vary in accordance with local wishes, it also means that those citizens in any area who find they dislike the services provided in their area can, if they feel strongly enough, move to another area that would suit them better. As Tiebout (1956, 422) explained, "just as the consumer may be visualized as walking to a private market to buy his goods...spatial mobility provides the local public goods counterpart to the private market's shopping trip".^{1} It is true that most people have ties with their jobs and families that make it hard for them to move very far, but they may be willing to move from one subcentral authority to another one nearby.

Improved Signalling

Important as the first advantage of multi-level government is, it is important to stress that there are at least three other advantages.^{2} One is that having multi-level government rather than a wholly centralized system may result in improved *signalling*, that is an improvement in the extent to which voters are able to convey their preferences to politicians. A major reason for this is that when public services are provided by two or more tiers of government, rather than by the central government alone, there should be more frequent elections, and each election will be fought over a smaller number of issues. So it may be easier for politicians to discover what voters really want. It is fair to add, however, that governments might make more efforts to ascertain electors' preferences by having occasional referenda, as occur in the United States and Switzerland.

Facilitating Experiment and Innovation

A second additional argument for multi-level government, noted by Oates (1972, 12), is that entrusting some services to subcentral governments may encourage more experimentation and innovation with service provision. One reason for believing this is that each area will have a separate manager for each service, whereas there will be only one manager for each service when there is central provision; and, arguably, the more managers there are for any given service, the more likely it is that one of them will have a new idea for the service and the way in which it is delivered.

Another reason why lower tier authorities may be more likely to try out new ideas is that an individual lower tier authority can overcome a political problem that a central government might face if it tried out a new idea in selected areas on an experimental basis. Suppose, for instance, that a central government, which is responsible for a national health service, thinks of a way of cutting hospital costs, perhaps by sending patients home sooner after an operation. If it tries this idea out in one city, then the citizens of that city will complain that they are getting a poorer service than citizens elsewhere even though they are paying the same tax rates as people who live elsewhere. But if health provision was a subcentral responsibility, then the city council could more easily persuade its citizens to try out the experiment, because it could reduce city taxes while costs were cut.

Improved Control of Bureaucrats

A third additional argument for multi-level government is that if the central government handled all government functions, there might be poor control of bureaucrats by politicians because there would be too many issues on which each politician would have to be informed to exert effective control. In contrast, multi-level government means that the politicians in each tier need to be informed only about the functions handled by their tier.

This issue has two aspects. First there is the situation of ordinary politicians who seek to ensure that their tier of government runs its departments responsibly. These politicians cannot be very effective if they are ill-informed. Secondly, there is the situation of the ministers who actually run the government departments. They may find that in the course of their careers they move from job to job and department to department at frequent intervals. The wider is the range of government activity, the wider is the range of posts that a minister may have to accept. How can ministers hope to become experts so quickly in a wide range of jobs? With decentralization, the government activities in any tier become narrower, so ministers will typically have fewer different posts in their careers.

Intervention With Subcentral Authority Services

It was argued above that a major argument for multi-level government is to enable the public sector to cater for varying preferences. Although this argument appeals to economists, it does not always appeal to politicians. Thus states in the United States frequently regulate the activities of their subordinate local authorities. Likewise, European central governments frequently regulate their local authorities, and the European Union (EU) has joined in too. For example, the EU now decrees how pure all EU public water supplies must be and how clean all EU beaches must be; and recently it has decreed that all EU local authorities must clear away any chewing gum that is deposited on their streets.[3]

At first sight, such intervention may seem reasonable. For while having subcentral authorities permits some variety between different areas - and may also improve signalling, facilitate experiments and improve the control of bureaucrats - having intervention means that a higher level of government, including the EU, can prevent "too much" variety and can protect citizens from the risk of having their authority run by local politicians with strange ideas.

However, although controls are widespread, it is hard to find many wholly satisfactory reasons why higher levels of government should intervene with the services that are provided by lower tiers of government. And yet, if subcentral authorities are run by people who have been democratically elected, then it seems reasonable to argue that intervention with their decisions should never be lightly undertaken.

Perhaps the clearest case for some intervention arises with subcentral services that provide *external benefits* to non-residents. Major roads are a widely quoted example. When an authority provides a service that creates external benefits, then it is likely that local citizens will ignore those benefits when deciding how much service they want their authority to provide. Thus under-provision may result and some intervention may be justified. The most appropriate type of intervention may often be the use of matching specific grants which, by subsidizing the service and so reducing the effective cost of the service to residents, should stimulate greater provision. However, this intervention may not work very well as it is hard for the higher tier authority paying the grants to gauge the correct level of grant or subsidy to give to each individual authority (see, for instance, Oates 1972, 95-104).[4]

It should be noted that the extent to which the benefits from any particular service are internal or external may often depend on the size of the jurisdictions that provide them. Thus the benefits of a major road provided by a small area may be enjoyed chiefly by non-residents, while the benefits of a major road provided by a large area may be enjoyed chiefly by residents. So one way of reducing the problem of externalities is to entrust provision of services such as major roads to large areas. This issue is considered further below in the discussion of optimum authority size.

Minimum Standards and Their Effects

In practice, higher tier governments may intervene with lower tier authorities for reasons other than external benefits. A common type of intervention is the imposition of minimum standards. In the United Kingdom, for instance, there are many minimum standard requirements for local authorities. Thus there are minimum standards over the provision of fire trucks and over the curriculum that must be followed in schools, and recently there has been pressure for minimum standards over street-lighting levels.

If a higher tier introduces minimum standards for one lower tier service, and if the lower tier authorities provide the service at that minimum level, then it is arguable that the lower tier is really acting as an agent of the higher tier. In turn, it is arguable that the higher tier should pay a lump-sum specific grant to meet the cost of providing the service at that level. The lower tier will then be free to use its own tax revenue to finance any improvement to the service that its citizens may desire.

At first sight, paying such a grant to meet imposed minimum standards may seem to make the standards quite harmless. But this is not the case. One reason is that the higher tier authority that pays the grants will have to finance its grants with extra taxes, and these extra taxes will be paid by the citizens of the lower tier authorities that receive the grants. So it is clear that, in aggregate, the citizens of the subcentral authorities will be no better off as a result of the grants scheme. In fact, the citizens in the typical lower tier authority will find that their authority's grant receipts are *less* than their extra tax payments. This is because some of their extra tax payments will be used up in administering the grants and, perhaps, in meeting extra administration costs that result from the increased taxes. A further disadvantage of the grant scheme to these citizens is that they may find that the extra taxes impose additional compliance costs on them and create distortions in their economic behavior.

While the citizens of the typical authority will certainly have no extra income at their disposal, despite the grants, they will be subject to an extra constraint in how they may spend their income. In general - that is unless they are ignorant or irrational - constraining their spending patterns cannot increase their utility. In these circumstances, it is worth asking what arguments can be adduced for imposing minimum standards. Three arguments are commonly cited.

One argument is to protect people in areas with "substandard" services. In particular, governments may be concerned about poor people who cannot afford to move to areas with "reasonable" services. But it seems unfortunate that any efforts made to protect these poor people mean that all the other people in their areas must be forced to pay for more subcentral services than they want.

A second argument is that minimum standards are needed in a mobile society to protect people who have to move by ensuring that they will be able to enjoy "reasonable" subcentral services wherever they go. But this outcome is secured only by forcing the citizens of many authorities to pay for higher levels of subcentral services than they would most like to have. It may be added that, rather paradoxically, this protection for migrants is likely to be unnecessary irrespective of whether the subcentral authorities in the tier concerned are large or small. If the authorities are large, then the variety of service provision between areas is likely to be modest, while if they are small, then mobile citizens should have plenty of areas to choose from wherever their work takes them.

A third argument for minimum standards is that some subcentral authorities may simply under-provide certain services, such as libraries, which may benefit only a minority of citizens, for some subcentral authorities may ignore minorities. This sounds a fair argument, but is there really any reason to suppose that subcentral authorities will be less concerned about minorities than the central government?

Intervention: An Alternative Approach

While the arguments for minimum standards are often weak, there could well be a case for a related concept of guidelines. Consider services such as water supply and fire services, which are frequently provided by subcentral authorities. These authorities must decide how pure their water will be and how many fire trucks they will have. So they need to consider how pure their water must be not to constitute a significant health hazard, and how many fire trucks they must have to ensure that fires can be put out reasonably quickly.

These are technical issues, and many subcentral authorities may be too poor to employ the technical experts who could answer them. Higher tiers of government could employ such experts and get them to issue guidelines. Then the lower tiers could decide how far they wished to meet these guidelines. But the lower tiers would become answerable to their own electors - and not to the higher tier - for any failure to meet the guidelines.

Intervention for Macroeconomic Reasons

So far, this chapter has considered reasons why higher tiers might wish to control subcentral spending on individual services. Sometimes central governments seek a different sort of control, namely one over total subcentral spending. A common argument for this sort of control is that subcentral spending must be controlled for macroeconomic reasons. The main fear is that a concerted change in subcentral spending could result in a significant change in aggregate demand and hence in the macroeconomic equilibrium. This fear is, in practice, a major reason why many governments, especially in unitary countries, allow little or no discretion over subcentral tax rates, or why they allow few subcentral taxes. Even in some federal countries, notably Austria and Germany, there is negligible scope at the state (or Länder) level for setting independent tax rates. Other federal countries are typically obliged by their constitutions to allow considerable tax power to their states, but the fear of subcentral spending rising in an uncontrolled way has led Switzerland, at least, to introduce a good deal of cooperation between the federal and canton governments to watch the level of public spending and tax receipts.[5]

Three points must be made about the fear that a concerted change in subcentral spending could cause macroeconomic problems. First, in terms of macroeconomic theory, there is little justification in controlling increases in subcentral spending that are financed by increases in subcentral taxes (or charges) because the expansionary impact of any increased spending will be almost wholly offset by the contractionary effect of the increased taxes: it may not be wholly offset if subcentral taxpayers meet some of their extra subcentral tax bills by cutting saving rather than spending. For members of the OECD, for example, spending by subcentral authorities averages about 18 percent of GDP.[6] If subcentral authorities raised their spending by a tenth, the extra spending would raise aggregate demand by just 1.8 percent. Against this, private spending might fall by an amount equal to about 1.6 percent of total spending. So the net effect on demand of a substantial increase in subcentral taxes would be a rise of a mere 0.2 percent.[7]

Secondly, as a point of economic practice, there is no evidence that countries with substantial subcentral tax powers have a poor macroeconomic performance.[8] Column (1) of Table 2.1 shows subcentral taxes as a percentage of GDP in 1993 for all the countries that were then members of the OECD. These 24 countries are given in the rank order of their column (1) figures, as shown in column (2). Column (3) gives each country's GDP per head while column (4) ranks these figures. The fact is that countries with substantial decentralized taxes seem generally - for some reason - to have more successful economies, not less successful ones, at least in terms of GDP per head. For example, looking at the top half of the table, it can be seen that of the 12 countries with the highest degrees of subcentral taxation, no fewer than nine are also in the top 12 as far as GDP per head is concerned.[9]

Thirdly, it must be allowed that if subcentral authorities decided to finance an increase in their spending by using extra borrowing rather than extra taxes, then there might be no direct offsetting fall in private spending. So the effect on aggregate demand could be much greater. This possibility offers a reasonable justification for central controls over the level of subcentral authority borrowing.

Aside from the fear that subcentral governments might change their spending levels and thus disturb the macroeconomic equilibrium, there is a further cause for concern over the macroeconomic effects of subcentral government. This is the possibility that, in a recession, subcentral authorities'

Table 2.1: The yields of state and local taxes as percentages of GDP, and GDP per head as percentages of the OECD average, 1993, OECD countries.

Country	Subcentral taxes as a % of GDP (1)	Rank of column (1) figures (2)	GDP per head as a % of the OECD average[a] (3)	Rank of column (3) figures (4)
Sweden	17.4	1.0	94	17.0
Canada	15.7	2.0	108	6.5
Denmark	15.5	3.0	107	8.5
Switzerland	12.3	4.0	130	3.0
Germany	11.3	5.0	103	12.0
Finland	9.8	6.0	87	18.0
United States	9.7	7.0	136	2.0
Norway	9.6	8.0	119	4.0
Austria	9.3	9.0	107	8.5
Japan	7.1	10.0	113	5.0
Australia	6.9	11.0	97	15.0
Iceland	6.5	12.0	105	10.0
France	4.4	13.5	104	11.0
Spain	4.4	13.5	74	21.0
Luxembourg	2.6	15.0	157	1.0
Belgium	2.2	16.0	108	6.5
Turkey	2.0	17.0	31	24.0
New Zealand	1.9	18.0	85	19.0
Portugal	1.8	19.0	66	22.0
Italy	1.7	20.0	99	13.5
United Kingdom	1.4	21.0	95	16.0
Netherlands	1.2	22.0	99	13.5
Ireland	0.9	23.0	77	20.0
Greece	0.4	24.0	60	23.0

Sources: Column (1) figures derived from OECD (1995), 197 and 199. Column (3) figures from (OECD) 1996, 197.

Notes: a. These figures are derived from conversions of national currencies that are based on purchasing power parities, which are rates of currency conversion that eliminate differences in price levels in different countries.

tax revenues might fall less than their spending so that their budgets might move into surplus and thus act in a pro-cyclical way. This fiscal perversity has been specially feared in the United States because it was believed in the 1930s that subcentral tax revenues were income inelastic. However, it seems that this fear is now groundless there because, in recessions, subcentral spending is likely to fall even less than subcentral taxes. The resilience of spending arises partly because much spending is devoted to items such as education and safety where spending cuts are hard, and partly because much spending is devoted to welfare programs and unemployment compensation, which actually tend to rise during recessions.[10]

MULTI-LEVEL GOVERNMENT IN PRACTICE

It would be agreeable to report that many countries have established systems of multi-level government in accordance with the rationale given above. But, in practice, systems of multi-level government have usually evolved in a fairly *ad hoc* manner. To illustrate this point, this section looks very briefly at the establishment of some OECD federations and then at the evolution of local government in two OECD unitary countries.

As a preliminary point, it may be noted that, in economic terms, decentralized governments in the OECD are typically rather more important in federal countries than they are in unitary countries. To measure their significance, the most convenient OECD data to use as a starting point are those for subcentral government revenues - though it should be noted that the OECD omits loans from its revenue figures on the grounds that loans merely represent a source of temporary revenues. Some people might argue that the significance of decentralized government is best indicated by expressing subcentral revenues as a percentage of GDP while others might argue that it is best indicated by expressing subcentral revenues as a percentage of total government revenues. Table 2.2 allows for both viewpoints by showing the two sets of percentages respectively in columns *(1)* and *(2)*. This table relates to 1992 and covers all the 18 OECD countries for which data are available.

Whichever column is examined, it will be seen that there is more decentralization in federal countries, for in them total subcentral revenue was, on average, 22.1 percent of GDP and 53.7 percent of total government revenues, while in unitary countries it was, on average, 15.3 percent of GDP and 30.2 percent of total government revenues. However, it may be noted that

Table 2.2 Taxes, grants and other revenues[a] for state and local authorities as percentages of GDP and as percentages of total general government revenues, 1992, OECD countries.[b]

Country	Subcentral revenues as a % of GDP (1)	Subcentral revenues as a % of total revenues (2)
Federal countries		
Australia	19.0	52.5
Austria	19.1	37.5
Canada	28.7	65.7
Germany	22.7	49.2
Switzerland[c]	23.1	61.1
United States	21.0	57.9
Unweighted mean	22.1	53.7
Unitary countries		
Belgium	6.1	12.9
Denmark	32.6	55.1
Finland	21.3	40.9
France	9.3	19.1
Iceland	9.2	23.9
Ireland	13.1	31.6
Luxembourg	7.9	17.4
Netherlands	17.1	31.1
Norway	21.3	36.1
Spain	7.4	18.6
Sweden	25.2	41.6
United Kingdom	13.9	34.2
Unweighted mean	15.3	30.2

Sources: OECD (1995), 252-3.

Notes: a. The figures exclude revenues from loans, which are disregarded by the OECD as temporary sources.

b. Greece, Italy, Japan, New Zealand, Portugal and Turkey are omitted because comparable data are not available.

c. 1990 figures.

the two of the countries where subcentral revenues formed the highest percentage of GDP were actually unitary countries, namely Denmark and Sweden, although the three countries where it formed the highest percentage of total government revenues were federal countries, namely Canada, Switzerland and the United States.

Federal Countries

As, typically, the states in federal countries have the most economically significant tiers of decentralized government, it would be tempting to suppose that these tiers had been established with particular care to perform a selected range of government functions in accordance with local preferences. But in fact, of course, the situation with many federations is that they are a group of previously independent states that came together and established a central or federal government to perform those functions that the states felt could be handled better on a larger scale. These functions typically included defense, the signing of treaties, and the coining of money.

The federation of the United States, and the later federations of Switzerland, Canada and Australia, were certainly inaugurated in this sort of way.[11] But while the lower tier authorities in these federations pre-dated the upper tier, the idea of multi-level government must presumably have evolved from considerations of the sort discussed above. In particular, it can be argued that the functions that were not and have not subsequently been entrusted to the federal government may be presumed to be ones where opinions vary between states sufficiently for the federation's citizens not to seek uniform policies.

There is a rather different scenario in the federations of Austria and Germany. These federations did not come about through a voluntary amalgamation of the states (or Länder) in line with the wishes of their inhabitants. Rather, these federations were imposed after World War II on two existing nations. In these two federations there is today, and perhaps always has been, a fairly widespread feeling that government services should be uniform - or at least fairly uniform - in all areas. In Germany, for instance, Spahn (1994, 148) notes that "the Germans strive for uniformity of living conditions in the whole nation, notably for national average standards in the provision of public goods". He concedes that this approach was put to a severe test by the merger of the two Germanies in 1990, but he insists that the uniformity of living conditions will remain a "cornerstone of German intergovernmental relations, being a constitutional right that will have to survive". And in Austria, Thöni (1994, 178) notes that "the basic philosophy behind the...federal arrangements can be summarised as having...like Germany...uniformities of living conditions". In each case, this desire for uniformity finds expression in the financial arrangements for the Länder, for they rely chiefly on tax-sharing and equalization grants rather than on autonomous taxes.

Unitary Countries

Many unitary countries in the OECD have longer histories than any of the OECD federations. It might be thought that, in these long-established unitary countries, the creation of local government could be traced back to a genuine desire for decentralized-decision making in order to cater for varying preferences. But in practice local government has usually developed over the centuries in a way that perhaps owed more to the expediency of the time. Examples of this *ad hoc* development can be seen in both England and France. In each country there was by the ninth and tenth centuries a single king. These kings had no interest in the decentralization of power, but they did have to decentralize their administrations.

In England, administration was decentralized dividing the country into counties, each of which was under the control of a sheriff who was appointed by the king to carry out government functions, chiefly the administration of law and order. Thus the ancient English counties were not established as local authorities. English local government actually began in 1130 when Lincoln and London were allowed to opt out of the control of the central government's sheriffs. Many other towns followed suit in the following centuries. But it is doubtful if kings created these independent boroughs out of enthusiasm for local autonomy. Instead, it seems that the kings who created them were motivated chiefly by money, for the boroughs had to pay for their privileges. Thus Lincoln paid 200 silver marks and 4 gold marks while London apparently negotiated a better deal and paid just 100 silver marks. So it seems likely that the chief reason for creating many local authorities was to reduce the central government's deficit! The result was a rather patchy system of local government that was initially confined to the boroughs. Local government was not extended across the whole country until the 1890s.

In France, too, kings gradually allowed many areas to opt out of the control of central government officials. The system of opting-out was

32

considerably more complex than in England, and by the time of the 1789 revolution there was a complex pattern in which some areas had some genuine local autonomy, some areas had merely limited rights and privileges, and some areas were still under the control of the king's officials. In those areas where there was a degree of local autonomy, it was sometimes enjoyed by local townsfolk and sometimes by local ecclesiastical bodies. Reforms were made after the revolution, and Napoleon consolidated these in 1800. His structure had four tiers - *départements*, *arrondissements*, *cantons* and *communes* - but these were conceived by Napoleon as existing to implement policies decided in Paris. By the 1870s, some of these tiers were allowed to elect their councils, and by 1983 a new higher tier of regional authorities had been established. Today, there are only three tiers, the new 1983 regions, the *départements* and the tiny *communes*.

SUITABLE FUNCTIONS FOR SUBCENTRAL AUTHORITIES

This chapter has argued that there is, in principle, a good case for entrusting some functions to subcentral authorities. But, in practice, which functions can be most suitably given to subcentral authorities? In answering this question, the conventional wisdom is that substantial problems would arise if subcentral authorities were allowed much part in the stabilization or redistribution roles of government, so subcentral authorities cannot be expected to participate much in these roles. In contrast, there might seldom be problems if subcentral authorities were allowed to take part in the resource allocation role of government, so subcentral authorities can expect to participate extensively in this role. This section looks briefly at this conventional wisdom. There is a further discussion of stabilization in Chapter 8, which examines intergovernmental aspects of growth and stabilization policy, and there is a further discussion of redistribution in Chapter 6, which examines intergovernmental relations and social welfare policy.

Stabilization

There are two reasons why it is frequently argued that subcentral authorities cannot play much part in stabilization. The first reason is that any authority that took actions to affect matters in its own area would find that most of the effects of its actions would spillover into other areas. Consider, for instance, an authority that tried to reduce unemployment in its area by reducing taxes. Certainly its citizens would spend more money, but given the high propensity to import that exists in any subcentral authority, most of the employment generated by this extra spending would be created in other areas.

The second objection to subcentral stabilization policies is that it is hard to find suitable instruments for subcentral authorities to use. For instance, if subcentral authorities were allowed to use monetary policy, each authority would need its own subcentral bank that could create money and lend new money to the authority. The problem is that each authority would be tempted to rely greatly on new money to finance its spending as it could thereby impose lower taxes. Of course the result would be highly inflationary, but each authority could reasonably argue that any inflationary impact created by its own new money would be felt largely in other areas; for when its citizens enjoyed their tax cuts, most of their extra spending would be likely to go on imports. Since the inflationary impact would be largely exported, individual subcentral authorities would not regard it as a reason to use taxes rather than new money to finance their spending.

It is not only monetary policy that cannot really be decentralized. It is also difficult to see how subcentral authorities could operate exchange rate policies as they would then have to have their own currencies; it is doubtful if this has ever occurred. And it is difficult to imagine subcentral authorities being allowed to use tariffs or quotas; for if they were allowed to use them, then there would have to be customs controls round each authority, and the administration and compliance costs associated with these controls would be enormous.

In contrast, there perhaps seems more scope for subcentral fiscal policy. For it seems arguable that subcentral authorities could be allowed to run budget deficits or surpluses. However, there could be a problem with deficits. It is likely that most of the debt issued by any subcentral authority would be taken up by non-residents. Consequently, the debt would be a burden to future citizens living in the area who would have to pay taxes in order for the debt to be redeemed. There is likely to be a widespread demand for tight controls on the extent to which subcentral authorities could impose burdens on their future citizens. Such controls would greatly limit the scope for subcentral deficit financing. Many countries do indeed control subcentral borrowing, but not always for precisely this reason. In the United States, for example, most states have limitations on the amounts that can be borrowed by both the state and its subordinate local authorities. However, Maxwell and Aronson (1977, 207-8) argue that while the limits on state borrowing are

34

indeed designed to prevent misguided over-borrowing, the chief reason for preventing it is to protect the solvency of local governments and the interests of their bondholders rather than to protect (presumably future) taxpayers.

The above arguments suggest reasons why subcentral authorities are unlikely to play much part in managing aggregate demand. Even so, they might be allowed to play a part in managing - or rather influencing - aggregate supply. For instance, they could be allowed to encourage in their areas the development of new industry or the expansion of existing industry, perhaps by using measures such as infrastructure improvements and advertisements that outlined the attractions of their localities. The worry here is that authorities might at times spend considerable sums competing in a zero-sum game. And Fisher (1993, 139-40) has argued that, while states may have some part to play in regional development, the central government has the responsibility for coordinating and assisting their policies.

Redistribution

The problem with allowing subcentral authorities to redistribute income is that any authority that tried to be more redistributive than other authorities would be likely to drive rich people out and attract poor people in. Indeed, all subcentral authorities might find themselves having to adopt redistribution policies that were very similar to those adopted by the least redistributive area. Thus the more generous English parishes in the sixteenth century were plagued by the problem of the itinerant poor (Foster, Jackman and Perlman, 1980, 51). And, arguably, a more recent example of problems with subcentral redistribution policies occurred in Australia. There, Queensland's decision not to tax inheritances has forced other states to follow suit - for fear of driving their wealthy retired inhabitants to Queensland - even though a majority of citizens in the other states would probably prefer inheritances to be subject to tax.

It must be allowed, though, that small differences in redistribution policies between areas would probably not cause migration problems, so some marginal adjustments to national redistribution policies could be made at the subcentral level. And indeed, there is a redistributive element implicit in all tax financed services, so that even when subcentral authorities participate in resource allocation, they are typically creating some redistribution.

Resource Allocation

While there seem to be fundamental problems with decentralizing stabilization and redistribution, the situation is quite different when it comes to resource allocation. Much of the resource allocation role of the public sector is concerned with the provision of services, and many of these services can be effectively provided by subcentral authorities. There are, in fact, many reasons why the public sector provides services, and this variety of reasons is reflected in the services that subcentral authorities may be empowered to provide.

For instance, subcentral authorities may provide some items, such as police services and street-lighting, that are essentially public goods in that consumption is non-rival and non-excludable. They may provide some items, such as parks and museums, where consumption, though excludable, is still non-rival so that there is a case for using tax finance to secure a zero price that equals the zero marginal cost of admitting an extra person. They may provide some items, such as minor roads, where exclusion through charging, though feasible, would be very costly and so create higher costs than benefits. They may provide some items, such as garbage collection and disposal, where charging would be reasonably easy - for instance they might collect rubbish only if it was placed in distinctive bags that were available at a high price from selected outlets - in order to prevent the external costs of garbage being dumped in streets or fields by people wishing to avoid the cost of the bags. And they may provide some merit goods such as education and health services.

Although subcentral authorities are arguably the most suitable authorities to provide many government services, there are two main circumstances in which they may be unsuitable. One is when the services provided by one authority provide external benefits elsewhere, as with major roads, where there is a possibility of under-provision. As noted earlier, this problem could be addressed either through matching specific grants or by entrusting the provision of the service concerned to a tier of larger authorities, or perhaps even to the central government.

The other circumstance is when there are substantial economies of scale in the production of services. Note, however, that subcentral provision does not always have to mean subcentral production. Thus small authorities could commission large-scale private firms to produce services where there were substantial economies in production. This possibility is explored further below.

A final point to note is that when externalities or economies of scale point towards provision by the central government or large subcentral authorities, the efficiency arguments of varying provision to meet varying preferences might point towards provision by small subcentral authorities. So to decide on the correct level of provision for any particular government service, an analysis is needed to show how these factors affect that particular service. The following section explores this issue of optimum authority size. Surprisingly, perhaps, this closer look indicates that subcentral provision may sometimes be justified even if there is no tendency for the distribution of voter preferences to vary from area to area.

OPTIMUM SUBCENTRAL AUTHORITY SIZE

This section outlines some of the main factors that determine the optimum size of subcentral authority for any particular function. Before discussing these factors, however, three preliminary issues need to be mentioned.

Three Preliminary Issues

The first preliminary issue is the question of whether the optimum size of authority should determined in terms of its population or its area. This section refers to population because, for most government functions, consumers' welfare probably depends more on the populations of their subcentral authorities than on the areas of those authorities.

The second preliminary issue arises because much of the analysis of optimum size hinges on the possibility that large authorities may have cost advantages over small ones. This possibility makes it important to distinguish between subcentral authorities as *providers* of services and as *producers* of services. Traditionally it has generally been assumed that if an authority was responsible for seeing that a service such as garbage disposal was provided, then the authority would actually undertake the provision of the service by employing and supervising the necessary staff. In recent years, however, more emphasis has been placed on authorities contracting private suppliers to do the actual production of many services. Contracting-out has introduced a new dimension to the debate on optimum size. When authorities were expected to provide the service, it was easy to argue that large authorities might enjoy economies of scale in production that gave them cost advantages. In a world of contracting out, this cost advantage seems to disappear. It would seem that even the smallest authority could have low costs by hiring some giant private firm to deal with its garbage at the lowest possible cost.[12]

The final preliminary issue is the fact that the discussion seeks to show how the optimum size could be determined for the provision of a particular service, such as street-lighting. In practice, the factors that affect the optimum size of authority for providing a particular service could point to a different optimum size for each government service. This would then raise the question of whether there should be a large number of tiers with a different tier for each major service.

Large numbers of tiers of subcentral government are not unknown. For example, they were to be found in England until the 1890s, and they were to be found in New Zealand until the 1990s.[13] And they can still be found in one or two states in the United States. However, there are arguments for instead having only a few tiers. These arguments include the possibility that administration costs could be cut with just a few tiers, the possibility that many tiers could confuse voters, and the fact that some services interact - for example street-lighting and roads, or garbage collection and street-cleaning - and that when this happens provision by the same tier may make for more effective services.

Consequently, most countries choose to have just one level of subcentral authorities, or very few tiers. Where this choice is made, it is probably best to estimate the optimum size for the main functions, set up one or two or three tiers as needed to ensure that these services are supplied by authorities of roughly the optimum size, and then give all the other services to whichever of these tiers seems most appropriate.

The Basic Approach

The approach adopted in this discussion is to recognize that any particular service - such as street-lighting - could be provided by minuscule subcentral authorities each with, say, one household. In other words, there could effectively be private provision. To determine the optimum size of authority, the approach is to consider what would happen if the authority size was progressively increased. Citizens might hope to realize some gains from the increase in size, and they might also find some losses from increased size to offset against the hoped-for gains. The essence of the argument presented here is that the size should be increased so long as the extra hoped-for gains exceed the extra losses.

The Hoped-For Gains From Large Group Provision

There are two main reasons why citizens might hope for gains if private provision was replaced by subcentral authority provision, and why their hoped-for gains might be greater with larger subcentral authorities than with small ones. One reason is that large groups may be able to provide services at a lower unit cost. The other reason is that groups internalize the externalities between people within the groups. The potential for reducing costs and for internalizing externalities can be best explained by considering some typical government services. Consider, first, some public goods, such as defense and street-lighting.

Citizens may want to have a system of defense to deter potential invaders, and they may want their streets to be lit. In principle, individual households could hire one private firm to operate a defense system - perhaps by having it install a system of early warning radar combined with anti-missile missiles - and they could hire another firm to operate a system of lights in their street. But each individual household may reckon that the cost of engaging a defense contractor (even if this were legal) or of paying someone to install and operate lights in the street where they live, would exceed the benefits that they would privately gain. Of course, there would be external gains to other households who would receive some protection from the defence services and some illumination from the lights, and thus the total benefits could well exceed total costs. But if the private benefits to the individual household fell short of that household's costs, then provision would not occur. So there would be under-provision.

Against this background, it is easy to see that one advantage of group provision, undertaken via a government, is that all the benefits to the people within the group will be taken into account when people vote on provision levels. So provision may become closer to the Pareto-efficient level. This advantage of group provision may be enjoyed more by large government areas than small ones. For instance, with subcentral provision, there might be no radar-cum-anti-missile defense systems as the costs to any subcentral authority that considered installing them would probably exceed the benefits to that authority. But the total benefits to the nation from these systems might exceed their costs, so the systems might well be provided if provision was organized at the national level.

Next consider why the unit costs of services might fall with group provision. There are several possible reasons. One of these reasons is the possibility of economies of scale in production. These might well occur if production was in the hands of the providing authorities, and they could also be relevant even if provision was always contracted out to efficient large-scale private firms. For example, the supplier of a radar-cum-anti-missile defense system would be able to offer a lower cost per person to a big city than it would to a number of small suburbs if the city area was split up - unless *all* the small areas agreed to participate - as the total cost might be the same in each case. And the supplier of street-lighting might charge a lower unit cost for providing lighting to a whole city than it would charge to each suburb if they had separate authorities; one reason for this is that the firm would expect to be asked to supply a uniform service to any one authority, but might have to provide rather different services to each of several smaller authorities.

Another reason why unit costs might fall with group provision, and especially with provision by large groups, concerns managerial economies. If all citizens effectively live in single household authorities, and if all these authorities provide street lighting, then every citizen must think about street lights and arrange for one or more lights to be installed and serviced. With group provision, lights still need to be installed and serviced, but there could be enormous economies of scale in management as a single person could act for a large number of citizens. Moreover, groups of citizens could appoint as managers for each service people who were highly skilled at managing that particular service.

Internalizing externalities and reducing costs can arise with government services other than public goods. Consider a merit good such as education. An individual household that was concerned that some of its neighbors did not educate their children might consider setting up and financing a school for those children. But it might well decide not to go ahead with the project on the grounds that the costs to the household would probably exceed the benefits it received from its altruism. But there would be additional benefits to other people who would be pleased if the children concerned were given schooling, and the total benefits of the school might well exceed its cost. These external benefits could be internalized with group provision and so lead to schools being provided. Moreover, there could be cost savings if large groups were better able to cater for the differing educational needs of different children.

Internalizing externalities would also come into play with services such as (uncrowded) museums and parks. Individuals or small areas might be aware of the inefficiencies of such services being provided privately and charged for given that the marginal cost of admitting an extra person is zero. But individuals or small areas might also feel that the costs to them of supplying the services at a zero-price outweighed the benefits to them. However, outsiders might also enjoy these services, so the total benefits might exceed the total cost. These external benefits would be internalized by large groups. Large groups might also enjoy lower costs, even if the services were contracted out to private suppliers. For a supplier of museums might find it much cheaper to build and maintain one large museum in a city center than to build and operate a host of smaller suburban museums, each of these smaller ones needing its own buying policy, its own security, its own publicity and so on.

Internalizing externalities would be even more important with services such as garbage collection and disposal which, as noted earlier, are chiefly provided by governments at a zero price in order to deter people from disposing of their rubbish in streets or fields. In this case, however, the externality benefits might not be much higher with large authorities than with small ones. However, there could be higher unit costs for small authorities, even if they could contract the service out to as large a private supplier as big authorities would use. A garbage disposal firm might offer a lower price per person for removing garbage in a subcentral authority with a population of 10,000 than it would offer to two authorities each with a population of 5,000, for it would provide the same type of service throughout the large area whereas it might be required to empty small bags twice weekly in one small area and to empty large bins once weekly in the other. Also, of course, there would be scope for managerial economies as large authorities could appoint the most highly skilled managers and might need proportionately fewer of them.

Losses From Large Group Provision

The main problem with moving from individual provision to group provision is that individuals would then lose control over the quantity and type of service that they consume. They would have to accept the defense and street-lighting policies, the museum and park policies, and the education and garbage service policies that are determined by the group. It will be assumed here that these policies are determined by the median voter in each group.

Relating the Hoped-For Gains to Group Size

In essence, the hoped-for gains from group provision may increase with every increase in group size. This is partly because larger and larger groups may result in ever lower unit costs, and it is partly because larger and larger groups should result in more and more internalization of external benefits. Admittedly the evidence for economies of scale is modest, but even if economies of scale cease at a certain point, increasing size should still secure greater hoped for-gains through the increased internalization of externalities. The most likely reason why increased size might eventually cease to lead to extra hoped-for gains is that, at some point, administrative diseconomies of scale might set in that more than offset any other advantages of larger size.

All citizens will hope for some gains as a result of falls in unit costs. The gains they will hope for are measured by the extra consumer surplus they will enjoy if consumption rises from the level they enjoyed with individual provision to the higher level they would desire with the lower unit cost made possible with group provision. But the reason that most citizens will not secure all these hoped-for gains is that few citizens will end up consuming the precise quantity that they would choose at the new lower unit cost. This is because, with group provision, the level of consumption is determined by the median voter. So all voters whose preferences diverge from those of the median voter will have different quantities from the ones they want. If the median voter wants less then they do, they will consume less than they wish and so secure less extra consumer surplus than they hoped for. If the median voter wants more than they do, they will consume more than they wish; they will gain all their hoped-for consumer surplus as consumption rises to their desired level, and then experience an offsetting loss as they are forced to pay in taxes for even more consumption than they want at the new unit cost.

Relating the Losses and the Net Gains to Group Size

There are actually three different scenarios that must be considered. One possibility is the remote one that everyone has identical preferences. In this case, everyone would agree with the median voter. So there would be no losses or shortfalls. In this case, the optimum size may well be central - or even international provision - unless the gains from increased size level out at some smaller size.

The second scenario is that, while preferences vary between individuals, the distribution of preferences in different areas is always the same. So every street, for instance, can be assumed to have the same proportion of people wanting high service levels, the same proportion of people wanting medium level services, and the same proportion of people wanting low level services. It is helpful to focus on this restrictive scenario before considering the implications of a scenario where this restriction is relaxed, so that, for example, some areas of the country are allowed to be dominated by seekers of high service levels while other areas are allowed to be dominated by seekers of low service levels.

In this second scenario, while the hoped-for gains may well rise continuously as group size rises, it is not obvious that the shortfalls will also do so. A single example will show why. Suppose that with individual provision, when the unit costs of street-lighting are high, there is some measure of disagreement about how much street-lighting to have. As group size increases, and unit costs fall, everyone hopes to gain through the lower unit costs. If the amount of disagreement increases as unit costs drop, then larger group sizes will bring about both higher hoped-for gains and higher shortfalls. In contrast, if the amount of disagreement falls as unit costs drop, then larger group sizes will bring about higher hoped-for gains and smaller shortfalls. Yet another possibility is that the amount of disagreement might initially fall as unit costs drop, and then rise.

If the amount of disagreement continuously fell, so that increasing size brought ever increasing hoped-for gains and ever smaller shortfalls, then central provision, or even international provision, would seem appropriate. But if the amount of disagreement increased, then increasing size might, at some point, lead to modest extra hoped-for gains combined with large extra shortfalls. In these circumstances, size should be increased only for as long as the extra hoped-for gains exceeded the extra losses. As a result, various optimum outcomes would be possible. For example, there could be a case for individual provision if replacing individual provision with even small groups led to hoped-for gains that were below the shortfalls. Such a situation might arise with, say, food; for here, if individual provision was replaced by group provision of standard food parcels, people would probably suffer greater losses through lack of choice than they would hope to gain through possibly lower food costs. Alternatively, there could still be a case for central or international provision if the shortfalls increased more slowly than the hoped-for gains. But equally, there could be an optimum size somewhere between individual provision and central provision, which would point towards subcentral provision.

The third scenario is one where the distribution of preferences varies in different localities. The same possible outcomes arise here as arise in the second scenario, but the extra losses from larger groups are likely to be higher, so the optimum size is more likely to be subcentral rather than central or international provision.

Implications

Four conclusions can be drawn from this analysis:

1. It is not possible to determine the optimum size of area for any service without knowing how much preferences vary, how much unit costs depend on group size, and how far increasing group size leads to externalities becoming internalized.

2. Even though cost savings may continue for all increases in group size, the optimum level of provision is not necessarily central provision. The hoped-for gains from increased size and reduced costs may sooner or later be more than offset by losses that arise from people's inability to control their own service levels.

3. If preferences vary between citizens, there could be a case for subcentral provision even if there is no variation in the distribution of preferences between areas. Clearly the case for subcentral provision is strengthened if there are variations in the distribution of preferences between areas.

4. The analysis implicitly assumed that people do not move between localities. In practice people can vote-with-their-feet. Those people who dislike the choices made by their subcentral authority's median voter can migrate to other areas. This, in turn, could increase the differences in the preference distributions between areas and so lead to a diminution in the optimum subcentral authority size.

VERTICAL BALANCES: THE LEVEL OF SUBCENTRAL TAXATION

This chapter ends by looking at two issues that concern the financial arrangements for subcentral authorities. The first of these issues is the question of vertical balances. This section looks at this issue; there is a further discussion in Chapter 3, which examines tax policy in an intergovernmental setting. The second issue is the question of horizontal balances, and this is considered in the following section.

Suppose a country's government functions have been allocated between two or more tiers of authorities. Then each tier will have certain spending needs. In principle, each tier could be given wide taxation powers that enabled it to finance its spending requirements wholly from its own tax revenues without it having to set tax rates for any of its taxes at levels that were deemed excessive. Such a situation might be termed one of vertical balance as there would be no need for any flows of money between tiers.

However, no OECD country enjoys a situation of vertical balance in this sense. Table 2.3 gives 1992 figures for the states and local authorities in the 18 OECD countries for which data are available; in each country, all the tiers of local authorities are aggregated together. In every country covered by the table, the lower tiers rely to some extent, often a considerable extent, on grants from higher tiers. There is, though, a significant difference between the situation of states and local authorities. On average, states receive 52.0 percent of their income from taxes, well over the 29.5 percent they receive from grants.[14] In contrast, local authorities receive only 40.8 percent of their income from taxes, a shade over the 38.2 percent they receive from grants. Despite this difference between states and local authorities, there is a substantial degree of vertical imbalance in each case. So it seems worth considering the arguments concerning financial autonomy for subcentral governments.

A Basic Choice - The "Localist" or "Centralist" Approach

Arguably, the key to deciding on the appropriate level of financial autonomy for lower tier authorities lies in deciding on the purpose of those lower tier authorities. This issue was highlighted in the United Kingdom in 1976 by the Layfield committee of inquiry into local government finance that was established to review the whole system of local government finance. Its chief recommendation (HMSO, 1976, 298-301) was that the government

Table 2.3 Taxes, grants and other revenues[a] for state and local authorities as percentages of total income, 1992, OECD countries.[b]

Country	Taxes	Grants	Other
States			
Australia	33.9	43.4	22.7
Austria	47.5	38.4	14.1
Canada	62.9	20.2	16.8
Germany	62.9	25.4	11.7
Switzerland[c]	54.8	27.1	18.1
United States	49.7	22.5	27.8
	52.0	29.5	18.5
Local authorities			
Australia	44.3	18.1	37.5
Austria	50.8	18.0	31.2
Belgium	37.3	54.5	8.2
Canada	39.2	44.9	15.9
Denmark	47.1	43.1	9.8
Finland	46.5	35.1	18.5
France	44.2	36.4	19.4
Germany	30.8	33.2	36.0
Iceland	71.4	9.8	18.8
Ireland	6.8	72.6	20.5
Luxembourg	32.1	36.2	31.7
Netherlands	6.4	72.8	20.8
Norway	44.9	41.1	14.0
Spain	59.3	27.8	12.9
Sweden	67.8	17.1	15.1
Switzerland[c]	52.9	15.6	31.6
United Kingdom	10.7	73.8	15.5
United States	41.0	37.8	21.2
Unweighted mean	40.8	38.2	21.0

Source: OECD (1995), 253.

Notes: a. The figures exclude revenues from loans, which are disregarded by the OECD as temporary sources.

b. Greece, Italy, Japan, New Zealand, Portugal and Turkey are omitted because comparable data are not available.

c. 1990 figures.

should make a choice between giving local authorities the main responsibility for raising the money they spend and deciding how that money is spent, or giving the central government the main responsibility for raising the money spent by local authorities and for deciding how that money is spent. The committee termed these two options the localist approach and the centralist approach.

It is important to stress that the issue hinges on which tier has the *main* rather than the *sole* responsibility for subcentral services. If the main responsibility lies with subcentral authorities, then the central government might intervene occasionally, especially perhaps when actions by one authority affect people elsewhere. Equally, if the main responsibility lies with the central government, then the central government might allow subcentral authorities a little discretion at the margin.

The committee went on to assert that the two approaches have very different financial implications. It justified this view by saying that "whoever is responsible for spending money should also be responsible for raising it so that the amount of expenditure is subject to democratic control". So the committee suggested that if the government opted for the localist approach, then it should ensure that the proportion of local spending financed by local taxes was well over half. In contrast, if the government adopted the centralist approach, then it should ensure that the proportion of local spending financed by grants was well over half. It is worth looking into the financial implications of these two options rather more fully than the Layfield committee did. For the committee gave little justification for its conclusions, even though they are certainly defensible.

Financial Implications of the Different Approaches

On the centralist approach, there are two main reasons for arguing that most subcentral government revenue should come from grants. First, the central government is likely to take a more responsible view about how much subcentral expenditure to require if it has to raise the money itself. Secondly, subcentral voters will be confused if they have to pay subcentral taxes to subcentral politicians who actually have negligible discretion over how that money may be spent. Nevertheless, even on the centralist approach there is a case for giving subcentral authorities a little tax power to enable them to finance any permitted marginal changes in spending levels.

On the localist approach, there are four main reasons for thinking that most subcentral authority revenue should come from subcentral taxes. First, subcentral taxes are necessary to enable subcentral authorities to vary the quantities and qualities of their services in accordance with local wishes. Secondly, when subcentral authorities rely on grants, subcentral politicians can spend the money inefficiently and blame the resulting poor services on under-funding. Thirdly, subcentral politicians, bureaucrats and voters may take more care with money that is raised locally than with money that has been given to them. Fourthly, when a government pays grants, it is likely to want to control how subcentral authorities spend them; indeed, arguably it *should* control how grant receipts are spent as it is accountable to its national taxpayers for this money.

It should be stressed that these four reasons for subcentral taxation really require that the subcentral taxes should be ones where subcentral authorities can set their own tax rates, at least within limits. This is clearly essential for the first reason, and it is virtually necessary for the others. If, for instance, subcentral authorities raise a large tax at a centrally decreed rate, they can still spend the money inefficiently and blame their poor services on their inability to raise enough money. Also, they may feel that their tax revenue is effectively given to them by the central government, so they may be less careful over how it is spent. Furthermore, the central government, by decreeing the tax rate, may feel it is effectively responsible for raising the money and so may feel it is giving its own money away; in turn it may feel entitled to control the way in which the money is spent.

Regarding the first of these four reasons, the central government might argue that subcentral authorities can alter their service provision even if they have only a small tax. Thus there is local discretion over local authority spending levels in both the Netherlands and the United Kingdom even though, as shown on Table 2.3, locally set taxes account for respectively for only 6.4 percent and 10.7 percent of local tax plus income. Writing about the Netherlands, Uhl (1994, 169) noted that not only do low local taxes permit variations in spending, they are also consistent with "efficient" spending levels because, to ensure such efficiency, people "need take account only of marginal tax burdens, weighing the cost of additional services against the additional tax burden they will entail".

However, relying for local discretion on taxes that raise only a small fraction of income seems unsatisfactory. Suppose that a typical authority in

48

the Netherlands wishes to raise its income by, say, 6.4 percent, a seemingly small amount. Then it must double the revenues from its taxes, which are a motor vehicle duty and a property tax. Such a rise could easily give misleading signals to local voters, for there is nothing else they consume where they would have to spend twice as much to get so little more. Moreover, it is possible that the tax increases needed would be opposed on the grounds that they would take the rates for the taxes concerned far above "reasonable" levels.

A Middle Approach

Ironically, the response to the Layfield committee of the United Kingdom government of the day was to reject both approaches! Instead, it advocated a "middle" approach with shared central and local responsibility for services (HMSO, 1977, 4-5). A middle approach may seem appealing because it suggests a compromise that will result in a partnership between central and local government. But the Layfield committee rejected this approach, and experience suggests that such an approach may be more likely to cause conflict and confusion than partnership and harmony.

With a middle approach, conflict and confusion can arise because subcentral voters may give their authority a mandate for one policy while the central government may have a mandate for the opposite policy. One example of such a conflict arose in the United Kingdom with the two Labour administrations of 1964-70 and 1974-79. In those years, some local authorities told the central government that their voters had given them a mandate to retain selective schools, but the central government over-ruled them saying that their voters had given it a mandate to force local authorities to have non-selective schools. Another example of conflict has arisen under the post-1979 Conservative administrations when some local authorities have told the central government that their voters have given them a mandate not to sell local authority homes to their occupants, but the central government has over-ruled them saying that its voters have given it a mandate to force local authorities to sell local authority homes to their occupants.

Democracy in subcentral authorities cannot easily flourish if a majority of the voters in an authority can express their preferences on important issues that concern their local authorities' services and then have their preferences over-ruled. To avoid conflict and confusion, it would be better to have clear demarcation lines for subcentral authorities' discretion, let the authorities' voters vote only on those issues where subcentral discretion was allowed, and then encourage the authorities to respect their voters' wishes.

So long as there are subcentral elections, subcentral voters and subcentral politicians need to know what discretion subcentral authorities have. This is possible on the localist approach: they have discretion except where stated otherwise. It is also possible on the centralist approach: they have no discretion except where stated otherwise. But it seems impossible on a middle approach. To operate a middle approach properly, it would be necessary to list every subcentral activity and say just how much, if any, subcentral discretion was permitted on each. But doing this would be very difficult, and it would almost certainly leave voters bewildered and confused.

This conclusion may seem unappealing to moderate people who instinctively favor partnership and co-operation between tiers of government. So it is worth re-iterating that the conclusion does not mean that one level must have complete responsibility for any broad area of government activity such as education. What it does mean is that it should be clear where the *main* responsibility for each aspect of an activity such as education lies. Thus the central government might have the main responsibility for the curriculum and the school-leaving age while lower tiers might have the main responsibility for providing schools and teachers.

The financial implications of the middle approach seem unclear. The United Kingdom's 1977 government argued that it implied that subcentral spending should be financed with subcentral taxes and grants each contributing roughly equally shares. But equal contributions can aggravate the conflict inherent in this middle approach. Subcentral authorities will claim that they should be able to spend subcentral taxes as they wish, while central governments will claim that they should be able to dictate how their grants are spent. As there is no way of saying which items of spending are financed by subcentral taxes and which items are financed by grants, both subcentral and central governments can claim the right to discretion on every particular item.

Choosing Between the Approaches

Given the inherent difficulties in the middle approach, it seems best for governments to choose whichever of the localist or centralist approaches they think best for their countries. However, it is worth noting that only the localist approach is likely to secure the advantages of subcentral government noted at the beginning of this chapter. In particular, only the localist approach facilitates variety of provision in different areas to cater for varying preferences. Logically, then, one might expect most countries to ensure that subcentral authorities are chiefly financed by taxes, or at least by taxes and other independent sources. But it was shown in Table 2.3 that grants to states and local authorities account for respectively 29.5 percent and 38.2 percent of their total revenues, with taxes accounting for only 52.0 percent and 40.8 percent.

It should also be noted that the tax revenue figures shown in the table do not always accurately measure the extent to which the localist approach has been adopted in the different countries. Most notably, the relatively high figures for state level taxes in Austria and Germany - 47.5 and 62.9 percent - are rather misleading. For, as noted earlier, these are countries where the attraction of subcentral authorities varying their provisions is little appreciated and where uniformity of services between areas is desired. In countries such as these where, effectively, the centralist approach is desired, there is little need for genuine state or local taxes. There is a choice between grants and tax-sharing, whereby certain percentages of certain nationally levied taxes accrue as of right to subcentral authorities. The Austrians and Germans rely greatly on shared taxes, and this probably creates more stability for the states and local authorities than would occur if they relied chiefly on grants. But for countries where uniformity is not desired, it seems most appropriate to adopt the localist approach and arrange for subcentral authorities to rely chiefly on their own taxes for their revenues.

HORIZONTAL BALANCES: EQUALIZATION

Suppose that a country has devolved a certain number of government activities to its subcentral authorities. A certain amount of money will be required to provide these services at reasonable levels. Either the central government will seek to create a vertical balance, where lower tiers can set reasonable tax rates on their permitted taxes and thereby raise the amount required. Or the government will seek to create a situation of imbalance where the lower tiers, if they set reasonable tax rates, cannot raise all the money required, but where their tax receipts will be topped up by grants, perhaps through the payment of equal per capita general grants in each area.

In each case, however, there will remain the possibility that some areas might need higher tax rates than others to secure the revenue that they require to provide services at reasonable levels. Equivalently, there is the possibility that two areas might set similar tax rates, and yet one would be able to provide higher service levels than the other. These equivalent situations reflect a situation of horizontal imbalance.[15]

Horizontal imbalances can arise for three reasons. They can arise when two areas differ in terms of their taxable resources per head, or in terms of needs per head, or in terms of unit costs. In each case, similar tax rates combined with similar efficiencies in respect of service provision will lead to different levels of services. It is important to distinguish between needs and unit costs. The concept of needs relates to the numbers of units of subcentral authority output in relation to population that are required to provide particular levels of services. The concept of costs relates to the costs of providing units of output. Suppose a tier of subcentral authorities provides primary education. Two authorities in this tier will differ in terms of needs if they have different numbers of primary age children in relation to population, for then they will need to provide differing numbers of school places per head. Two authorities in this tier will differ in terms of unit costs if, for example, one has to pay higher salaries than the other to attract comparable teachers.

Many countries seek to reduce such horizontal imbalances, or even to remove them completely, by paying grants, often general equalization grants, to the areas which would otherwise need the highest tax rates. This section looks briefly at the main reasons for having equalization grants. Equalization is discussed further in Chapter 4.

The Rationale for Equalization Grants

There are two reasons why it might be decided to address a situation of horizontal imbalance, perhaps by means of equalization grants. First, there is an equity argument: without grants, equals in different areas may pay the same rates of subcentral taxes but receive different levels of services in return. This case for equalization grants is really equivalent to saying that the system of subcentral government finance should provide the same sort of equity in respect of the provision of subcentral services that the system of central government finance does in respect of central services; for central governments generally levy equal tax rates in all areas and thus feel obliged to try to provide similar service levels in all areas. Of course, subcentral authorities may choose to set different tax rates and have different service levels: the crucial point is that *if* they set the same tax rates, then equity demands that they should be able to provide services at similar levels.

The second reason for equalization grants stems from an efficiency argument. The point is that inequalities in subcentral services accompanied by equal subcentral tax rates, or vice versa, could lead to migration from the unfavorable area to the favorable one. Such migration will in itself use up resources; moreover, it could lead to people locating themselves in areas where their contributions to output were less than before if the lower wages they received were more than offset by an improved subcentral fiscal package. It must be conceded, though, that there is also an efficiency argument against equalizing differences in unit costs. For if people move from areas where services are costly to areas where services are cheap, then the total cost of providing people with a particular level of services will fall.

Some Particular Problems With Subcentral Property Taxes

Even if the case for equalization is accepted, it is arguable that not all differences in resources should be equalized, particularly if the only subcentral tax is a property tax.[16] As such a tax is a particularly common subcentral tax, it is worth teasing out this particular point. To see the issue, it is necessary to begin by noting that there are three factors that could cause the property tax base (per head) of a particular area to be relatively low:

(a)   the area might have relatively little business property;
(b)   domestic properties in the area might be relatively small;
(c)   site values in the area could be relatively low.

In each case, the result of the low tax base is that the area will have to set a higher rate of tax to provide services comparable with services elsewhere. But does this mean that its citizens will actually pay more in taxes than people in equal-size homes elsewhere for comparable services? It certainly does mean this if the tax base differentials arise from factors (a) and (b), and so in these two cases there is a case for equalizing the differences concerned.

But with factor (c), it seems there is no special need to equalize for tax base differentials. It is true that this factor will cause tax rates to be higher in the area concerned, but these higher rates will be applied to lower property values. Consequently, people in the area may well find that they are paying no more in tax than people elsewhere who live in property of a similar size and type. In turn, there seem to be no problems of inequity or possible migration to address.

However, the situation is more complex than it initially seems. To see this, suppose that factor (c) was the only one that varied between areas. This can be most easily envisaged by supposing that the property tax applies to domestic properties alone, so that factor (a) is irrelevant, and by supposing that all localities have comparable mixes of large and small domestic properties, so that factor (b) is irrelevant. Then the only reason why tax rates would vary between areas with comparable service levels and comparable degrees of efficiency in service provision would be if some areas had higher site values than others.

The crucial point to appreciate is that site values, and hence property values, are likely to vary *within* areas as well as *between* areas. Within any area, there will be a uniform tax rate, which means that people in low site value properties of a certain size and type pay less tax than people in high site value properties of the same size and type. Thus there is, implicitly, full equalization within areas simply because there is a uniform tax rate and a uniform level of service provision.

If this intra-area system of implicit equalization is felt acceptable, then it would seem logical to extend the idea of equalization to the nation as a whole by having an explicit scheme of equalization grants to ensure that areas with, on average, low site values, can still provide similar service levels as other areas with similar tax rates. If, however, the implicit intra-area equalization is felt inappropriate, then not only would the case for explicit equalization grants to disadvantaged areas disappear. So also would the case for implicit equalization within areas. The appropriate policy would seem to be to replace a property tax on property values with a property tax that excluded site values.

Equalization and Capitalization

It is sometimes argued that there is no need to equalize at all on the grounds that capitalization adjustments in home prices will prevent migration from taking place and will also preserve equity. Thus if one area is disadvantaged with low resources, high needs or high costs, and if as a result people seek to leave, then home prices there will fall while home prices in relatively attractive areas will rise. These home price changes could act so that the total cost of living in each area was the same - taking both home costs and subcentral service costs into account - and thus there would be no inequity and no incentive to migrate.

There are, however, two reasons for not placing too much reliance on this capitalization process as a reason for not having a system of equalization. First, it is really land prices that will alter. In the long run, at least in rural areas, the prices of land for homes may be set at the levels determined in the markets for agricultural land. Thus the supply of land for homes may be perfectly elastic in rural areas at the levels of agricultural land prices. If so, land price differentials may not emerge as a result of subcentral fiscal differences so that migration and inequity will occur.

Secondly, even if the supply of residential land was perfectly inelastic, as it might be in built-up areas, so that appropriate price differentials could occur, there would still be an equity case for equalization grants. For without such grants, home owners would face windfall gains and losses whenever the resources, needs or costs in their areas altered, and these gains and losses would occur in a capricious and hence arguably inequitable way.

Despite the arguments for equalization, few countries attempt anything like full equalization. Some countries, such as the United Kingdom, Denmark, Sweden, Canada and Australia, have pursued equalization quite assiduously. Others, most notably perhaps the United States, have done relatively little. In general, schemes of equalization grants usually seek not only to tackle the problems of horizontal imbalance but seek also to tackle simultaneously the problem of vertical fiscal imbalance. So the usual type of grant scheme is one which pays grants to all areas, but which gives the highest grants to those areas with low resources, high needs and, perhaps, high costs.

Vouchers as an Alternative to Equalization

An alternative to full equalization has recently been presented by Oakland (1994). His paper raises some interesting issues that cannot be explored here. But his main recommendation is that, instead of paying equalization grants, the central government should give vouchers to poor people who would hand them to their local authorities who could in turn redeem them for central funds to help them meet the costs of their services. If subcentral authorities rely chiefly on an income tax and/or a property tax, then this scheme would certainly ease the problem of low resources in areas where there were many people on low incomes or in low value properties. But, in essence, this proposal is not quite as radical as it sounds, for it is equivalent to giving partial equalization grants directly to authorities where there are many poor households. So Oakland is, implicitly, arguing merely for a particular scheme of partial equalization grants in which the only criterion for payment is the number of poor households in an area. Thus it is an equalization scheme that would ignore both cost differences and needs differences, and that would tackle resource differences only indirectly.

It was noted above that there are sound efficiency reasons for not equalizing cost differences. But it was also argued that there are reasons for equalizing differences in resources and needs. Oakland objects to fully equalizing these differences partly because he feels that doing so doing denies areas with natural resources access to the benefits from taxes on them, a policy which he regards as contentious, and partly because he feels that doing so can be seen as pursuing an egalitarian distribution of public services, a policy which he finds hard to defend. Positive economics cannot say whether natural resources should be taxed locally or nationally; nor can it say whether service levels should be comparable in all areas. But it can say, as was argued above, that there will be inefficiency and inequity if some areas have superior fiscal packages to others. Perhaps the question that should be put to people who object to full equalization of differences in tax resources and needs, and hence who object to the notion that local authorities with equal tax rates should usually be able to provide comparable services, is whether they also object to the implicit equalization that usually occurs with central government services. Do these people argue that, despite having equal tax rates in all areas, central governments should provide services in a discriminatory way to give the most benefit to those areas with the highest tax yields and the lowest needs?

NOTES

1. Tiebout's analysis has since been the subject of an extensive literature whose chief aim has been to see how far migration might help create an efficient level of public good output in each area. For an overview of this literature, see Fisher (1988, 66-81).

2. In addition to the arguments mentioned in the text, it is also sometimes claimed that multi-level government may be useful in situations like Quebec in Canada, the Basque region in Spain and Scotland in the United Kingdom where there is widespread support for political separation. If such areas are given their own provincial or regional assemblies, then their citizens can enjoy a degree of autonomy without having to become separate nations.

3. This piece of EU legislation is mentioned in *The Times*, 3 August 1995, 2.

4. Paradoxically, applying the correct level of matching specific grants might actually reduce the overall level of service provision in the nation as a whole. This issue is discussed by King (1984, 127-9).

5. For the Swiss experience, see Gygi (1994).

6. This figure is derived from Table 2.2.

7. Admittedly there would be a multiplier effect on output as a result of this increase in aggregate demand. But against this it should be allowed that there would also be upward pressure on interest rates, which would soften the impact.

8. This may be in part because subcentral authorities with access to substantial tax power do not necessarily use that power to raise their aggregate spending levels. For example, Lotz (1991, 253) showed that, during the 1980s, local authority spending grew less rapidly in both Denmark and Sweden, where local authorities had considerable freedom to raise tax revenues, than it did in both Norway and the United Kingdom, where local authority tax rate powers were much more restrictive.

9. In an earlier but extended discussion of this issue, King (1993, 286-90) argued that OECD members with substantial decentralized tax power also tend, if anything, to have both lower unemployment and lower inflation rates. Of course, these empirical observations do not necessarily imply a causal link.

10. For a fuller discussion of this issue, see Fisher (1993, 131-7).

11. Wheare (1946, 4 and 45-6) notes, for example, that the 1787 United States constitution gave the federal government responsibility for

defense, foreign representation, treaties and coinage, while the 1848 Swiss federation regularized the relationships between the cantons whose numbers had grown after Napoleon's expansionism.

12. There may be some subcentral services - such as most aspects of police activity - where contracting-out is difficult or impossible to introduce.

13. For a discussion of local government in New Zealand before the. recent reforms, see Scott (1979).

14. It will be noticed that the states with the lowest degree of tax revenue are those in Australia. Taxes there raise just 33.9 percent of state incomes, a lower percentage than applies on average to local authorities in the OECD. The lack of state tax power in Australia is currently a much debated issue. For a discussion of this problem, see the papers in Collins (1993).

15. For a fuller discussion of equalization, see King (1984, 140-99) and Bramley (1990).

16. Analogous issues can arise with other taxes. Suppose, for example, that subcentral authorities levy an income tax. An individual area might have a low base either (a) because it has large numbers of people on low-paid jobs or (b) because wage rates for many types of job in the area are low, perhaps because the area has a good climate and can attract workers with lower wages than those applying elsewhere. There would be a case for equalizing in case (a) but not in case (b), for there, if workers pay higher tax rates on lower incomes, they would not actually pay any more for their subcentral services.

REFERENCES

Anderson, J. (ed.) *Fiscal Equalization for State and Local Government Finance.* Westport, CT: Prager, 1994.

Bennett, Robert J. (ed.) *Decentralization, Local Governments and Markets: Towards a Post-welfare Agenda.* Oxford: Clarendon Press, 1990.

Bramley, Glen. *Equalization Grants and Local Expenditure Needs.* Aldershot: Avebury, 1990.

Collins, David J. (ed.) *Vertical Fiscal Imbalance.* Sydney: Australian Tax Research Foundation, 1993.

Fisher, Ronald C. *State and Local Public Finance.* Glenview, Illinois: Scott, Foresman and Company, 1988.

Fisher, Ronald C. "Macroeconomic Implications of Subnational Fiscal Policy: The Overseas Experience." In Collins (1993), 125-52.

Foster, C.D., R. A. Jackman and M. Perlman. *Local Government Finance in a Unitary State.* London: Allen and Unwin, 1980.

Gygi, V. "Maintaining a Coherent Macro-economic Policy in a Highly Decentralised Federal State: The Experience of Switzerland." In King and Owens (1994), 253-8.

HMSO (Her Majesty's Stationery Office). *Local Government Finance.* (Report of the Committee of Enquiry, chairman Frank Layfield, Cmnd. 6453.) London: HMSO, 1976.

HMSO (Her Majesty's Stationery Office). *Local Government Finance.* (Green Paper, Cmnd. 6813.) London: HMSO, 1977.

Hodge, Patrick. (ed.) *Scotland and the Union.* Edinburgh: Edinburgh University Press (for the David Hume Institute), 1994.

Hutchinson, Gladstone. "The Budget Process and Fiscal Federalism in Canada." In Ott (1993), 145-67.

James, Denis W. *Intergovernmental Financial Relations.* Sydney: Australian Tax Research Foundation, 1992.

King, David N. *Fiscal Tiers: the Economics of Multi-level Government.* London: Allen and Unwin, 1984.

King, David N. "Australian Reform Options: a European View." In Collins (1993), 265-300.

King, David N. "Economic Independence and Political Independence." In Hodge (1994), 30-49.

King, David N., and Jeffrey P.Owens. (eds.) *Fiscal Federalism in Economies in Transition,* Paris: OECD (conference proceedings), 1994.

Lotz, Joergen R. "Controlling Local Government Expenditures: The Experience of Five European Countries." In Prud'homme (1991), 249-62.

Maxwell, James A., and J. Richard Aronson. *Financing State and Local Governments.* Washington DC: The Brookings Institution, 1977.

Oakland, William H. "Recognizing and Correcting for Fiscal Imbalances: A Critical Analysis." In Anderson (1994), 1-19.

Oates, Wallace E. *Fiscal Federalism.* New York: Harcourt Brace Jovanovich, 1972.

Organisation for Economic Cooperation and Development. *Revenue Statistics of OECD Member Countries 1965-94.* Paris: OECD, 1995.

Organisation for Economic Cooperation and Development. *Main Economic Indicators.* Paris: OECD, February 1996.

Ott, Attiat F. *Public Sector Budgets: A Comparative Study.* Aldershot: Edward Elgar, 1993.

Prud'homme, Rémy. (ed.) *Public Finance with Several Levels of Government.* The Hague: Foundation Journal Public Finance, 1991.

Schumacher, Ute. "Fiscal Federalism in the Federal Republic of Germany." In Ott (1993), 168-207.

Scott, Claudia D. *Local and Regional Government in New Zealand: Function and Finance.* Sydney: George Allen and Unwin, 1979.

Söderström, Lars. "Fiscal Federalism: The Nordic Countries' Style." In Prud'homme (1991), 37-53.

Solé-Vilanova, Joaquim. "Regional and Local Government in Spain: Is Fiscal Responsibility the Missing Element?" In Bennett (1990), 331-54.

Spahn, P. "The Choice of Own Taxes, Shared Taxes and Grants to Finance State Governments: The Experience of Germany." In King and Owens (1994), 147-60.

Thöni, Eric. "Financing Federal and State Government: The Experience of Austria." In King and Owens (1994), 173-86.

Tiebout, Charles M. "A Pure Theory of Local Expenditures." *Journal of Political Economy,* 64 No. 5, (October 1956) 416-24.

Uhl, G. "The Experience of the Netherlands." In King and Owens (1994), 167-72.

Wheare, Kenneth C. *Federal Government.* London: Oxford University Press, 1946.

3 TAX POLICY IN AN INTERGOVERNMENTAL SETTING: IS IT TIME FOR THE U.S. TO CHANGE?

Daphne A. Kenyon

By 1950, the basic structure of the United States intergovernmental tax system was established.[1] The national government had adopted its major revenue raisers---the personal and corporate income taxes---decades earlier; property taxes had long served as the fiscal mainstay of local governments; and by 1950 three-quarters of the states eventually adopting individual income, corporate income, or general sales taxes had done so (U.S. ACIR 1995: 32). The intergovernmental tax system in 1950 could be characterized, as it can be now, by minimal federal constraints on state taxing powers and maximum interstate diversity, so much so that one observer from another federal country has labeled the United States a "tax jungle."

The vintage-1950 intergovernmental tax system now operates in a very different world. The U.S. economy is much more open; exports and imports as a percentage of GDP are double what they were fifty years ago. Multinational corporations whose economic interests span the globe play an increasingly important role in our national economy. Advances in transportation and communication have greatly increased the mobility of capital, goods, services, businesses, and individuals. In the 1950s when the Interstate Highway System was built, the birth of the personal computer was two decades away. Now the internet is growing at an exponential rate and Americans look forward to its evolution into an "information superhighway." Advances in telecommunications have been so dramatic that *The Economist* predicts that, "the demise of distance as the key to the cost of communicating may well prove the most significant economic force shaping the next half century." (1995: 15). As this chapter is written, land use changes in Wall Street serve as an apt symbol of the historic economic changes taking place. Because of improvements in telecommunications, financial firms no longer require a physical location in Wall Street---the long-time center of finance in the U.S.---leading to substantial office space vacancies and the need to convert real estate at the tip of Manhattan to other uses, such as housing.[2]

The major question addressed in this chapter is whether the United States can successfully enter the 21st century with the same intergovernmental tax system it had fifty years ago or whether major modifications are called for. In order to address this question a review of the important dimensions of intergovernmental tax policy and of recent theoretical and empirical research is conducted. The chapter looks not only at the U.S. record, but at the tax structures of three other federal countries: Australia, Canada, and Germany.[3] The paper concludes by arguing that the U.S. intergovernmental tax system will have to move closer to either the Canadian or German model in certain particular dimensions if it is to support rather than impede the U.S. economy and governmental system in the next century.

GENERAL PRINCIPLES OF INTERGOVERNMENTAL TAX POLICY

Since Adam Smith's *Wealth of Nations*, economists have judged tax systems according to a standard set of criteria, the most important of which are equity and efficiency.[4] The traditional principles of taxation still apply when considering tax policy in an intergovernmental setting, but new dimensions of those traditional principles become important because new variables or considerations are introduced. Let us first consider the implications of having multiple state or local governments. This introduces the potential for mobility among jurisdictions: businesses or individuals may be induced to move from one jurisdiction to another by tax differentials. Spillover effects are introduced in that one jurisdiction may export taxes to residents or firms in other jurisdictions. Multiplicity of jurisdictions also introduces the issue of disparities in tax capacities among jurisdictions.

Each of these issues can be labeled horizontal intergovernmental tax policy issues.

In an intergovernmental context, relations between the central government and the state governments or between a state government and its local governments also become important. What restrictions on revenue-raising powers, if any, should a higher level of government impose on a lower level of government? How should access to revenue sources be allocated among the levels of government?

Equity and efficiency take on new meaning in an intergovernmental context. When considering efficiency of taxes, special notice must now be paid to potential locational distortions created by variations in tax policies among states or local governments. When considering equity, one can now consider whether tax exporting is fair or not. To what extent does tax exporting match exporting of the benefits from public services, and to what extent is it unrelated to benefit spillovers? Further, one can focus on the extent to which an individual in a relatively rich jurisdiction might pay one tax bill for a particular public service, at the same time that an otherwise identical individual in a relatively poor jurisdiction pays a higher tax bill for the same public service.

An important new consideration arises when tax policy is considered in an intergovernmental context---how tax arrangements affect the health of the intergovernmental system. Some analysts argue that a federal system serves to prevent tyrannical government because competition between governments at different levels as well as competition among governments at the same level limits government power and provides more choice for citizens (Dye, 1990; Kenyon and Kincaid 1991: 1-2). If this view of federalism is accepted, then the division of taxing powers among the levels of government, as well as the character and degree of competition among the states become important issues.

FOCUS OF CHAPTER

The following pages will divide intergovernmental tax policy issues into vertical and horizontal issues[5]. Within the section on vertical tax issues, the issue of vertical fiscal balance is considered first. That is, what proportion of the power to raise revenues should be given to each level of government (central, state, and local)? Next tax assignment is considered:

which taxes should be assigned to which levels of government? Should more than one level of government be allowed to use the same tax base? Also, to what extent does tax assignment in practice correspond to theories of optimal tax assignment? Other vertical tax issues include the benefits and costs of tax sharing, tax limits and other forms of tax coordination imposed by higher levels of government on lower levels of government.

Consideration of horizontal issues begins with the theory of tax choices made by state and local governments. To what extent do state and local governments export taxes, and to what extent should they export taxes? Analysis of tax exporting depends crucially on understanding tax incidence in an intergovernmental setting. Other horizontal issues include the pros and cons of tax competition and tax harmonization, and the existence of disparities in tax capacities and the appropriate policies for ameliorating such disparities. A major role of the central government is to set the appropriate framework for competition among states and to optimally compensate for disparities in tax capacities among states (states perform the same functions vis-a-vis local governments.)[6]

The issues in this chapter on tax policy in an intergovernmental setting are closely tied to issues of service provision and intergovernmental grants, which are addressed in other chapters. At the most basic level, tax capacity should be tied to service responsibility. In order for a government to be responsive to its citizens and be held accountable by its citizens, it should have revenues that neither greatly exceed nor greatly fall short of expenditure responsibilities. Many analysts agree that division of service responsibilities should logically come before tax assignment decisions.

To the extent that a state or local government's tax capacity falls short of its service responsibilities, intergovernmental grants from a higher level of government can serve to balance its budget. In some cases the distinction between taxes and grants is hard to make. Tax sharing arrangements, whereby two levels of government draw revenue from the same tax source, are very much like revenue sharing grants. To the extent that the shared tax is administered by the higher level government, and that the amount of revenue provided to the lower level government is dependent upon an annual decision by the higher level government, such tax sharing appears even more like a revenue sharing grant.

Throughout this paper I will use four large, mature federal systems as examples: Australia, Canada, Germany and the United States.[7] Each of these countries has a long tradition of federal government, but each is currently facing important challenges. In Australia, the dominance of the central government in tax policy (known as vertical fiscal imbalance) is currently receiving much attention. The major current issue in Canada's federation is the possibility that Quebec might secede from the union. Germany faces the opposite issue in its efforts to bring the five former East German laender (states) into a reunified Germany. The United States is going through a second decade of devolution of fiscal responsibilities to the states, that seems to be intensifying as the federal government continues its efforts to reduce the federal budget deficit. In recent years, there has also been substantial discussion of fundamental federal tax reform, generally focusing on proposals to replace federal income taxation with some form of consumption tax. Such major federal tax reform, if enacted, would likely have important impacts on state and local governments.

The intergovernmental tax systems of Australia, Canada, Germany and the United States differ in many important respects, as the discussion that follows will illustrate. It is beyond the scope of this paper, however, to attempt to explain why each country adopted the particular intergovernmental tax system that it did. Explaining the existing intergovernmental tax structure would require a history of each country, touching on constitutional, political and economic issues. For example, the intergovernmental tax system of the United States is deeply affected by the fact that the country is divided into 50 states, instead of some much smaller number as in the other mature federal countries. But explaining this institutional fact would likely require a paper in itself. Suffice it to say that the U.S. system of fiscal federalism:

> is neither constitutionally prescribed not politically inevitable; and it is not the outcome of any intentional design or national consensus. Instead, it is the outcome of policy-by-policy responses to...many democratic demands and global crises...(Kenyon and Kincaid 1991b: 4).

Because the United States intergovernmental tax system has changed dramatically over the course of our nation's history, there is no reason to assume that it cannot undergo further, even dramatic, changes. An examination of alternative models of federalism can provide a useful guide to alternatives the United States might choose from in the future.

At the same time that one can learn much from the intergovernmental systems of other countries, there are reasons to be cautious in applying lessons from other countries to one's own. First, as noted above, governmental structures differ dramatically among countries. Horizontal intergovernmental tax policy issues will inevitably be much different in the United States with its 50 states and 86,000 local governments than those in Australia where there are eight states and approximately 900 local governments. (See Appendix Table 1.) Second, the values of citizens in different countries will lead them to make much different tradeoffs when choices between opposing principles must be made. For example, in choosing between local autonomy and maintaining equal access to public services across the country, the United States has emphasized the former and Germany, the latter (See Kenyon and Kincaid 1991b). Equality is valued in Germany to such an extent that the federal government is given power under the German constitution (Basic Law) "to legislate as needed to maintain 'uniformity of living conditions,' "a provision that would be unthinkable in the United States (Bird 1986, 78).

VERTICAL TAX ISSUES

Vertical Fiscal Balance

The issue of vertical fiscal balance, or the balance of revenue-raising power between the central government and the states, has been a longstanding and contentious issue in Australia. Largely because of constitutional provisions and the courts' interpretations of those provisions, states in Australia are not allowed to levy individual income, corporate income or general sales taxes (Groenewegen 1983). As Charles McLure, Jr. describes the Australian system:

> the States are forced to rely on payroll taxes and a hodge-podge of other revenue sources which can best be described as nuisance taxes, such as stamp taxes, taxes on financial transactions, and taxes on gambling, most of which should not have an important place in a modern tax system. They rely on grants from the Commonwealth for roughly half their financial resources...To me this does not sound like a description of a sensible federal system in which States have

fiscal sovereignty approaching that of the federal government. At best it sounds more like an essentially unitary government, with the States being little more than administrative agents for the Commonwealth (1993: 251).

It is unclear, however, whether the near-monopoly on revenue sources is the source of the purported vertical fiscal imbalance in Australia, or whether it is the relationship between revenue-raising powers and expenditure responsibilities (expenditure responsibilities for Australian states far exceed revenue-raising powers).

As can be seen in Table 3.1, federal taxes account for 77.5 percent of total taxes at all levels in Australia. This percentage exceeds the 68.2 percent for federal taxes in the United States, 70.9 percent in Germany, and 56.5 percent in Canada. By this simple measure, in Australia the balance of revenue-raising power leans most heavily towards the central government, and in Canada, the balance of revenue-raising power leans most heavily towards the provinces.

Table 3.1: **Attribution of Tax Revenues to Sub-Sectors of General Government as Percentage of Total Tax Revenue, 1991**

	Central	State	Local
Australia	77.5	18.5	3.9
Canada	56.5	34.1	9.4
Germany	70.9	20.5	7.7
United States	68.2	18.8	13.0

Source: Organization for Economic Cooperation and Development, *Revenue Statistics of OECD Member Countries, 1965-1992*, p. 196.

Note: Central entry includes social security taxes. 0.9 percent of total German tax revenue is attributed to the European Union.

A growing literature on competitive federalism has argued that a balance of power between different levels of government, and even competition between those governments, is good because it checks the potential monopoly power of any particular government (Breton 1987, Dye

1990, Walsh 1989). This literature has not, however, offered empirical guidelines regarding a reasonable proportion of total revenue-raising power that should be allocated to each level of government to ensure a well-functioning intergovernmental system. There is however, some empirical evidence on the relationship between the degree of centralization of revenue-raising and the size of government. Wallace Oates used data on 43 countries from the early 1980s (including Australia, Canada, West Germany and the United States) to run regressions testing for a relationship between government size (measured as total public revenues divided by GDP) and revenue centralization (the proportion of total revenues going to the central government). The revenue centralization variables are not statistically significantly different from zero, and Oates concludes that he cannot reject the null hypothesis that "centralization and the size of government have little to do with one another" (Oates 1985: 756).[8]

The concept of vertical fiscal balance might also apply to the relations between states and local governments. In the United States, state revenues account for between 51 percent and 82 percent of total state-local general revenue (U.S. ACIR 1994: 90, 104). Do the states at either end of the spectrum suffer from vertical fiscal imbalance? That is, are New Hampshire, Illinois, Florida, Georgia, Texas, and Colorado too fiscally decentralized and Delaware, West Virginia, New Mexico, Alaska, and Hawaii too fiscally centralized? If vertical fiscal imbalance obtains, what are its symptoms and how serious are they?

Tax Assignment

A second very important vertical tax issue is that of tax assignment; that is, which level of government should be allowed to levy which tax? An Australian conference of public finance experts held in 1983 addressed this issue, and the major conclusions of those experts apparently still stand. The theory of tax assignment was approached from four viewpoints: traditional public finance, optimal taxation, public choice and tax effectiveness. The conclusions these approaches had in common included these basic principles of tax allocation:

(1) Taxes on highly mobile factors should be assigned to central governments, whereas taxes on immobile factors should be reserved for local governments. This implies, for example, that death taxes

should be levied by central governments, while property taxes are an appropriate source of revenue for local governments.

(2) Taxes used to redistribute income (such as progressive income taxes) should be levied by central governments.[9]

(3) Taxes used for stabilization purposes or taxes with very unstable revenue patterns should be levied by central governments. (This principle and the previous principle follow Richard Musgrave's traditional assignment of redistribution and stabilization tasks to the central, not to sub-national governments.) Because changes in individual income taxes can easily be used for stabilization purposes, this would tend to imply that individual income taxes should be a central government tax. Further, because corporate tax revenues are likely to be unstable over the business cycle, this implies that the corporate income tax is most appropriately used as a central government revenue source.

(4) "Residence-based taxes, such as personal income taxes and retail sales and other indirect taxes, are more likely to be appropriate for subnational governments than are source-based taxes such as origin-based value-added taxes and corporation income taxes" (McLure 1983a, xiv). This recommendation arises, in part, from the difficulty of having independent governments attempt to allocate the tax base of multistate or multinational corporations.

(5) Taxes that operate like private sector prices for services rendered (e.g., user charges) can be used at any level of government.

The consensus regarding tax allocation between central, state and local governments, presented by type of tax, is shown in Figure 3.1. Table 3.2 presents a summary of the tax allocation for major taxes in practice in the four federal systems. The allocation of 100 percent of individual and corporation income, and most of the goods and services tax revenues to the central government, and the payroll and property taxes to state and local governments in Australia violates none of the principles of tax allocation stated above. This allocation, as noted in the previous section, does appear to many, however, to create a fiscal imbalance in Australia's intergovernmental system favoring the central government. For Canada and Germany there appear to be clear departures from the principles of tax

70

Table 3.2:   Percentage of Particular Taxes Raised by Level of Government, 1989

	Federal	State and Local
Individual Income Tax		
Australia	100.0%	---
Canada	61.6%^{a}	38.4%
Germany	40.2%	59.8%
United States	82.0%	18.0%
Corporation Income Tax		
Australia	100.0%	---
Canada	65.8%	34.2%
Germany	38.3%	61.7%
United States	80.0%	20.0%
Social Security		
Australia	---	---
Canada	100.0%	---
Germany	100.0%	---
United States	100.0%	---
Payroll		
Australia	18.3%	81.7%
Canada	---	---
Germany	---	---
United States	---	---
Property		
Australia	3.6%	96.4%
Canada	---	100.0%
Germany	6.8%	93.2%
United States	5.4%	94.6%
Goods and Services		
Australia	76.3%	23.7%
Canada	42.9%	57.1%
Germany	71.7%	28.3%
United States	20.4%	79.6%

	Federal	State and Local
Other[b]		
Australia	---	---
Canada	34.6%	65.4%
Germany	---	100.0%
United States	---	---

Source: U.S. Advisory Commission on Intergovernmental Relations. 1992. *Significant Features of Fiscal Federalism, Vol. 2.* Washington, DC: Author: 27.

Notes: [a] This figure indicates that 61.6% of all individual income taxes in Canada were raised at the federal level.
[b] Includes unclassified income taxes, unclassified business taxes, and unallowable taxes.

allocation described above. About one-third of corporate income tax revenue flows to state and local governments in Canada, while nearly two-thirds of individual income and corporation income tax revenues go to German state and local governments. However, as will be described below, special features of each tax system---tax sharing in Germany and tax collection agreements in Canada---make such tax allocations more palatable. In the United States, the fact that 20 percent of corporation income tax revenues are contributed to state and local coffers is a concern, particularly in light of the absence of any strong mechanism to coordinate such taxes among the subnational governments.

Empirical Effect of Particular Tax Assignments. Given that some taxes are more income elastic than others, one would expect that the tax assignments in a federal system would make a difference to the long term revenue raising capabilities of the different levels of government. To take a stylized example, suppose that in a mythical federal system the central government levied a progressive non-indexed income tax, whereas the states were limited to levying per unit excise taxes. Over time one would expect that a larger proportion of total government revenue would go to the central government and less to the states because of the large degree by which the elasticity of the income tax would exceed that of the per unit excise taxes. In the real world, this distinction is not so clear cut because, for example, some income taxes are more elastic than others, and although income taxes are generally considered to be more elastic than sales taxes, some sales taxes can be more elastic than flat rate income taxes (Dye and McGuire 1991). Further, governments can alter the elasticity of a tax by, among other

Figure 3.1: Optimal Tax Assignment

Tax	Appropriate Level of Government to Levy Tax
Individual income tax	
generally	C
non-progressive	C or S
Corporate income tax	C
Value added tax	C
Retail sales tax	S
Excise taxes	C or S
Natural resource taxes	C or S
Customs duties	C
Estate taxes	C
Property taxes	L
User charges	C or S or L
Payroll tax	C or S
Environmental taxes	C or S

Sources: Bahl (1994), McLure (1983a) and Musgrave (1983).
Note: C = central, S = state, and L = local.

policies, indexing certain provisions of an income tax. Nevertheless, one would expect that, all else equal, having access to an elastic tax source would increase revenue growth for a particular government.

Although this makes sense from a theoretical standpoint, so far empirical investigations have not found evidence supporting this hypothesis. Neither Feenberg and Rosen (1987) nor Oates (1975) found that the elasticity of a state's tax system affected the level or growth of state spending. However, one might be skeptical of their findings, given the logic of the theory, and given certain methodological weaknesses of these two studies (Gold 1995: 16-17).

Separation of Tax Assignments. Do the basic principles of tax allocation among levels of government imply that a tax source assigned to one level of government should not also be assigned to another level of government? Richard Musgrave definitively argues in the negative:

> A sense of orderliness might suggest that multiple use is undesirable. In the U.S., for instance, opponents of a federal sales tax tend to argue that the consumption base already 'belongs' to the states and should hence not be 'invaded' by the federal government. At closer consideration, however, this concept of belonging has little merit. If consumption is held to be a good tax base for more than one level, why should it not be subject to multiple use?...There is a case against multiple use only to the extent that there is a case against excessive utilization of any one tax base (1983: 14).

Musgrave further argues that in the case of multiple use of one tax, uses by the different levels of government should be coordinated in some way to simplify administration. World Bank researchers advising Russian officials would appear to agree with Musgrave. When a new law regarding intergovernmental fiscal relations was passed in Russia assigning all taxes to one or another level of government, it was not praised by the researchers. Instead, they argued in favor of retaining some part of the current intergovernmental fiscal system in which various taxes are shared between governments at different levels (Wallich 1994: 10-13).

An alternative point of view is stated by Thomas J. Nechyba (1995: 2):

> By dividing tax bases clearly between different levels of government, voters know exactly where each of their tax dollars is going: property taxes are collected locally and compared by voters to local government output; similarly, state and national taxes are

collected by state and national authorities and compared to the level of state and national outputs.

Based on this logic, Nechyba argues forcefully that tax bases should not be shared by more than one level of government. Nechyba's conclusion depends crucially on the weight he places on government accountability and his faith that tax separation would ensure such accountability. There is room for reasonable people to disagree on such matters. We now turn to an explicit description of tax sharing, as alternative way to organize vertical fiscal relations.

Tax Sharing

An alternative to assigning tax sources to particular levels of government is for two or more levels of government to share revenue from common taxes. Because Germany relies on tax sharing to a much greater extent than these other federal countries, the German system is described first, then the applicability of tax sharing arrangements to other countries is considered.

Tax sharing dominates the German fiscal system; in 1991, 72 percent of total tax revenues raised by all levels of government were raised via shared taxes (Schumacher 1993: 182). The most important taxes are shared taxes: individual income, corporate income and value added taxes are all shared taxes. Tax sharing is mandated by the constitution (Basic Law) (Furkel, et al, 1991: 3-4).

Specifically, the law provides that the federal government and the laender each receive 50 percent of corporate income taxes. The individual income tax is split among all levels of government with 42.5 percent allotted to the federal government, 42.5 percent to the laender, and 15 percent to municipalities as of the late 1980s. The division of the value added tax between the federal government and the laender is determined by federal legislation that must be approved by the Bundesrat (the house of the national legislature representing the laender). There also is a capital yields tax that is split between the federal government and the laender on a 50-50 basis. Finally, localities are required to give 15 percent of the revenues from their business tax to the federal government and the laender (Schumacher 1993: 203).

Taxes that are not shared include the taxes of more minor importance. At the local level, governments have exclusive rights to revenues from real property taxes, licensing taxes, and municipal beverage taxes, among others. The laender have exclusive rights to revenue from personal wealth, motor vehicle, real property, and inheritance taxes. Taxes that are exclusively federal include insurance, stock exchange, and some selective excise taxes and customs duties (Schumacher 1993: 203).

The German constitution did not originally provide for this extensive system of tax sharing. Sharing of individual income and corporation income taxes was introduced in 1955; sharing of value-added tax revenues was added in 1969 (Schumacher 1993: 206).

Some tax sharing takes place in other federal systems, but not to the same extent as in Germany. In the United States, there is no tax sharing between the federal government and the states, although it has been proposed (Rivlin 1992). In some states there is tax sharing between the state government and local governments. For example, the state of Maine shares about 5 percent of its sales and income tax revenues with local governments to help relieve property tax burdens. These funds are distributed among municipalities according to a formula based on population and property tax burden. However, in times of fiscal stress, the state government has unilaterally reduced the amount of tax sharing funds given to localities (Maine Municipal Association 1993: 8,26,27).

Some of the main advantages of tax sharing are that interjurisdictional tax competition is lessened, economies of scale in tax administration and collection are achieved, and each level of government may find its revenues to be more stable over the business cycle than if it had sole rights to revenues from a smaller number of taxes. On the other side, tax sharing considerably reduces the autonomy of state and local governments. They no longer have control over which taxes to raise, how to specify the tax base, or at what level to set tax rates. Tax sharing may also reduce government accountability.

Joint Tax Collection Agreements

A less coercive alternative to tax sharing of the German form is joint tax collection agreements, such as are used in Canada. Since 1962, Canada's federal government has agreed to collect individual and corporate income taxes for each province that entered into a tax collection agreement. As part of the bargain, the province must use the federal base and rate structure. Provinces have the option of setting their own tax rates, and recently, of adding certain tax credits, such as tax credits exempting low income families from taxation (Boadway and Hobson 1993: 37-40).

As part of the tax collection agreements, the federal government has reduced the rates of the individual income and corporate income taxes in order to provide "tax room" for the provinces to tap into the same revenue base. Equalization payments are also made from the federal government to selected provinces with lower than average tax capacities. Most provinces have participated in the tax collection agreements, but Quebec has levied its own individual income and corporation income tax, and Ontario has levied its own corporate income tax (Boadway and Hobson 1993: 37-40).

In the United States, no state takes advantage of current law that provides for the federal government to collect income taxes on the state's behalf if the state levies a so-called piggyback income tax (Rivlin 1992: 136). In many cases, however, state income taxes are linked in some way to the federal income tax, but that linkage is quite variable. Some states have no explicit linkage to the federal income tax, some link to federal adjusted gross income, some link to federal taxable income, and a few express their state income tax liability as a percentage of federal income tax liability (U.S. ACIR 1994: 58-59.) At least one state has instituted a form of tax collection agreement between the state and its local governments. In Maryland all counties and Baltimore City impose local income taxes as a percentage of state income tax liability (U.S. ACIR 1994: 78).

Tax collection agreements occupy a middle ground between unbridled tax competition among lower level governments and the uniformity inherent in tax sharing arrangements. States can decide on their own tax rates, but must leave tax base decisions to the federal level. For some states, though (Quebec, Ontario and states in the United States), autonomy regarding tax rates alone does not appear to be sufficient.

Should the U.S. Federal Government Enact a Consumption Tax?

In light of the preceding discussion of vertical tax issues, it is appropriate to make some preliminary comments about the wisdom of adoption of a consumption tax by the U.S. federal government. I will leave aside any discussion of whether a consumption tax base would be preferable to an income tax base, and will concentrate on the intergovernmental dimensions of this question.[10]

The most important question is whether a federal consumption tax would substitute for an income tax or supplement an income tax. If the consumption tax would substitute for income taxation several problems would be created. Marginal tax rates for the entire intergovernmental system would have to be higher because of the rejection of one previously heavily used base by the central government. Governmental accountability may suffer as the central government and the states come to share the consumption base as their most important tax base. State governments who now rely on income taxation would no longer benefit from income tax information provided by the federal government and other federal assistance with income tax administration. Furthermore, if state and local taxes were not deductible, then one useful mechanism for reducing effective interstate tax differentials would be lost.

If, on the other hand, federal tax reform involved adoption of a consumption value added tax used to supplement the current income tax system, evaluation of the tax reform is much more positive. Many of the problems noted above would no longer apply. Furthermore, to the extent that a tax sharing arrangement could be set up with the states, the tax reform could reduce two current problems with the U.S. intergovernmental tax system: excessive diversity and interstate tax competition. Rivlin (1992) makes a persuasive case for such a tax package as part of a reform of the federal system that involves sorting out of expenditure responsibilities as well.

HORIZONTAL TAX ISSUES

Tax Incidence

Some very complex issues of tax incidence arise when considering tax policy in an intergovernmental setting. Specifically, the theories of the incidence of property and corporate income taxes are among the most complex areas of public finance. The consensus of the conventional wisdom about thirty years ago was that the corporate income tax was a progressive tax and the property tax was regressive. State and local policymakers to some extent rely on these outmoded ideas, even though the public finance literature has moved far beyond the partial equilibrium theories that underlay these conclusions.

When considering property or corporation income tax incidence there are no longer any simple answers (Fisher 1996: 356-368, 451-454). When asking who bears the burden of each of these taxes, one first must distinguish between the burden of these taxes in a country on average or the burden of the tax imposed by a single jurisdiction within a country. One must also take into account the mobility of all factors of production and the long-run elasticities of the supplies of these factors. One has to choose between incidence based on the concept of annual income or permanent income.

As a further complexity, the property tax, under certain circumstances, can be considered a benefit tax. For example, consider one of many suburbs in a metropolitan area that decides to raise property taxes in order to pay for improved public safety in a manner desired by voters. To ask whether this tax change is progressive, proportional, or regressive makes no sense. The tax change must be considered together with the proposed improvement in services. Under certain simplifying assumptions, this increase in the property tax can be considered an efficient charge for improvement in public services desired.

The phenomenon of property tax capitalization also complicates tax incidence questions. When considering a program of property tax relief, one must distinguish between long-time citizens of a community and recent arrivals. The recent arrival will have paid a somewhat reduced price for housing if property taxes are heavy; this person would appear not to be so needful of property tax relief. The long-time resident, whom we assume arrived in the community before the run up in property taxes, did not receive this form of compensation.

The primary complication that is added when considering state, rather than federal, corporation income taxes is the necessity to apportion the net income of multistate corporations. In the United States, such corporate income is usually apportioned among the states based on the proportion of sales, property, and payroll in each state (although not all states use the same formula). To the extent that this three-factor formula is used, the corporation income tax is converted from a tax on corporate profits to taxes on sales, property, and payroll whose rates are set in proportion to a corporation's profit level (McLure 1981).

In recent years, computer microsimulation models have been built for individual states in the United States to answer complex questions of tax incidence. At their core, such models contain: 1) a database of information on a sample of taxpayers; 2) a tax calculator (or a number of tax calculators) that can calculate income tax liability, for example, for each of the taxpayers in the database; 3) a means of projecting estimates for several years into the future; and 4) a way to change some tax information in response to tax policy changes (e.g., wage income might be made dependent on tax rates) (Plesko 1995). The simpler microsimulation models provide revenue and distributional information about a single tax. The tax most commonly analyzed with microsimulation models is the individual income tax (McCarty and Marks 1993).

More sophisticated models can analyze the distributional effects of several taxes by, in effect, linking several separate microsimulation models together. Thus, a state could ask questions regarding the distributional impact of all of its major taxes---individual income, sales, and property taxes---with such a combined model. With rapid advances in computer technology such models can be run on personal computers with fairly user-friendly software. These models have their downside, however. The builder of the model will have entered as a default option certain assumptions regarding incidence of corporate and property taxes, which may not be sensible for the state at hand, and if currently reasonable, may not be reasonable in future years. However, there is no easy way for the user to ascertain such problems. More likely the user may blithely maintain the model-builder's default options despite changes in the state's economy.

Tax Exporting[11]

Both state and local governments often succumb to the understandable temptation to try to shift tax burdens to either individuals or businesses from other states. Donald Phares studied tax exporting in the U.S. several years ago and estimated the proportion of each type of tax that was exported by each state (1980). He divided tax exporting into two types: tax exporting via federal deductibility of state and local taxes and price/migration exporting. He defined the latter as "the spatial shifting of taxes among states due to market conditions that allow them to be passed on to owners of factors of production or consumers of taxed commodities, as reflected in higher prices, or due to the movement of taxpayers" (1980:64). This would include Nevada's ability to shift taxes to out-of-state tourists who indirectly bear the burden of some of the state's gaming taxes, or Alaska's ability to shift the burden of oil taxes to out-of-state consumers of that oil.

Phares' estimates of tax exporting through federal tax deductibility are now dated, so only his estimates of tax exporting through the price/migration avenue will be described here. According to Phares, those taxes with the highest average rate of tax exporting are severance taxes (34.7 percent exported) and corporation income taxes (43.7 percent exported), and with the lowest average rate of exporting are tobacco taxes (3.8 percent exported) and alcohol taxes (3.8 percent exported) (1980: 67). When considered for all avenues of price/migration exporting by state, the average rate of exporting was estimated to be 8.5 percent. Nevada and Delaware, however, export over 20 percent of their total taxes, and at the other end of the spectrum, South Dakota exports less than 5 percent of its total taxes.

Robert Tannenwald has computed estimates of the rate of tax exporting through federal tax deductibility for 1985 (Tannenwald 1989: Appendix Table). He finds that the average rate of state tax exporting through deductibility was 14 percent, with a range from 9.2 percent for South Dakota to 19.3 percent for New Jersey. These estimates are also dated given the reduced benefits from federal deductibility of state and local taxes enacted in the Tax Reform Act of 1986 and subsequently.

Dennis Zimmerman used Phares' estimates of state-by-state tax exporting to examine the potential subsidy to state and local spending and the potential welfare loss (1983). Zimmerman estimated that public spending for all states combined was about 10 percent higher because of the reduced price of state and local services inherent in tax exporting opportunities. He noted that any estimates of potential welfare losses arising from this stimulus to spending are problematic until there is sufficient information to judge the extent to which exported taxes correct for exported public sector benefits.

There appear to be several productive avenues of research here. Updated estimates of potential and actual tax exporting by tax and by state would provide a much clearer picture of how tax burdens are shifted among the residents of different states. Equally useful would be estimates of the match between exported taxes and exported public service benefits. Once these empirical data were generated, an updated estimate of the consequences of tax exporting could be done. A final link would be an analysis of the constitutional and legal constraints on tax exporting and the extent to which these constraints serve to maximize social welfare.

Tax Choices of State and Local Governments

Several studies have examined the determinants of state and local tax mix (Gade and Adkins 1990, Hettich and Winer 1984, Metcalf 1993, and Sjoquist 1981). These studies are based either on a median voter, average voter, or maximizing bureaucrat model of state and local government behavior. Most studies test the assumption that state or local governments tend to rely more heavily on taxes that can be exported outside the jurisdiction than taxes that cannot be exported, all else equal. Because of the lack of good measures of tax exporting, however, most studies rely on crude proxies to measure exporting, which limits the quality of the empirical work. One advance in a recent paper by Metcalf (1993) is the use of the National Bureau of Economic Research TAXSIM tax calculator to estimate individual tax prices. This at least refines the measurement of tax exporting through federal deductibility of state and local taxes. Metcalf is still restricted to crude measures of price/migration tax exporting, however.

An interesting contribution to the state tax choice literature is some work by Timothy Besley and Anne Case (1995) which examines copycatting behavior by states. They assume that state voters use information from neighboring states when deciding whether or not to reelect an incumbent governor. Besley and Case find that "voter are sensitive to the tax changes they face, relative to those observed in neighboring states, and that this sensitivity translates into votes against an incumbent whose tax changes are high by regional standards" (p. 36). States are copycats when the incumbent governor is planning to run again: according to their empirical results, when neighboring states increase (decrease) taxes by one dollar, the home state will increase (decrease) taxes by 20 cents.

Tax Diversity

Table 3.3 and Appendix Table 3.1 together provide some information about tax diversity in these four federal countries. Appendix

Table 1 shows the very large number of governments in the United States, many of which have independent taxing powers. Table 3.3 shows the range in top tax rates for major state taxes in Australia, Canada and the United States. Recall that most taxes are shared in Germany, which greatly diminishes the potential for tax diversity. In addition, the Canadian tax collection agreements enforce a significant degree of tax base uniformity, which is not illustrated in either table. Australian states are severely limited in their potential tax bases, so only the range in state payroll tax rates is shown in Table 3.3. After taking into account number of taxing authorities, potential tax bases, range in tax rates, and special institutions such as tax

Table 3.3: **Range in Top Tax Rates for Major Taxes of States of 3 Federal Countries**

	Australia	Canada	United States
Personal Income Tax	---	8.4 -- 27.03%	0 -- 12%
Corporate Income Tax	---	3.45 -- 10%	0 -- 12.25%
Retail Sales Tax	---	0 -- 12%	0 -- 7%
Payroll Tax	5 -- 12%	---	---

Source: Taryn A. Rounds. 1992.
Note: Data for Australia are from 1987-88, data for Canada are from 1989 and U.S. data are from 1991.

sharing and tax collection agreements, it is clear that tax diversity in the United States far exceeds that in Australia, Canada or Germany.

One consequence of intergovernmental tax diversity is higher administrative and compliance costs. Daniel Shaviro, who has written a book calling for greater uniformity in taxation among American governments, summarizes this problem as follows:

> The existence of multiple separate tax systems, each with its own set of rules and enforcement personnel, imposes a number of different costs on the national economy. It adds substantially to taxpayers' costs of tax planning and compliance. It increases the costs of tax administration, as each state hires its own bureaucracy and, in many cases, conducts its own audits and imposes its own reporting

requirements. It leads to more litigation, in the state courts as well as through federal constitutional challenges. It means that more legislative bodies spend time considering tax law changes and are lobbied by a host of different interests. *The aggregate costs* of all the tax planning, compliance, administration, litigation and politicking attributable to state and local taxation *cannot readily be estimated but are plainly enormous* (Italics added) (Shaviro 1993: 30).

Administration and compliance costs are particularly high for the state corporate income tax (See McLure 1980 and Strauss 1992). As multinational corporations grow in importance in our national economy, administration and compliance costs associated with the state corporation income tax are guaranteed to increase.

Another corollary of tax diversity is the possibility that tax differentials will create locational distortions. There has not been a great deal of discussion of such locational distortions, perhaps because of a long standing controversy regarding the extent to which taxes do influence business location decisions (McLure 1980: 344). In the United States, the number of econometric studies of the determinants of business location, including taxation as well as other factors, has mushroomed in recent years. Bartik (1991), who has compiled one of the most recent and comprehensive surveys of such studies, reviews 57 studies of interstate or interregional location and 14 studies of intraregional location, all published or released since 1979. Most researchers have concluded that at least for some industries, states, and time periods, taxes can influence location. They further agree that taxes have a greater impact on locational decisions within metropolitan areas than among states. Given economic trends that are likely to further enhance mobility of capital and businesses, locational distortions are likely to be magnified, in the absence of any policy changes that lead to reductions in interstate tax diversity.

Tax Competition[12]

Another important consequence of interstate tax diversity is tax competition. When there are multiple governments with independent tax powers, some degree of tax competition is inevitable. There are two major forms of tax competition: active rivalry and implicit competition. In active rivalry, governments consciously seek to export tax burdens to businesses and individuals in other states, or they use tax exemptions or abatements in order to attract businesses or high income individuals to their state. In implicit competition, states or local governments are constrained in their tax policies by the free movement of goods, services, people and capital. When a state decides not to pursue as progressive a tax policy as it would like because of the fear of driving businesses or individuals from the state, there is implicit tax competition.

Each of these federal countries has been concerned with tax competition among states or local governments at some time. In Australia, state death and gift taxes met their demise through apparent tax competition. Queensland abolished its death and gift taxes, and the remaining states subsequently abolished their death and gift taxes as well (Grossman 1990). Even in Germany, in which most taxes are levied jointly by the federal government and the states, commentators have argued:

> State parliaments have...nearly no possibility to raise taxes...It is widely agreed that this is not a satisfactory situation and it has therefore been suggested to change the federal constitution at least enabling states to decide on surcharge rates of income or wealth taxes. However, this could, it is feared, lead to fierce tax competition and rich states could be tempted to offer tax incentives to investors, whereas financially weak states would not be able to do this (Furkel, et al, 1991: 6).

However, tax competition is clearly a much more visible and contentious issue in the United States than in the other three federal countries considered. The form of tax competition that has received the most attention in the popular press is the crafting of special packages of tax abatements to particular firms to entice them to locate in particular states or cities. Journalists seem fond of reporting the apparently extravagant implicit prices paid per job gained by cities and states willing to engage in the tax abatement competition. Press coverage is also given to tax rivalries between neighboring states such as New York and lower tax New Jersey, or Massachusetts and its fiscally frugal neighbor, New Hampshire. Again, given the economic forces favoring greater mobility of taxpayers and resources, one should expect that tax competition will increase in the future, barring structural changes in U.S. fiscal federalism.

Tax Cooperation

Although tax cooperation receives much less attention than does tax competition, it does exist. In 1967, the U.S. Multistate Tax Commission was created to help increase coordination in corporate income taxation. The impetus behind organization of this commission was the difficulties states have had in taxing multistate and multinational corporations, and the particular concern that certain multistate and multinational corporations are able to escape state tax liability through astute use of tax laws, tax advice, and locational decisions. There has been some, limited success in this cooperation:

> ...this voluntary association has only nineteen members and fourteen associate members, and even they have not adopted a uniform tax code. Although thirty-three states employ a similar corporate-tax base, substantial diversity still exists in the definition of corporate income, in apportionment formulas, and in tax rates (Rounds 1992: 109).

There have been suggestions that joint state action should be taken a good deal further in reforming state tax systems. A recent report published by two influential state-local groups, the National Conference of State Legislatures and the National Governors' Association, proposes joint state action to solve the tax loophole created by sales taxation of mail order sales, or possible use of an interstate compact to enact a uniform state system of value added taxes (Snell 1993: 102-103).

Disparities in Tax Capacity

In a federal system, with a number of independent states, the issue of disparities in tax capacity among those states inevitably arises. Some states will have higher per capita incomes that others; some states will have more access to revenue from tourism or from severance taxes than others. Tax capacity is a measure developed by the U.S. Advisory Commission on Intergovernmental Relations to measure these differences (U.S. ACIR 1991). Tax capacity estimates the potential revenue-raising power of a state if the state were to levy taxes at the national average tax rate for a specified number of different tax bases.

Recent figures for the United States and Canada show that disparities in tax capacity are somewhat greater in the United States. In 1991, in the United States, the tax capacity in the state with the highest capacity (Alaska) was 2.6 times that of the state with the lowest tax capacity (Mississippi) (U.S. ACIR 1994: 182). If one discounts Alaska, because of its anomalous fiscal situation, the tax capacity of Hawaii (now the highest state) was 2.1 times that of Mississippi. In Canada, in 1989-90 the own-source tax capacity for Alberta (the province with the highest tax capacity) was 2.1 times that of Newfoundland (the province with the lowest tax capacity) (Hutchinson 1993: 161). In Canada, unlike the United States, a strong effort is made to equalize fiscal capacities of the provinces. After equalization grants, the fiscal capacity of Alberta was only 1.3 times that of Newfoundland (Hutchinson 1993: 161).

ROLE OF CENTRAL AND STATE GOVERNMENTS IN MONITORING HORIZONTAL TAX ISSUES

Although the sections above have divided intergovernmental tax policy issues between vertical and horizontal tax issues, in reality there is a great deal of overlap between the two. In particular, tax rules set by the central government affect state, and to a lesser degree, local tax policies. Likewise, states set the framework within which local tax policies are formed. Some of the ways in which the central government can affect state and local tax policies have been considered in sections above. For example, mandating tax sharing places restrictions on tax policies of lower levels of government. Likewise, tax collection agreements, although providing advantages for lower levels of government, also constrain allowable tax policies of those governments. In this section other means by which higher levels of government can place restrictions on tax policies of lower levels of government are discussed.

In the United States, federal deductibility of state and local taxes has traditionally played an important role in reducing interjurisdictional tax differentials and thus moderating horizontal tax competition. The central government can also use a tax credit to affect state tax policies. An interesting example in the United States is the tax credit against federal death (gift and estate) taxes for state estate taxes paid. "The federal tax code permits the decedent's estate to take a credit against estate taxes paid, up to certain amounts, based on the total size of the estate. All states have at least imposed a tax equal to the allowable credit. This tax is known as the "pickup" tax" (U.S. ACIR 1994: 153). That is, because imposing state estate tax liability up to the amount of the federal credit costs the state's taxpayer nothing, but effects an equal dollar reduction in federal tax liability and increase in state tax liability, the federal credit acts as a floor on state estate taxes across the U.S.

Finally, central governments can impose limits on taxes raised by states and local governments, while state governments can limit the tax powers of local governments. An example of the first type of limitation was noted above when discussing the limitations the Australian constitution places on state tax powers. The types of limits states in the U.S. place on local taxes include limitations on property tax rates, on property tax revenues, on property tax assessments and on general revenues (U.S. ACIR 1993: 20).

RECOMMENDATIONS FOR U.S. INTERGOVERNMENTAL TAX POLICY

My review of the intergovernmental tax structure of the U.S., compared to that of Australia, Canada and Germany, and synthesis of descriptive, prescriptive, theoretical and empirical literature leads me to these recommendations for U.S. intergovernmental tax policy in the 21st century:

1. The major problems with the current intergovernmental tax system are excessive diversity and an unproductive degree of tax competition. These problems are likely to worsen with increased economic integration of our global economy.

2. The federal government should not enact a tax reform package that would exacerbate the current problems in our intergovernmental tax system. Replacement of the federal income tax with a consumption tax would create additional problems by eliminating federal deductibility of state and local taxes and forcing states to "go it alone" with respect to income tax administration.

3. I don't believe there is any need for the U.S. to make a clear division between those taxes levied by federal, state and local governments. I find the arguments for sorting out tax sources by level of government to be unpersuasive.

4. There is a need to achieve greater uniformity in state and local tax policy. Solutions that are unlikely to be successful are: drastic solutions such as mandated tax sharing, purely voluntary solutions such as optional piggyback arrangements, and interstate tax compacts given the large number of governments that would have to be party to any effective agreement. My current favorite is an optional tax credit for states that agree to take part in a joint corporate tax collection agreement and forgo levying their own corporate income taxes. This would use a carrot rather than a stick, and work towards eliminating the state corporate income tax, probably the most troublesome of the current U.S. state-local taxes. A close runner up would be Rivlin's proposed enactment of a new national value added tax shared between the federal government and the states, but not replacing income taxes.

NOTES

1. Many thanks to Christine Collins and Lora Slomich for their valuable help as research assistants. I also appreciate the support and forbearance of my husband, Peter, and my daughter, Elizabeth, while I hid myself in my office to write this paper. I appreciate the helpful comments of Ronald Fisher and Michael Wolkoff on an earlier draft. I would also like to thank the Simmons College Fund for Research for supporting this work.

2. "Where once almost one in every two brokers or other securities industry workers was located here [Wall Street], now only one in every four is, the figures show. And where once 15 percent of all the insurance agents, adjusters and executives in the country worked here, now a mere 3 percent do (Gosselin 1996: 4).

3. Although I focus on four specific countries, issues of intergovernmental tax policy have a much broader applicability across the world, as government decentralization in developed, developing, and transition economies appears to be very much in vogue. At present, intergovernmental issues in transition economies that are teetering between growth and disaster appear most salient. As Christine Wallich states, "In most economies in transition, the design of fiscal federalism [including the design of tax systems] is crucial because it affects almost all of the key goals of reform, including macroeconomic stabilization, the effectiveness of the social safety net, and private sector development" (1994: 1-2).

4. Adam Smith's four maxims for taxation were: equality, certainty, convenience of payment, and economy in collection (Heilbroner 1986: 313-314). Smith's maxims are broadly similar to Musgrave and Musgrave's principles of a good tax system: revenue adequacy, equity, efficiency, facilitation of fiscal policy for stabilization and economic growth objectives, ease of administration, transparency to the taxpayer, and low compliance costs (1989: 216).

5. I use the terminology of different levels of government and of vertical tax issues vs. horizontal tax issues with some trepidation. I feel that it is more clear than any alternative descriptors I have found, but am aware that certain scholars strenuously object to any reference to levels of government in the federal system, particularly when referring to state and federal governments. Daniel Elazar argues that, "to the extent that those involved in governance now conceive of the American federal system as a pyramid with federal, state, and local 'levels,' they have opened the door to the

transformation of cooperative federalism into coercive federalism. In a hierarchy, the top is expected to have more authority and power that the middle or bottom. Such an arrangement contradicts the basic principles of federalism" (Elazar 1991: 72).

6. One could make the argument that the tax capacity issue also belongs among the list of vertical tax issues. This is because of the crucial role of the central government in either lessening or creating fiscal disparities among state and local governments. I have somewhat arbitrarily chosen to list tax capacity among the horizontal tax issues even though it has important vertical aspects.

7. Throughout the paper, when I am speaking of federal countries generally, I speak of state and local governments, despite the fact that middle level governments in some countries are not called states. In Germany, middle level governments are called laender, and in Canada, they are called provinces.

8. A more recent article by Marlow, finds that expenditure decentralization in the United States from 1946 to 1985 has a statistically significantly negative effect on government expenditure as a share of GNP and annual growth in total government expenditure as a share of GNP (Marlow 1988).

9. One dissenter to this statement is Timothy Goodspeed, who found in one paper that "the efficiency loss that would result from migration induced by local ability to pay taxation is likely to be quite small for the United States" (Goodspeed 1989 as quoted in Goodspeed 1990: 1). He found in another paper that local governments in some countries do levy income taxes, contrary to conventional advice, and that such fiscal choice may make sense depending upon: "different views concerning the importance of intra- as opposed to intercommunity redistribution, different demands for redistribution regardless of the level of government, and different costs in terms of the trade-offs between equity and efficiency at the local level" (Goodspeed 1990: 2).

10. But for a comprehensive and scathing criticism of the current infatuation with movement to a consumption tax see Strauss (1995).

11. This draws extensively from U.S. ACIR 1991: 36-37.

12. Some of this section follows U.S. ACIR 1991 closely.

REFERENCES

Bahl, Roy. "Revenues and Revenue Assignment: Intergovernmental Fiscal Relations in the Russian Federation." In *Russia and the Challenge of Fiscal Federalism,* edited by Christine I. Wallich. Washington, D.C.: The World Bank, 1994.

Bartik, Timothy J. *Who Benefits from State and Local Economic Development Policies?* Kalamazoo, Michigan: W.E. Upjohn Institute for Employment Research, 1991.

Besley, Timothy and Anne Case. "Incumbent Behavior: Vote-Seeking, Tax-Setting, and Yardstick Competition." *The American Economic Review* 85 No. 1 (March 1995): 25-45.

Bird, Richard M. *Federal Finance in Comparative Perspective.* Toronto: Canadian Tax Foundation, 1986.

Boadway, Robin W. and Paul A.R. Hobson. *Intergovernmental Fiscal Relations in Canada.* Toronto: Canadian Tax Foundation, 1993.

Break, George F. *Financing Government in a Federal System.* Washington, D.C.: The Brookings Institution, 1980.

Breton, Albert. "Toward a Theory of Competitive Federalism." *European Journal of Political Economy 3* No. 1 + 2 (1987):263-329.

Dye, Richard F. and Therese J. McGuire. "Growth and Variability of State Individual Income and General Sales Taxes." *National Tax Journal* 44 No. 1 (March 1991): 55-66.

Dye, Thomas R. *American Federalism: Competition Among Governments.* Lexington, MA: Lexington Books, 1990.

Elazar, Daniel. "Cooperative Federalism." In *Competition Among States and Local Governments: Efficiency and Equity in American Federalism,* edited by Daphne A. Kenyon and John Kincaid. Washington, D.C.: The Urban Institute Press, 1991.

Feenberg, Daniel R. and Harvey S. Rosen. "Tax Structure and Public Sector Growth." *Journal of Public Economics* 32 (1987): 185-201.

Fisher, Ronald C. *State and Local Public Finance.* Chicago: Irwin, 1996.

Furkel, Rudiger, Wolfgang Forster, Dieter Carl, and Roland Kramer. "Background Paper" provided for the Colloquium on Intergovernmental Fiscal Relations hosted by the Saarland Ministry of Finance, Saarbrucken, Germany, November 8-9, 1991.

Gade, Mary N. and Lee C. Adkins. "Tax Exporting and State Revenue Structures." *National Tax Journal* 43 No. 1 (March 1990): 39-52.

Gold, Steven D. "The Income Elasticity of State Tax Systems: New Evidence." New York: Center for the Study of the States, The Nelson A. Rockefeller Institute of Government, State University of New York, April 1995.

Goodspeed, Timothy J. "A Re-Examination of the Use of Ability to Pay Taxes by Local Governments." *Journal of Public Economics* 38 (1989): 319-342.

Goodspeed, Timothy J. "The Assignment of Ability to Pay Taxes in the OECD Countries: Different Approaches to Redistribution." Presented to the International Institute of Public Finance, 46th Congress, Brussels, 27-30 August, 1990.

Gosselin, Peter G. "Wall Street Hits the Wall: As Financial World Spins, Leading Firms Depart the Nation's Economic Capital." *Boston Globe*, June 28, 1996, pp. 1,4.

Government of the District of Columbia, Department of Finance and Revenue. *Tax Rates and Tax Burdens in the District of Columbia: A Nationwide Comparison.* Washington, D.C.: June 1994.

Groenewegen, Peter. "Tax Assignment and Revenue Sharing in Australia." In *Tax Assignment in Federal Countries,* edited by Charles E. McLure, Jr. Canberra: Centre for Research on Federal Financial Relations, The Australian National University, 1983.

Grossman, Philip J. "Fiscal Competition Among States in Australia: The Demise of Death Duties." *Publius: The Journal of Federalism 20* (Fall 1990): 145-159.

Heilbroner, Robert L, ed. *The Essential Adam Smith.* Oxford: Oxford University Press, 1986.

Hettich, Walter and Stanley Winer. "A Positive Model of Tax Structure." *Journal of Public Economics 24* (June 1984): 67-87.

Hutchinson, Gladstone. "The Budget Process and Fiscal Federalism in Canada." In *Public Sector Budgets: A Comparative Study,* edited by Attiat F. Ott. Brookfield, Vermont: Edward Elgar, 1993.

International Monetary Fund, *Government Finance Statistics Yearbook 1995.* Washington, D.C.: International Monetary Fund, 1995.

KPMG Peat Marwick Policy Economics Group. "A Study of the New Hampshire State and Local Revenue Structure." Washington, D.C.: February 13, 1992.

Kenyon, Daphne A. and John Kincaid, eds. *Competition Among States and Local Governments: Efficiency and Equity in American Federalism.* Washington, D.C.: The Urban Institute Press, 1991.

Kenyon, Daphne A. and John Kincaid. "Fiscal Federalism in the United States: The Reluctance to Equalize Jurisdictions." Draft, October 30, 1991.

Krelove, Russell. "Efficient Tax Exporting." *Canadian Journal of Economics 25* No. 1 (February 1992): 145-55.

McCarty, Tanette Nguyen, and Thomas H. Marks. "The Use of Microsimulation Models for Policy Analysis: The New York State Personal Income Tax." In *Proceedings of the Eighty-Sixth Annual Conference on Taxation, 179-185. Columbus, Ohio: National Tax Association-Tax Institute of America, 1993.*

McLure, Charles E., Jr. "The Elusive Incidence of the Corporate Income Tax: The State Case." *Public Finance Quarterly 9 (October 1981): 395-413.*

McLure, Charles E., Jr. "Introduction: The Revenue Side of the Assignment Problem." In *Tax Assignment in Federal Countries,* edited by Charles E. McLure, Jr. Canberra: Centre for Research on Federal Financial Relations, The Australian National University, 1983a.

McLure, Charles E., Jr., ed. *Tax Assignment in Federal Countries.* Canberra: Centre for Research on Federal Financial Relations, The Australian National University, 1983b.

McLure, Charles E., Jr. "Assignment of Corporate Income Taxes in a Federal System." In *Tax Assignment in Federal Countries,* edited by Charles E. McLure, Jr. Canberra: Centre for Research on Federal Financial Relations, The Australian National University, 1983c.

McLure, Charles E., Jr. "A North American View of Vertical Imbalance and the Assignment of Taxing Powers." In *Vertical Fiscal Imbalance and the Allocation of Taxing Powers,* edited by D.J. Collins. Sydney: The Australian Tax Research Foundation, 1993.

McLure, Charles E., Jr. "The State Corporate Income Tax: Lambs in Wolves' Clothing." In Henry J. Aaron and Michael J. Boskin, eds. *The Economics of Taxation.* Washington, D.C.: The Brookings Institution, 1980: 327-346.

Maine Municipal Association. *The State of Maine's Municipalities 1993.* Augusta: Maine Municipal Association, 1993.

Marlow, Michael L. "Fiscal Decentralization and Government Size." *Public Choice* 56 (1988): 259-269.

Metcalf, Gilbert E. "Tax Exporting, Federal Deductibility, and State Tax Structure." *Journal of Policy Analysis and Management 12* No. 1 (Winter 1993): 109-35.

Musgrave, Richard A. "Who Should Tax, Where, and What?" In *Tax Assignment in Federal Countries,* edited by Charles E. McLure, Jr. Canberra: Centre for Research on Federal Financial Relations, The Australian National University, 1983.

Musgrave, Richard A. and Musgrave, Peggy B. *Public Finance in Theory and Practice.* New York: McGraw Hill, 1989.

Nechyba, Thomas J. "Tax Base Assignments in a Federal System." Presented at the Eighty-Eighth Annual Conference on Taxation, Sponsored by the National Tax Association, San Diego, CA, October 8-10, 1995.

Nowotny, Ewald. "Tax Assignment and Revenue Sharing in the Federal Republic of Germany and Switzerland." In *Tax Assignment in Federal Countries,* edited by Charles E. McLure, Jr. Canberra: Centre for Research on Federal Financial Relations, The Australian National University, 1983.

Oates, Wallace E. "'Automatic' Increases in Tax Revenue---the Effect on the Size of the Public Budget," in Wallace E. Oates, ed., *Financing the New Federalism.* Baltimore: Johns Hopkins, 1975: 139-60.

Oates, Wallace E. *Fiscal Federalism.* New York: Harcourt Brace Jovanovich, 1972.

Oates, Wallace E. "Searching for Leviathan: An Empirical Study." *American Economic Review* 75 (September 1985): 748-758.

Organization for Economic Cooperation and Development, *Revenue Statistics of OECD Member Countries, 1965-1992.* Paris: Organization for Economic Cooperation and Development, 1993.

Ott, Attiat F. *Public Sector Budgets: A Comparative Study.* Brookfield, Vermont: Edward Elgar, 1993.

Phares, Donald. *Who Pays State and Local Taxes?* Cambridge, Massachusetts: Oelgeschlager, Gunn and Hain, 1980.

Plesko, George. "Assessing Maine's Tax Data and Modeling Needs and Capabilities." In *A Preliminary Outlook on Maine Tax Policy,* edited by Daphne A. Kenyon, George Plesko, Roy Kelly, and Therese McGuire, mimeo, September 21, 1995.

Rivlin, Alice M. *Reviving the American Dream: The Economy, the States and the Federal Government.* Washington, D.C.: The Brookings Institution, 1992.

Rounds, Taryn A. "Tax Harmonization and Tax Competition: Contrasting Views and Policy Issues in Three Federal Countries." *Publius: The Journal of Federalism 22* No. 4 (Fall 1992): 91-120.

Rubinfeld, Daniel. "Tax Assignment and Revenue Sharing in the United States. In *Tax Assignment in Federal Countries,* edited by Charles E. McLure, Jr. Canberra: Centre for Research on Federal Financial Relations, The Australian National University, 1983.

Schumacher, Ute. "Fiscal Federalism in the Federal Republic of Germany." In *Public Sector Budgets: A Comparative Study,* edited by Attiat F. Ott. Brookfield, Vermont: Edward Elgar, 1993.

Shannon, John. "Federalism's Invisible Regulator--Intergovernmental Competition." In Daphne A. Kenyon and John Kincaid, eds. *Competition Among States and Local Governments: Efficiency and Equity in American Federalism.* Washington, D.C.: The Urban Institute Press, 1991.

Shaviro, Daniel. *Federalism in Taxation: The Case for Greater Uniformity.* Washington, D.C.: The AEI Press, 1993.

Sjoquist, David L. "A Median Voter Analysis of Variations in the Use of Property Taxes Among Local Governments." *Public Choice 36* (1981): 273-285.

Snell, Ronald, ed. *Financing State Government in the 1990s.* Washington, D.C.: National Conference of State Legislatures, December 1993.

Strauss, Robert P. "The Effects of a Flat Federal Consumption Tax on the States." Presented at the 88th Annual Conference on Taxation, National Tax Association, San Diego, CA, October 8, 1995.

Strauss, Robert P. "Federal Collection of State Corporate Income Taxes." In Thomas F. Pogue, ed., *State Taxation of Business: Issues and Policy Options.* Westport, Connecticut: Praeger, 1992: 69-87.

Tannenwald, Robert. "The Changing Level and Mix of Federal Aid to State and Local Governments." *New England Economic Review* (May/June 1989).

Tanzi, Vito. *Taxation in an Integrating World.* Washington, D.C.: The Brookings Institution, 1995.

The Economist. "The Revolution Begins, at Last." September 30, 1995: 15.

Thirsk, Wayne R. "Tax Assignment and Revenue Sharing in Canada." In *Tax Assignment in Federal Countries,* edited by Charles E. McLure, Jr. Canberra: Centre for Research on Federal Financial Relations, The Australian National University, 1983.

U.S. Advisory Commission on Intergovernmental Relations. *Studies in Comparative Federalism: Australia, Canada, The United States and Germany.* Washington, D.C.: November 1981.

U.S. Advisory Commission on Intergovernmental Relations. *Intergovernmental Tax and Policy Competition: Good or Bad for the Federal System?* Washington, D.C.: 1991.

U.S. Advisory Commission on Intergovernmental Relations. *RTS 1991: State Revenue Capacity and Effort.* Washington, D.C.: 1993.

U.S. Advisory Commission on Intergovernmental Relations. *Significant Features of Fiscal Federalism, Vol. 1.* Washington, D.C.: 1993, 1994, and 1995.

Vaillancourt, Francois. "Subnational Tax Harmonization, Canada and the United States: Intent, Results, and Consequences." In *Canada-U.S. Tax Comparisons,* edited by John B. Shoven and John Whalley. Chicago, The University of Chicago Press, 1992.

Wallich, Christine I., ed. *Russia and the Challenge of Fiscal Federalism.* Washington, D.C.: The World Bank, 1994.

Walsh, Cliff. "An Economic Perspective." In *Australian Federalism,* edited by Brian Galligan. Melbourne: Longman Cheshire, 1989.

Walsh, Cliff. "Vertical Fiscal Imbalance: The Issues." In *Vertical Fiscal Imbalance and the Allocation of Taxing Powers,* edited by D.J. Collins. Sydney: The Australian Tax Research Foundation, 1993.

Zimmerman, Dennis. "Resource Misallocation from Interstate Tax Exportation: Estimates of Excess Spending and Welfare Loss in a Median Voter Framework." *National Tax Journal 37* No. 2 (June 1983): 183-201.

Appendix Table 3.1: Number of Government Units

	Australia	Canada	Germany	United States
State	8	10	16	50
Local	900	8,000	16,100	86,692

Sources: *Statistical Abstract of the United States, 1995,* p. 297, and International Monetary Fund, *Government Finance Statistics Yearbook 1995*, pp. 645, 660, and 683.

Note: German data are after reunification.

4 TRANSFERS IN FEDERAL SYSTEMS: A CRITICAL SURVEY

Jeffrey Petchey, Perry Shapiro and Cliff Walsh

INTRODUCTION

Federations are characterized by an extensive and usually complex system of grants from their central (federal) governments to otherwise autonomous sub-national governments. Many of these transfers are purely redistributive while others are designed to stimulate additional subnational spending in certain functional areas, such as education and health. The transfers may be aimed at providing equity or economic efficiency, but they are commonly influenced by purely political considerations as well. For this reason there is a wide divergence between what the fiscal federalism literature has to say about what grants should be made on economic grounds and what actually occurs in practice. Nevertheless, the literature identifies three instances where transfers are justified.

The first is based on the view that because of certain advantages in having centralized tax systems, combined with advantages from decentralized expenditure decisions, a fiscal gap, defined here as an excess of revenue collections by the center over what it needs for its own purposes, is optimal. This, in turn, necessitates that lump sum, unconditional, tax reimbursement grants be made by the center although in practice some form of revenue sharing is often utilized. The second is based on the premise that sub-national expenditures generate externalities unaccounted for by states resulting in inefficiency and under or over - provision of public goods. It is argued that in these circumstances specific purpose, open ended and matching grants can be used by the central government to ensure that states expand (contract) provision of such goods to the socially optimal level. The third is based on the belief that centrally mandated interstate transfers can promote both equity and efficiency. These 'fiscal equalization' transfers should be lump-sum.

US writers rely, to a large extent, on externality arguments to prescribe specific purpose, open ended, matching transfers. They have been much less concerned about fiscal gaps and inter-regional efficiency and equity arguments for transfers. Because of the apparent concern for externalities, the US literature has tended to concentrate on issues surrounding such transfers, in particular, whether the matching rates are appropriate (see Gramlich 1985). This is in contrast to Canada and Australia where there has been much greater concern with the equity and efficiency cases for equalization transfers, and fiscal gap considerations.

The literature on transfers is vast and we cannot hope to provide a comprehensive analysis of all the relevant arguments in the space available. Therefore, while we attempt to make mention of the major results to be found in the literature for completeness, we concentrate on three issues which, we believe, have received less attention but which are, nevertheless, of considerable importance.

First, we argue that while the literature has presented a case for specific purpose transfers based on externalities, in practice such transfers have also been used by central governments to exert a general influence over expenditure decisions made by the states. We argue this using Australia as an illustrative example and examine the way that the center, the Commonwealth Government, has used specific purpose transfers to facilitate a centralization of expenditure powers well beyond what was ever intended at federation and the division of powers implied by the Australian Constitution. In other words, specific purpose transfers have been used to shift the balance of expenditure powers.

Second, we provide a critique of some of the latest ideas on equalization transfers and in particular whether states would undertake voluntary equalization. We emphasize equalization transfers, first, because they have become so controversial in Australia which has the most comprehensive system of horizontal fiscal equalization in the world, second, because they are also very important in Canada, and third, because although the US does not have an explicit system of equalization, it can be argued that the implicit aim of transfers from the center to the states is to redistribute between states (since this is what they seem to do). In discussing equalizing transfers we mention not only the traditional equity and efficiency cases but also discuss some relatively unconventional rationales for inter-state redistribution, such as compensation for the effects of federation and citizenship/ nationhood arguments.

The outline is as follows. Section 2 discusses the fiscal gap argument for untied tax reimbursement grants. Section 3 examines specific purpose open - ended transfers while Section 4 looks at fiscal equalization. Conclusions are presented in Section 5.

UNCONDITIONAL TAX REIMBURSEMENT TRANSFERS

The rationale for untied tax reimbursement transfers rests on analysis of the tax and expenditure assignment issue. Specifically, it is argued that tax powers should be relatively centralized and expenditure powers relatively decentralized so that the central government collects more revenue than it needs for its own expenditures and distributes the surplus through lump-sum unconditional grants to the states who collect less revenue than they need to discharge their spending obligations. The difference between what is raised at the central level and what is required by the center for federal expenditures is known as the optimal fiscal gap . We now briefly examine the case for an optimal fiscal gap, fiscal gaps in practice and how they affect state behavior.

The argument for centralized tax powers rests on the following. First, it is claimed that most of the major tax bases are highly mobile across states, and state taxes are inherently inefficient because of problems caused by tax competition and tax exporting. Second, it is argued that centralizing taxes yields benefits because of scale economies from national collection of revenues. Third, it is argued that the center needs to have control of certain major tax instruments for macroeconomic policy. Finally, some have suggested that the center needs control over major tax bases to enable it to undertake primary responsibility for income redistribution, which it is argued, if left to the states, will be sub-optimal because of migration externalities (see Gordon 1983, Wildasin 1991).

With regard to expenditure powers, it is commonly argued that if there are significant externalities the center should undertake provision. This is based on the premise that the center is beneficent and able to implement fully efficient outcomes. On the other hand, it is argued that if externalities are limited, and there is considerable inter-state diversity in terms of preferences or incomes, then subnational provision is preferable (see Oates 1972, Gordon 1983).

The case for centralizing tax powers is seen to be much stronger than the case for centralizing expenditure powers. Accordingly, the usual recommendation is that tax powers be relatively centralized while expenditure powers be relatively decentralized. As noted above, a consequence is that there will be a fiscal gap, that is, the center will have an excess of revenue over expenditure. This surplus must be returned to the states as unconditional tax reimbursement grants and in most federations such transfers are made.

But as pointed out by Boadway and Keen (1994), because of the complexities of modeling interaction between levels of government almost nothing has been done to measure the size of the optimal fiscal gap, and hence the optimal lump-sum transfers needed to support such a gap. This is despite the rather extensive literature on the role and structure of intergovernmental grants. They take a preliminary step in this direction and model the relative efficiency of raising taxes at the different levels of government. Brennan and Pincus (1994) also do this by analyzing the fiscal gap using analogous considerations.

It seems to us that this is an important line of continuing research. However, measuring an optimal fiscal gap is only part of the broader research agenda aimed at determining what powers to centralize and what powers to decentralize (an issue that is again addressed below).

Regardless of the theoretical arguments about fiscal gaps, they exist in practice more from the historical assignments of tax and spending powers in constitutional arrangements and the subsequent policy evolution of taxing powers to the center and expenditure responsibility to the states. For example, in the Australian federation most indirect taxes, such as the sales and excise tax, and the income tax power, rest exclusively with the central government. As a consequence, the states rely on a range of relatively inefficient taxes. They have no access to the income tax base and only very restricted access to a few indirect taxes. However, the states still have responsibility for major spending programs in health, education, law and order and public infrastructure .

This combination of centralized tax powers and decentralized tax powers means that there is a relatively large fiscal gap in Australia that has evolved as a consequence of the centralization of taxing powers rather than any appeal to theoretical ideas about tax and spending assignment. There is also in Australia a large transfer of surplus revenue to the states, and this is the case in most federations. We do not go into differences in fiscal gaps across countries here. These results are well-known and for further analysis see Walsh (1993).

There is also a literature on the effect that reimbursement transfers have on the expenditure decisions of states. For a discussion of these arguments, all of which show how recipient behavior is distorted by such grants, see Walsh and Petchey (1992). One argument is that such transfers create inefficiencies through a flypaper effect. The anomaly is that economic theory suggests that lump sum grants from the federal government to states are equivalent to an exogenous increase in state income. As such, the fractional changes in state public spending caused by the grants depend on the income elasticity of public expenditure demand, the fractional increase in income and the tax price. Gramlich (1977) found that predictions based on these theoretical considerations were grossly below the actual outcome. Lump sum grants appear to have an effect 40 to 50 percent greater than predicted by the theory. The explanation proffered by Gramlich was that state public expenditures were attracted to and stuck to the federal grant: thus the flypaper effect.

One explanation for this conflict between theory and empirical results is that voters are subject to fiscal illusion: they do not see the link between the taxes they pay and the grants that come back to the state from the center. Other explanations are, one, bureaucrats have an incentive to over-expand spending in response to central government grants, two, the relatively high excess burdens of state and local taxes predispose states to spend relatively more from unconditional grants and, finally, the evidence is not inconsistent with theory when general equilibrium effects are accounted for (see King 1984 for discussion).

Brennan and Pincus (1991) have argued that while there are no explicit conditions attached to unconditional grants, suggesting that they should be treated as lump sum transfers, there are implicit conditions because of the presence of implicit contracts between donors and recipients. What appear to be unconditional tax reimbursement grants, are actually conditional grants and have a substitution as well as an income effect that explain the flypaper result. This analysis highlights the importance of public choice theory to explain the effects of grants on recipient government behavior.

SPECIFIC PURPOSE, OPEN ENDED MATCHING TRANSFERS

The existence of spillovers or externalities created by subnational decisions is cited in the conventional fiscal federalism argument in support of specific purpose, open ended, matching grants. In particular, if the provision of local public goods involves benefit spillovers unrealized by the decision-making state and, thus, not taken into account, then national under-provision is the result. An equilibrium in which local public goods are under provided in the presence of benefit spillovers is often characterized as an inefficient Nash equilibrium.

Inefficient non - cooperative equilibria are used to justify a role for the central government. It can provide open ended and targeted matching grants to the states in which the center gives a grant of $x if the state also provides $y to be spent on a particular local public good such as health, education or other public infrastructure. As a result, the relative price of the specific local public good is reduced. Such grants create an income effect, which tends to expand consumption of all goods at the state level because the states are free to pass on the benefits of a transfer to citizens as tax cuts, but also a substitution effect that tends to cause spending to switch in favor of the public good in question. If the grant is optimally designed, it encourages increased provision to an extent that just offsets the tendency of states towards under-provision through strategic behavior (in the case of positive externalities).[1]

But in practice specific purpose matching grants have also been used by central governments to exert a more general control over state behavior in order to centralize decision-making power, not simply to take account of externalities. We now illustrate this by discussing the Australian experience with conditional transfers and centralization. We believe this story is of general interest as it highlights a public choice rationale for such transfers. Australia is also an interesting contrast to what appears to be happening in Canada, which is currently decentralizing some powers. In the US too, the Republican majority in Congress has a program of devolving powers to the states.

In the last century, the Australian states have lost two important tax powers: excise and income taxes. Customs and excise powers were relinquished to the Commonwealth at federation in 1901 (see Section 90 of the Constitution). But the intended meaning of excise was not made clear. As a consequence, the Australian High Court has interpreted it broadly, thus baring states from the use of any sales taxes.[2] This interpretation of excise has been highly contentious in Australia. Whatever the theoretical debate, the practical implication is that it has kept the states out of much of the indirect tax base.

Compounding the problem of state autonomy is the absence of a state income tax as well. In 1942 federal legislation granted the Commonwealth the sole authority to impose income taxes for the duration of World War II, and one year thereafter. This legislation invalidated all state income taxes and established a uniform Commonwealth income tax across all states, which remains in force today. Although there have been several legal challenges to this legislation by the states, all have been unsuccessful.

However, most expenditure powers remain relatively decentralized. Section 51 of the Australian Constitution gives about forty powers to the Commonwealth. All powers not listed in Section 51 are, by implication, left to the states as a residual although they are not specified explicitly as other constitutions. This effectively gives the states responsibility for big spending items such as education, health, law and order, and public infrastructure.

With highly centralized tax powers and relatively decentralized spending powers, Australia has the largest fiscal gap of all the major federations. In addition, because of High Court decisions the central government is able to attach any conditions to the large transfers necessitated by this fiscal gap, whether or not such conditions have anything to do with the center's constitutional powers.

At first only light use was made of this flexibility. But starting in the 1960s there came a considerable expansion of specific purpose transfers to

106

the states in line with the more general growth in the relative size of the public sector that occurred in most western economies during this time. Indeed, this growth in conditional transfers has continued unabated, at least in Australia, since then. Specific purpose transfers as a proportion of total payments to the states have increased from 25% in the early 1960s to 55% in 1993-94. There are now extensive Commonwealth and state bureaucracies devoted to conditional transfers, and their extensive coverage is a contentious issue in state-federal relations.

The end result is that in Australia the size and pattern of conditional transfers bears little relationship to externalities, a situation that is also found in many other federations, the US included. Thus, although externalities stand in the theoretical literature as the justification for conditional grants, in practice they have served other purposes. Principally, they have been used to secure a general shift in t};e distribution of power over spending and public policy - making in favor of central governments regardless of constitutional assignments of such powers.

This has led some people to question conditional transfers and the general centralization process at work in federations. For example, Petchey and Shapiro (1994) have examined the economic costs of this 'back-door' centralization. In a model of a federation where states provide local public goods with externalities, preferences differ within and between states and there are informational constraints so that states and central governments act inefficiently, the welfare effects of three policy regimes, including non-cooperative state provision, cooperative provision by states in treaty arrangements and, finally, centralization, are examined. They argue that excessive centralization, aided by conditional transfers, can create conflicts between state and national interests and a loss of self-determination by states.[3]

Therefore, while there may be theoretical justifications, based on the presence of externalities, for centrally mandated specific purpose transfers from the center to the states, in practice there are other reasons why such transfers are made. They have also been used to achieve back door centralization of expenditure powers and hence get around constitutional and other limitations on the reach of central powers. If the centralization that occurs through the use of specific purpose transfers creates costs such as loss of self-determination by states, then we may need to rethink arguments suggesting that they have a purely efficiency enhancing role (the externality argument). Indeed, the costs of losing self-determination at the sub-national level (assuming there are any) must be weighed against any benefit that such transfers yield in terms of correcting for externalities.

INTER-STATE REDISTRIBUTION (EQUALIZATION)

In many federations, particular importance is attached to transfers designed to achieve horizontal fiscal equalization. Equalization transfers are administered as stand alone interjurisdictional grant programs (through the auspices of the federal government as in Canada, or directly between states as in Germany), as well as adjustments to states' shares of grants within revenue sharing arrangements. The transfers are meant to facilitate nationally uniform assessment, administration and collection for major taxes (as is explicitly the case in Germany, and implicitly so in Australia). The fiscal equalization payments are intended to transfer resources between sub-national jurisdictions ("states") to ensure that they all have the capacity to provide similar standards of services with similar tax burdens.

The degree to which "fiscal equalization" is achieved or attempted in different federal systems reflects unique societal values. These, in turn, are reflected in different practices and procedures for assessing and implementing equalization transfers. In particular, there is considerable variation in the degree of attachment to the independence and autonomy of subnational governments and the degree of tolerance of differences in outcomes between regions, and between individuals in different regions.

The standard economics literature on federalism and fiscal equalization pays little attention to these differences in values. The case for decentralization of fiscal decision-making and equalization of fiscal capacities that emerges in the literature reflects a recognition of differences in preferences for service levels or qualities, not of differences in preferences for political structures or administrative procedures. Most of the literature reviewed in the following survey ignores a number of practical and political issues that influence decisions about fiscal equalization procedures. To the extent that these issues are overlooked, the review is limited in perspective.

Even within its own economics-oriented perspective the extant literature should be regarded with caution. Much of the economics literature on fiscal equalization, like other aspects of the fiscal federalism literature, is based on a presumption that federalism and fiscal decentralization in otherwise unitary systems are analytically equivalent. From this perspective the central issue is to identify what intervention (e.g. through central government taxes or grants) might be required to correct for efficiency and equity distortions inherent in the decentralization of some fiscal decisions in an otherwise unitary system.

In our view, this perspective is misleading. Federations can be thought of as a compact between autonomous political units to create a central government to which certain powers are ceded to secure the benefits of economic, fiscal, social and political union. Principal among these benefits are the creation of a common system of defense and foreign relations, the creation of a customs union and single economic market, and the building of a common sense of nationhood and of shared (but dual) citizenship, while allowing independent and potentially diverse decisions over policy development and the levels and patterns of service delivery in a range of functional spending areas at the sub-national level. Although it is subject to potential misinterpretation, the slogan "unity in diversity" captures something of the flavor of the proclaimed benefits of a federal system.

Even where the initial formation of the federal compact is subject to the will of the people (as also may be subsequent changes to it, e.g. through referendums), the federal system exists and operates as a set of dealings and relationships between governments, each autonomous in their own agreed sphere. Correspondingly, political and procedural phenomena such as the provision for interjurisdictional equalization transfers need to be seen and understood to be inherently associated with the conditions necessary for the existence and stability of the federal compact, and for securing the benefits to the nation from its existence, as much as about interpersonal equity and individual efficiency.

This does not mean that comparisons with unitary systems, and analysis of the consequences of fiscal decentralization within them, are irrelevant. Federal systems represent an alternative way of achieving the efficiencies (economic, fiscal and political) perceived to attach to the formation of unitary nation-states from formerly independent political units while preserving the advantages of subnational autonomy. This makes the benefits and efficiencies achieved through the unitary alternative an appropriate benchmark for assessing the value and virtues of federal arrangements. But in the end, it is the value and the virtue of the differences between federal and unitary systems that really are at issue and, to evaluate them, federal systems have to be seen as being much more than just unitary systems with fiscal decentralization.

In this connection, it is important to observe that in unitary systems a great deal of interregional fiscal equalization occurs— indeed, on some estimates more so than in the major federations. But much of it is different from the formula-based interjurisdictional transfers that dominate the fiscal equalization literature. In highly centralized unitary systems, central governments use uniformly applied national taxation systems (e.g. income tax) to fund not only uniform provision of national public goods and services, such as defense and foreign relations, and welfare benefits, but also to fund broadly uniform access to many of the public services such as education, health and hospitals, law and order that are the province of autonomous subnational governments in federal systems. Centralized provision of these services in unitary systems is a way to ensure broadly equal access to them for residents of all regions. This leads to potentially significant implicit transfers between states that have different average per capita taxable capacities (e.g. because average per capita incomes differ or because of different costs of service provision). Brosio (1992) has estimated that in Australia these implicit transfers exceed in magnitude explicit equalization transfers.

In practice, of course, even unitary systems decentralize at least administrative provision of services, and often (and increasingly) give a degree of autonomy in decision-making to regional governments over the delivery of services. In some cases, the funding of local governments from a mixture of local taxes and central government grants involves a degree of limitation on local discretion, which ensures that the system as a whole remains essentially centralized unitary. In this event, an explicit (comprehensive) equalization component usually will be contained in central government grants, often combined with strict guidelines about service delivery standards. Even where a greater degree of regional or local discretion in the levels or patterns of service delivery is permitted, unitary systems with fiscal decentralization can be expected to put considerably more emphasis on equalization grant arrangements than in federal systems. This, again, makes the conventional horizontal equity and locational efficiency arguments more directly and immediately relevant to them.

In federal systems, by comparison, the autonomy of sub-national governments over functional areas within their agreed spheres, the capacity for diversity of outcomes in their autonomous political choices, and the innovation and competition in policy development and service delivery are essential and highly valued features of political and fiscal arrangements. The central concern in the design of fiscal equalization arrangements is to preserve autonomy and the capacity for diversity and incentives for productive policy innovation, while ensuring that differences in outcomes are the consequence of political choices that reflect differences in preferences, not the consequence of unacceptable differences in fiscal capacities among subnational jurisdictions.

In the analysis that follows we emphasize the essential features of federal systems while presenting the conventional arguments about the inefficiencies and inequities of decentralized decision making and we assess these arguments against the background of an understanding and assessment of arguments that go to the very heart of questions about the conditions necessary for the existence, stability and vitality of federal systems. What emerges is a strong emphasis on the role of interjurisdictional equalization transfers in the formation of federal unions. The transfers may also meet the requirements of common citizenship and nationhood that are a vital component of the federal solution.

Our detailed analysis starts with a view of federations as compacts between member-states to form a unifying federal government to which certain powers are ceded. Simultaneously, responsibility for a wide range of functional policy areas is reserved (either as a residual, or explicitly) to the member-states, whose powers in these regards remain fully autonomous, protected by a constitution and a constitutional court. Usually this involves a clearer division of powers over expenditure and regulatory functions than over taxation and other forms of revenue raising, which must be shared in order to sustain the autonomy of both the federal and state spheres.

We begin with the compact itself, and the possibility that a federal stability case for interjurisdictional transfers may exist, both to secure federation in the first place and to maintain it in effective operation. The collection of arguments that make up the nationhood/citizenship case considered next focus on suggestions that equalization is required to ensure the financial independence of states. We then turn to consider a case that provides a rationale based on the need for a degree of economic convergence and social cohesion in federal systems. Finally, we examine the inter-state equity and efficiency in migration cases for equalizing transfers and draw a link between these arguments and the federal stability case.

Federal Stability

One of the more important branches of the fiscal federalism literature deals with why we might wish to have federal-type structures. This issue usually has been addressed by asking why decentralization of functions should take place within a mature centralized nation-state. Important contributions to this literature have been made by Stigler (1957), with his menu approach, and Oates (1972), who developed the notion of perfect correspondence and the related decentralization theorem. In addition to these ideas, the theory of club goods has something to tell us about optimal jurisdiction formation (Cornes and Sandler, 1986). There are arguments in favor of decentralization that rely on appeals to imperfect information on the part of the central government over local preferences: the idea that local governments are closer to the people and know their preferences better (Oates, 1972 and Tresch, 1988). Yet another case, put forward by Brennan and Buchanan (1980), is that decentralization limits the power of governments in the interests of citizen-voters by introducing inter-governmental competition. For an overview and discussion of all these arguments see Tresch (1981) and Walsh and Petchey (1992).

While a detailed discussion of this extensive literature would take us too far afield for present purposes, it should be noted that, although considerable effort has been put into justifying decentralization within an existing unitary-state or federation, comparatively little attention has been given to why politically independent states choose to cooperate through explicit contractual arrangements (constitutions) and federate. There are many examples of federations formed from previously independent member-states (or colonies), rather than through decentralization within a given single nation, and the literature has overlooked some of the more interesting and more relevant questions.

What analysis has been undertaken on this latter question has tended to argue that federation can yield the benefits to member-states of (i) gains from trade as internal trade becomes free; (ii) tax price and scale economy benefits in the provision of national public goods; (iii) the pooling of risk between heterogeneous member-states; and (iv) increased bargaining power with other nations. On the other hand, federation can bring with it costs for any particular member-state. One of these is that the centralized functions are provided uniformly to all member-states regardless of possible differences in preferences. Uniformity of provision might lead to a loss of well-being for some states residents. For example, every resident of the federation will have to contribute to, and consume uniform levels of provision of, defense (a centralized function in all federations) even though, within different member-states, they may have different preferences for levels and quality of common defense. Of course, it is possible that the functions centralized in federations will be those for which there is little diversity of preferences, in order to minimize this cost. Moreover, this uniformity cost is not a problem for those functions that remain decentralized.

Federation can yield a distributable social surplus of an excess of benefits over these uniformity and other costs, but not all of the parties to federation will necessarily benefit, or obtain what is perceived to be a fair share of the benefits. Thus, in order for federation to be attractive to all participants it may have to be accompanied by lump-sum transfers between member-states. These transfers from the winning to the losing states are needed to facilitate the formation of the federal system itself. Each participant has a participation constraint in the sense that a state will not join the federal process if its welfare suffers from doing so. This is the basis of the compensatory argument for lump-sum transfers between states. They are equalization payments in the sense that they either partially or fully equalize the net social benefit from federation and are necessary in the interests of obtaining and sustaining federal unity.

A recent analysis along these lines is undertaken by Burbidge and Myers (1994a) who model the benefit of federation as the gains from forming a custom union between previously independent and competitive nations. Using the notion of the Shapley value and the Nash Bargaining Solution they characterize the social surplus from federation under certain conditions.

Shapiro, Petchey and Coram (1996) also address this issue and ask, what constitutes a stable federation? They attempt to answer this in a model that utilizes the theory of the core where the benefit of federation is a lower tax price for the supply of a public good and the cost of union is an inefficient level of provision of the public good in the presence of diverse preferences. It is then shown under what conditions such a federation will be stable in the sense that no subcoalition of participants will wish to secede. The authors extend this analysis to allow for interparticipant transfers and show that transfers enhance federal stability and also allow a federation to achieve efficient supply of public goods. Thus, inter-participant transfers have a clear efficiency role.

Another issue the authors explore is the potential need, under certain circumstances, for there to be costly secession from federal systems rather than the costless secession argued for by Buchanan (1990). The reason is that efficiency enhancing transfers may not be feasible in a world of costless secession. Only if secession is costly can the member states commit to the transfers necessary to ensure federal stability and efficient supply of public goods. Thus, the analysis shows that transfers are an integral part of maintaining federal stability and are intertwined with the issue of secession.

Shapiro, Petchey and Coram (1996) also use the theory of the core to examine the stability of tax sharing arrangements entered into by state and central governments within existing federations. They argue that such arrangements would have similar features to federation itself, that is, no incentive for a participant to break away or secede from the arrangement. By using the theory of the core they show which types of coalitions will be stable under particular assumptions about the tax sharing arrangement. In particular, they examine the conditions under which there will be support for the central government imposing a tax at a uniform rate across states and returning surplus revenue to the states according to a formula. This is, as noted above, exactly what equalization processes actually do. The uniform tax case is especially interesting because many constitutions, Australia's included, contain explicit constraints that force central governments to tax regions uniformly regardless of differences in preferences and technology.

Although arguments for equalizing grants among the Australian states were many and varied and predated the tariff compensation (or federal stability) issue, it can be argued that stability and the compensatory motive explain the creation of the system of equalization in existence today. The principle of needs actually adopted as the basis for equalization payments to the states was a feasible-best way of introducing and sustaining compensatory equalization (for further discussion of this point see May (1971) and Shapiro, Petchey and Coram (1996).

In summary, the idea that transfers between states are necessary to secure federal union and stability is an attractive one because it supports a theory of inter-state transfers linked to a theory of federation formation. However, as yet only tentative moves towards such a theory have been made. It would be fruitful, in our view, for more research effort to be into this issue.

Nationhood and Citizenship

According to Courchene (1984) there are a variety of arguments for interjurisdictional transfers in federations associated with the fundamental requirements for state autonomy, and the common (shared) aspects of national as well as state citizenship rights and aspirations. Although these arguments sometimes are suggested to be non-economic, they do have strong connections with economic arguments concerning the potential instability of political competition and horizontal equity.

In a federation the constitutional duties assigned to states requires that they have financial security. Ensuring the required degree of financial security for all states requires the existence of a mechanism for providing unconditional transfers between the states according to their varying fiscal needs. In meeting their constitutional obligations without interstate transfers, differences in their access to resources would lead to excessive (relative) tax burdens and/or levels of indebtedness for some states.

The nationhood and citizenship rationales shift the focus more directly onto the implications for state residents as a consequence of variations in financial security and capacity. Federation brings with it shared expectations and aspirations concerning access to public sector services. This is most immediately and obviously seen in the centralization of some spending and taxing decisions in the hands of the federal government, with associated uniformity. Over time, however, there also may be a growing expectation that core state-type services should be available on similar terms across states. More specifically, differences in levels or patterns of state-type services should be the result of democratic political decisions reflecting differences in preferences across states, not differences in capacities to fund similar service levels. To assure this, a case again emerges for unconditional transfers to equalize fiscal capacities across member-states.

At the time many of the major federations were formed, a lesser role existed for governments in the delivery of social services and welfare benefits than is expected of them today. Over time the interpretation of the nature of the social union embodied in the federal contract has expanded to incorporate a wider meaning and deeper attachment to equality of opportunity. There seems little doubt, even in those federations embodying values that tolerate a much higher variation in outcomes than is the case in Australia, Canada or Germany, common citizenship expectations and aspirations have expanded in federations. This is a consequence of the expansion of the notion of the welfare state supported by central (federal) government. It probably also reflects learning (by governments, bureaucrats, and informed and/or mobile residents) from the diverse experiences and experiments of the different member states.

In his analysis of these motives, Courchene (1984) also adds a cautionary note, based on his earlier (1971) work. In particular, he points out that, in the context of the economic and monetary union that is an integral part of overall federal arrangements, the member-states do not have access to an explicit exchange rate mechanism to assist in the process of adjusting to shocks affecting their relative competitiveness. Regional economic adjustment could occur, however, alternatively through changes to relative wages and prices between regions, if this were allowed to happen. However, if national wage-setting arrangements and regulations prevent wages falling in adversely affected regions, and the state facing adjustment problems is receiving substantial equalization payments completely justified by their initial intended purposes, then these transfer will, in effect, at least offset the affected states current account deficit and minimize required adjustments in other ways. Courchene called this transfer dependency. It is a disease he associates with the Atlantic provinces in Canada, where unemployment insurance arrangements further compound the dependency problem.

It is clear, however, that the source of the problem lies in obstacles to the ability of wages and prices to adjust appropriately (possibly compounded by welfare payments which also may be uniform nationally, or, as in Canada's unemployment insurance case, perverse in effect). The appropriate response is not to attack equalization payments, which may meet their objectives appropriately and effectively, but to remove other blockages to regional adjustment.

116

In Australia there is not, to our knowledge, any evidence of the extreme form of transfer dependency that afflicts Canada's Atlantic Provinces (or the depressed regions of southern (unitary) Italy, which receive transfers through the EU Structural Funds), although current changes to the competitive positions of the states, given the extent of wage uniformity, conceivably could result in similar problems. However, the solution, we repeat, would lie with freeing up relative wages between states, rather than with adjusting equalization arrangements for the wrong reasons. Indeed, during a period of transition to new economic policy regimes, provided adjustment mechanisms are allowed to work effectively, fiscal equalization transfers may help to maintain financial security for states coping with difficult economic adjustments.

If transfer dependency is a risk, it is incidental, and in general not logically connected to equalization transfers that meet the requirements of federation, nationhood and citizenship.

Convergence and Social Cohesion

There are substantial interregional transfers in all federations, even ones that do not appear to attach much weight to redistributive transfers for explicit equalization of fiscal capacity among regions. The MacDougall Report (1977) on public finances in the EU suggested that even among advanced countries such as the USA and UK in which transfers play a modest role, implicit and explicit interregional transfers reduced initial disparities in regional per capita incomes by 28 per cent (USA) and 36 per cent (UK).

The MacDougall Report focused on prospects for the existence, stability and cohesion of the emerging European federal-type arrangement in the face of the loss of the exchange rate mechanism and independent monetary policy adjustment, and the need for common economic policies. The report put particular emphasis on the importance of securing and maintaining some degree of convergence in the economic performance of member-states of federal systems to ensure a sustainable degree of economic integration. It indicated that explicit interregional transfers were desirable, and should be targeted at reducing interregional differences in capital endowments and productivity, through support for economic infrastructure, education and training.

The objectives put forward in the report led to the establishment of so-called Structural Funds, which make substantial transfers to lagging regions amounting to the equivalent of between 2 and 3 per cent of national GDP in several recipient countries (EC, 1993). The Maastricht Treaty proposed a new Cohesion Fund to provide additional interregional transfers to secure greater political and social stability, as well as economic convergence, under the conditions of macroeconomic and microeconomic reforms that will underpin a single market and common currency.

Equity and Efficiency

The conventional equity and efficiency arguments for equalization are based on treating fiscally decentralized unitary systems of government as equivalent to federal systems. What is distinctive about these conventional arguments is that they focus their attention on the consequences for individuals of the decentralization of fiscal decision-making in what, alternatively, would be centralized unitary political and fiscal systems. In particular, they focus, first, on the horizontal equity of treatment of individuals who are equal in economic terms before sub-national taxation and expenditure policy decisions, but (potentially) differentially affected by those decisions. Second, they examine how the locational decisions of individuals may be affected by fiscal decisions of subnational governments in ways at variance with those which would maximize national efficiency and well-being.

Horizontal Equity. It commonly is argued that horizontal inequities may be created in federal economies for at least two reasons. The first is that the taxing and expenditure decisions of state (or sub-national) governments create net fiscal benefits (NFB) for citizens such that otherwise identical individuals receive different levels of net benefits in different states. The second is that the tax and expenditure decisions of the central government also may create NFBs that differ between states. Consequently, the tax/ expenditure mechanisms of the states and central government combined may lead to horizontal inequities between individuals in different states who, before the effects of state and central government decisions, would be regarded as economic equals. It is argued that these inequities should be corrected using interpersonal equalization transfers.

Buchanan (1950) highlighted the way in which the redistributive policies of sub-national or state governments can create inequities between states. The following example illustrates the argument. Consider a federation of two states, i = 1, 2. In state 1, there are three individuals, two rich and one poor. In state 2, there are also three residents; one rich and two poor. Everyone in the federation has the same preferences, the rich in state 1 are identical to the rich in state 2, and the poor in state 1 are the same as the poor in state 2. There is no migration between states.

Suppose states provide pure local public goods with no externalities, each state funds its provision of public goods with a residence-based proportional (flat) state income tax and the income tax rates are the same in both states.[4] Although Buchanan chose an income tax, presumably because states in the USA (and Canada) impose significant income taxes, other residence-based taxes could be assumed (for example, payroll taxes, property taxes, sales and excise duties), as long as they are taxes that are approximately proportional to income (or wealth), and hence the absolute amount of taxes paid varies according to the presence of high income (or high wealth) residents.

Define the net fiscal benefit for a state i resident, NFB_i, as the difference between what individuals contribute in taxes to the state where they live and what they receive in state-provided goods and services. NFB_i (an externality) is added to a resident's wage income, w_i, (assuming for convenience, without making any qualitative difference to the results, that individuals receive only wage income) to make up 'comprehensive income' defined as CI_i. Hence, we have for state i = 1:

$$CI_i = w_1 + NFB_1 \tag{1}$$

In the example constructed, Buchanan shows that NFBs, in general, will differ between identical individuals living in different states. To see this, assume that the rich in states 1 and 2 have a zero NFB, in the sense that the higher absolute amount of tax they pay (relative to the poor) is exactly matched by the benefits they derive from the level of public good provision. On the other hand, the (sole) poor resident of state 1 receives a positive NFB in the sense that this person's absolute tax contribution is lower (than each of the two rich persons), but they receive the benefit of the greater level of public good provision due to the presence of the two rich residents. The two poor individuals in state 2 also receive a positive NFB because of the presence of the rich resident in state 2, but their NFB is lower than for the poor in state 1 because there is only one rich resident in their state. Hence, the NFB for the poor in state 1 is higher than for the poor in state 2 because of the presence of more high income residents in state 1.

Horizontal equity, a somewhat cherished principle in public finance, is violated here because individuals who are identical in terms of preferences and incomes are not treated equally by the two state governments (due to the presence of a greater number of high income people in state 1).

Buchanan's conclusions are the direct consequence of two conditions: (i) taxes paid by individuals are progressive in the sense that those with above average incomes contribute more in absolute taxes than residents with below average incomes; and (ii) expenditure by the state is distributed among residents on a uniform per capita basis. These two assumptions, combined, imply that state budgets are progressive: that is, they redistribute income from the rich to the poor.

Progressivity has two general implications for NFBs. First, in general residents with above average incomes have negative NFBs because their tax contribution is greater than what they receive in services. Second, those with below average incomes receive positive NFBs since what they receive in services exceeds their tax contribution.

Thus, the residence-based state income tax used by Buchanan (or other state taxes such as payroll and property taxes to the extent that they are proportional to income or wealth), combined with state expenditure that is distributed on a per capita basis, can cause horizontal inequity in a federal system due to variations in the location of high and low income residents across states. Of course, if all state budgets were distributionally neutral then the amount of residence-based taxes paid by individuals would be equal to the benefits they receive. This might be so also if all state services were provided on a user-pays basis, that is, all state fiscal activities correspond to the benefit taxation principle where residents are taxed according to the benefit received (as we will see later, in this case there is no need to equalize on horizontal equity grounds).

The central government may also contribute to NFBs across states by not including NFBs created by state policies in their own tax bases. However, we do not pursue this issue here.

Buchanan saw horizontal inequity as a fundamental problem in federal systems and proposed that the central government impose a higher personal income tax on the rich in state 1 (relative to the rich in state 2) and redistribute the additional revenue to the rich in state 2. This lowers the NFB received by the poor in state 1 and raises the NFB for the poor in state 2. Effectively, the transfer equalizes per-capita residence based income taxes paid by the rich in states 1 and 2.

However, Buchanan recognized that geographically discriminatory central government income taxation would face constitutional and political barriers in the USA as it would in Australia and elsewhere. He, and others since then, have proposed transfers between state governments as the feasible-best alternative.

Apart from residence-based taxes [and the Buchanan (1950) arguments], the fiscal federalism literature has argued that source-based taxation of rents on natural resources (undertaken by states) can also create differences in NFBs.[5] The conclusion is that if some states have within their boundaries substantial natural resources over which they have sovereignty; (ii) rents from these resources accrue largely to non-residents; and (iii) the rents are taxed by the state and the benefits of these taxes are distributed to residents on the basis of residency alone, then these resources will contribute to NFBs. Moreover, the rents, and the NFBs created by them, will vary across states according to differences in resource endowments. Therefore, they also contribute to horizontal inequity.

How can fiscal equalization transfers be used in practice to correct for horizontal inequities? Accepting that inter-state differentials in NFBs exist, what should be done to correct for them depends upon the normative view of horizontal equity considered appropriate to federal systems. There are two notions of horizontal equity in federations. One is broad-based horizontal equity and the other is narrow-based. The broad-based view is that individuals who are equals in the absence of central and state government budget activities, should also be equals after the tax and expenditure actions of both the state and the central government are in place. If the central government takes this broad-based view of horizontal equity, then all NFBs should be equalized so as to completely undo residual horizontal inequities arising from both state and central government policies.

The narrow view of horizontal equity is that persons otherwise equal in the presence of state government policies should also be equal after central government policies are in place. The central government should only correct for differentials in NFBs caused by central government actions and differentials created by state policies would remain.

If the broad-based view is adopted, to the extent that they are approximately proportional to income (and expenditures are on a uniform per capita basis), all residence-based taxes should be equalized—in principle, through inter-personal transfers, although interjurisdictional transfers probably are the feasible best available option. If states rely on source-based taxes whose incidence falls on non-residents, including foreigners, these too should be equalized, as should the effects of: (i) explicit state redistribution policies; (ii) income differentials caused by infrastructure spending; (iii) dents earned by state business undertakings; (iv) income differences caused by the pricing policies of state business undertakings; and (v) differences in expenditures required to provide public goods across states. With the broad based view the federal system behaves as a unitary system in that differences arising from state policies which have a distributional consequence, especially if they result from differences in per capita incomes and expenditure needs, are offset by central government equalizing taxes or transfers. Note, however, that the equivalence of the unitary and federal systems applies only if the transfers are paid to individuals, the payment of the transfers as capacity-equalizing grants to state governments within a federation is distinctly different from the policies of a unitary state. States are given equal capacities but allowed diverse expenditure choices.

Alternatively, if the narrow-based view is adopted, the central government only need ensure that its own policies are neutral with respect to their effect on horizontal equity. Under this view, for ethical, constitutional or moral reasons, states are assumed to have the property rights to the NFBs generated by their own fiscal and expenditure activities and equity considerations do not dictate that differences across states be equalized. If one state is resource-rich and derives considerable fiscal benefit from taxing resource rents, under the narrow-based view of horizontal equity, these fiscal benefits belong to the people of that state and should not be equalized. Indeed, in Canada the narrow-based view is partially adopted for source-based taxation of resource rents. The Canadians equalize only a proportion of state taxes from minerals. State residents have the property rights to the remainder.

Thus, opinions about the proper degree of equalization undertaken depends upon views about sovereignty and property rights in federal systems. This is a normative issue.

Again, however, how these questions are viewed depends on whether equalization is, in practical terms, to be pursued among individuals or among states. The seemingly more federalist nature of the narrow view of horizontal equity disappears when states, rather than their residents, are to be the recipients of (unconditional) equalizing transfers—as would be supported both by the practical infeasibility of interpersonal equalizing taxes or transfers and by the broader arguments about the nature of federal systems and the compacts which underlie them. Moreover, as we point out later, the narrow based view fails to address adequately the problem of inefficient, fiscally-induced migration.

In practice, therefore, equalization is achieved by intergovernmental grants, both because calculation of required interpersonal transfers would be horrendously complex and because central governments in federal systems typically are precluded from discrimination between states, at least in their taxation policies. Moreover, although the inter-state nature of the federal compact does not, in itself, convert the equity argument directly into one between states rather than individuals, the need to secure federal stability points to another reason why inter-state equalization transfers might be the preferred option.

All equalization schemes adopt inter-state transfers as the feasible best way of implementing equalizing transfers. For example, in Australia the Commonwealth Grants Commission (CGC) was established in the 1930s to make recommendations on equalization transfers. The CGC has since become the dominant institution in Australian federalism and large inter-state transfers are undertaken. The US in contrast has no comprehensive centrally-based equalization system although the principles are applied in specific areas such as education.

While some have argued that the CGC in Australia was originally established for federal stability reasons, it is generally considered that the main motive for its retention is equity. Moreover, Australia's equalization is more comprehensive than in most federations in the sense that it equalizes for revenue and expenditure differences across states, unlike Canada, which equalizes for revenue differences only.

Efficiency. The literature on the efficiency of equalizing transfers has two strands. The first (see Boadway and Flatters 1982) argues that because of fiscal externalities and location specific rents, free migration of labor between states leads to equilibria that are inefficient because average rather than marginal products are equated in equilibrium. This is thought to support a case for centrally-mandated transfers between states to establish an optimal population distribution and achieve production efficiency where marginal products are equated. The second strand to the efficiency case, developed in a series of papers in the first half of the 1990s, beginning with Myers (1990), argues that if given access to their own inter-state transfer instruments, states would voluntarily make such transfers, thus negating any role for centrally mandated equalization. Hence, the literature now prescribes transfers for efficiency but does not necessarily give a role for the center in facilitating these transfers.

A simple two state model, as the one previously considered, illuminates the efficiency motive for interstate transfers. Added to that model is the assumption that residents are free to migrate between states. They do so to maximize their comprehensive income. It is argued [see Buchanan and Goetz (1972), Flatters, Henderson and Mieszkowski (1974), Hartwick (1980) and Boadway and Flatters (1982a, 1982b)] that in the absence of appropriate equalizing transfers residents migrate to capture a share of NFBs, which are externalities and hence introduce the potential for economic inefficiencies.

Individuals seek to maximize their comprehensive incomes, and in an equilibrium in which no individual will wish to move, the comprehensive income in the two states are equalized

$$CI_1 = W_1 + NFB_1 = CI_2 = W_2 + NFB_2 \qquad (2)$$

If NFBs are higher in state 1 than in state 2, as our previous example supposed, the equilibrium wage rate in state 1 must be lower than in state 2. If not, individuals will migrate to state 1, even if it means accepting a lower wage than in state 2, as long as comprehensive income is higher. The higher NFB in state 1 makes up for the lower wage. Because wages are assumed to be equal to marginal product (MP), this also means that MPs are not equated in equilibrium (except, perhaps, by chance). Any equilibrium where MPs are not equal is inefficient because a reallocation of people between states yields increased total output. In our example, too many residents migrate to state 1, attracted there by the relatively higher NFBs. Note that, if NFB 1 = NFB2, the equilibrium is efficient because the equilibrium wage rates, and thus the marginal products, are equal. Observe that it is the presence of differential NFBs, not NFBs per se, which leads to inefficient migration equilibria.[6]

Centrally mandated inter-state transfers can be made that increase per-capita well-being for residents in both the recipient and contributing states by achieving a population distribution where marginal products are equated and national income is maximized. The transfer equalizes per capita NFBs between states (and hence marginal products), or per-capita residence and source-based taxes, and is the same as the transfer required in the broad-based equity case. This result is applied within the context of a federation with different resource endowments across states in Petchey (1993) and for states that face different production costs and resource endowments in Petchey (1995).

Myers (1990) extended this analysis in a model with fiscal externalities in which rents are shared equally by all citizens in the nation. His model allows states to make transfers among themselves. The result is voluntary inter-state transfers will be a part of a decentralized and efficient Nash equilibrium. This means that, while transfers are still necessary for efficient outcomes, they do not have to be undertaken by the center. If the states have access to transfers they can do as well as a fully efficient beneficent central planner. An implication of these results is that there is no equity or efficiency role for the center in correcting for the effects of migrational externalities, or location specific rents, at the subnational level. Effectively, the states can replicate an efficient central planning solution. The Myers (1990) results challenged the need for efficiency or equity based centrally mandated equalization transfers.

This result is shown by Shapiro and Petchey (1996) to depend on coincident interests between states. This arises from the assumption of a homogenous and freely mobile population that allocates itself between states until per capita utility is equated for the marginal person. It is then assumed that each state government maximizes the utility of a representative freely mobile individual. This structure implies, therefore, that state governments choose their level of public good provision in the face of an equal per capita utility constraint and that the objective of one state is exactly coincident with the objective of the government in the neighboring state. States independently act in the broader collective interest in such a world.

Mansoorian and Myers (1993) continued with this theme in a model with no fiscal externalities but location specific rents, and introduced the notion of attachment to place so that mobile individuals derived utility from where they live independently of the tax and expenditure decisions regional government. They still get the result that voluntary transfers will be made at the Nash equilibrium and that this equilibrium will be efficient. Again, there is no role for a central authority. Burbidge and Myers (1994b) generalized the Myers (1990) result slightly to allow for two mobile types where each state has a social welfare function defined over the two types. Again, it is shown that as long as each state has the same welfare function, that is, puts the same weights on each mobile type so that incentive equivalence is maintained, optimal transfers are part of a Nash equilibrium. While this result should also hold for n mobile types, Burbidge and Myers (1994b) only consider the generalization to two types.

In a paper on income redistribution and migration, Wildasin (1994) obtains results somewhat similar to those of Myers (1990) on voluntary inter-state transfers. However, the Wildasin model differs from Myers (1990) in that it introduces an immobile factor within each state which undertakes income redistribution in favor of the mobile factor (which is freely mobile between the two states). Wildasin (1994) then considers, broadly, two cases. In the *first*, the immobile factor undertakes income redistribution (denoted by s) in favor of the mobile factor within its borders. In order to facilitate the analysis an income distribution frontier is employed. This frontier, which is equivalent to a utility possibility frontier between the immobile and mobile factors, shows all the possible combinations of income achievable between the fixed and mobile factor.

In undertaking income redistribution in favor of the mobile factor, a migration distortion is created, and hence some degree of production inefficiency also results for moves along the frontier. The migration inefficiency arises because, as the immobile factor in state 1 (for example) transfers income to the mobile factor, mobile labor is attracted into state 1. In general, equilibria with free migration and redistribution within each state will not equate marginal products. In the *second* part of the paper Wildasin

(1994) shows that if the immobile factor (in state 1) is also able to make transfers (denoted by σ) to the mobile factor in state 2, then it can achieve *any* income distribution it wants within state 1, while at the same time stopping the unwanted migration from state 2. In short, state 1 is able to achieve different points on the income distribution frontier between the immobile and mobile factor within its own borders, without the efficiency costs of migration in response to the income distribution chosen by state 1. It can do this by increasing s and σ by the same amounts so that $s-\sigma$ is constant and hence there is no migration response to redistribution within state 1.

But as noted, the Myers (1990) result depends on there being a coincidence of interests between states so that they act in the common interest without any need for coordination or central intervention. There are reasons why a coincidence of interests may not occur. One is if states have different weights over the mobile groups in the social welfare functions modeled in Burbidge and Myers (1994b). Another would be to allow a richer model of public choice in each state resulting from heterogeneous preferences. This is the approach taken by Shapiro and Petchey (1996). They argue that if one considers classes of models where states have conflicting interests there is an efficiency and equity role for the center in undertaking transfers. In their model a conflict of interest between states arises because the public choice process in each state is dominated by an immobile landed class who earn income from the rent generated by a mobile disenfranchised class (hence there are three types). The landed class provide a public good which is redistributive in favor of the mobile group but which also creates utility for themselves. Thus, in choosing the level of public good to provide they are cognizant of the fact that it provides utility directly but also attracts mobile labor to their state and hence raises rent income. The two landed classes therefore have opposing interests: an increase in one state's mobile population makes that state's landed class better - off but makes the landed class in the other state worse-off. This is in contrast to Myers (1990), Mansoorian and Myers (1993) and Burbidge and Myers (1994b) where states have coincident interests.

Apart from introducing conflicts between the interests of states to re-establish an equity and efficiency role for the center, one could also restrict the tax instruments available to the states, for example, by taking away the ability to make inter-state transfers. Doing so puts us back into the world of Boadway and Flatters (1982b). It is such restrictions that seem to be of most analytical interest in a federalism context because, in practice, states do not have access to such transfers and therefore cannot replicate a central planning solution even if they do have coincident interests.

More generally, it seems to us that this literature needs to proceed by placing meaningful restrictions on state and central behavior, such as the conflicts of interest modeled in Shapiro et al, restrictions on policy instruments, and informational constraints if we are to derive clear results about whether inter-state redistributive transfers should be undertaken by the center or by states. While we work with models where the states can achieve what an efficient central planner can do (i.e. a full social optimum) with no policy restrictions and coincidence of interests, we are unable to draw any conclusions about assignment and optimal transfers.

One other paper of interest here is Petchey (1995) in which there is free inter-state migration and location specific rents. Rather than address the issue of which level of government can undertake efficient equalizing transfers in this world, Petchey examines the direction that efficient transfers should take when states face both different production costs and have different resource endowments.

This model is of interest in Australia where the equalization system equalizes for differences in costs of providing public services between states and differences in tax bases (the latter picks up the effects of differential resource rents and hence can be thought of as revenue equalization). States that have higher costs are said to face a cost disability, and the existing system compensates such states with additional equalization grants. This is unlike Canada, another major federation with an equalization system in place, where only revenue equalization is undertaken. Including cost disabilities in the equalization formula creates, so it has been claimed, inefficiencies.

Thus, Petchey (1995) sets out to examine whether efficient transfers should take into account these so-called cost disabilities between states, as well as the effects of differential resource rents. It is found that optimal transfers should account for cost differences and, somewhat surprisingly, that under some circumstances, transfers should be made in favor of high cost resource rich states, depending on what one assumes about interstate diversity in production technology relative to diversity in resource endowments.

128

An issue raised here is that the property market is generally suppressed in the analysis of the efficiency and equity cases for inter-state redistribution. But in a model with a property market, it is possible that NFBs might be capitalized into the price of fixed factors such as land. To the extent that such capitalization occurs, there is a lessened significance of NFBs as a source of continuing economic inefficiency and inequity. Although migrants share in the NFBs generated by a state when migrating, they also incur a cost for residing there by paying higher land prices. Capitalization of NFBs into the price of land means that residents are charged a price for the NFB they receive.

But migration patterns and hence property values reflect variables other than fiscal inducements—for example, better employment prospects and/or climatic considerations. Moreover, to the extent that capitalization of NFB s occurs, this must be due to fiscally-induced migration. Unless interstate differences in property values equal the differences in NFBs the resulting equilibrium is not efficient. If comprehensive income is adjusted for property costs it is

$$CI_i = w_i - r_i + NFB_i \tag{3}$$

where r_i is the price of property. Migration equilibrium requires

$$w_1 - r_1 + NFB_1 = w_2 - r_2 + NFB_2 \tag{4}$$

Efficiency requires $w_1 = w_2$ (equality of wage rates and hence marginal products) but for this to be met we need $r_1 - r_2 = NFB_1 - NFB_2$ which in general will not hold. Thus, even with capitalization there is still a migration inefficiency which needs equalizing.

The question of whether capitalization is an empirically significant self-policing mechanism is unresolved. Nevertheless, on a priori grounds, one would expect some degree of capitalization to occur and more so the more fixed (or inelastic) is the supply of land. It is only differential NFBs, to the extent that they are not capitalized, which further distort migration decisions and create horizontal inequities.

The Efficiency Case and Federal Stability

When independent states federate they remove barriers to labor (and capital) mobility. Putting aside all the other costs and benefits of union, if the federating regions have differing resource endowments and concentrations of rich residents one might expect there to be inefficient migration following union as residents seek to equate comprehensive incomes. Without any equalization this can be counted as an efficiency cost of federation as it results in a distribution of labor which may not maximize national income. This cost detracts from the net benefits of union and lowers the distributable surplus from federation.

But if federation occurs with a system of efficient equalization transfers this cost is avoided, making a larger distributable surplus available. This expands the class of feasible unions. Hence, the federal stability and efficiency cases for equalization transfers are related as equalization has the potential to eliminate a cost of union between disparate states and hence contribute to the stability of a given union.

CONCLUSION

We have provided a selective critique of the main arguments for lump-sum tax reimbursement grants, as well as specific purpose (matching transfers) and redistributive (equalizing) transfers in federal systems.

It has been shown that the case for tax reimbursement grants is based on a view that tax powers, for various reasons, mainly to do with the negative effects of tax competition at the subnational level and the need for central control over macroeconomic policy and income redistribution, should be relatively centralized, and expenditure powers relatively decentralized. This implies that there should be a fiscal gap on efficiency grounds and hence lump sum transfers of excess revenue to the states. The case for specific purpose transfers is commonly supposed to depend on the presence of direct externalities associated with the provision of local public goods which also have spillovers. Justifications for equalization transfers that redistribute income from one state to another have been built on many grounds, including compensation for the net welfare effects of federation, citizenship/nationhood and the more standard migration efficiency and equity arguments. We have concentrated on certain aspects of specific purpose transfers and equalization grants.

We wish to conclude by emphasizing that most of the rationales for transfers derive from analysis of the expenditure and tax assignment question - the two are inextricably linked. It is also crucial to understand the kind of theoretical world the assignment question, and hence the rationales for transfers, are built on. In particular, the conventional rationales for transfers, be it the tax reimbursement analysis, specific purpose transfers or redistributive equalizing transfers, are based on models in which central governments are beneficent, act efficiently, have full information on preferences (so that they know exactly who should receive transfers and who should pay), and can implement Pareto optimal outcomes, either through transfers or through direct central provision of public goods or control over tax instruments. States, on the other hand, act inefficiently for a variety of reasons, most of which have to do with externalities of some kind (e.g. direct externalities or those generated by migration of people or capital, or mobility of tax bases themselves).

Therefore, the literature concentrates on how the center can, through the use of transfers, make the states act as it would, that is, efficiently. Thus, the choice is between efficient centralized provision of public goods or control over tax instruments, versus decentralized provision (or taxation) with optimal transfers of various kinds in place to correct for the inefficiencies of decentralization and replicate the central (efficient) solution. The two choices are seen as equivalent and both are Pareto optimal. In addition, if, as the work of Myers (1990) suggests, states can make these transfers themselves there is not even any need for central intervention. Efficient centralization is equivalent to decentralization (which is also efficient because states will correct for any inefficiencies themselves). Thus, again there is no difference between sub-national provision and central control - both are efficient. It is just that in the Myers (1990) world there is no need for the center to mandate the efficiency enhancing transfers they are made by the states themselves. However, as we argued, the Myers (1990) result does not hold in a world of heterogeneous preferences and conflicts between state interests and in this sense is not general.

This, then, is the view of a federal system on which the conventional arguments for transfers are developed and it has, we believe, been extremely valuable in generating important insights into efficiency and equity rationales for federal transfers. But it seems that in order to move forward in our understanding of transfers, we need to develop richer models of federalism and the expenditure and tax assignment issue. This will, in turn, require that we move on from models where decentralization with optimal transfers (undertaken by states voluntarily or mandated by the center) is equivalent to centralization, with both being fully efficient.

One fruitful path is to examine the assignment issue and hence the question of transfers in models where governments do not have perfect information on preferences and must use suboptimal collective choice mechanisms. This means thinking about assignment and transfer issues in a world with inefficient public choice processes. Another possibility is to analyze transfers in a world where states and the center face constraints on the instruments they can use. Further, it seems that it would be fruitful to break the coincidence of interests that these models of voluntary transfers depend on and examine transfers in models where states have conflicting interests. It is unlikely that we will generate the same rationales for efficiency transfers in such models.

Another promising way forward, especially with regard to transfers that redistribute between states, is to develop a better theory of the federation process itself, that is, obtain a better understanding of what it is that makes independent political entities give up sovereignty and form federal unions. We have pointed to some early work considering this issue and derive results suggesting that inter-state transfers are necessary for federal stability and may play a role in enhancing the efficiency with which centrally provided public goods are provided. These ideas are relatively new and we believe may eventually offer considerable additional insight into the reasons why we observe the sizable inter-state transfers that seem to be a feature of most federations.

NOTES

1. For more detailed discussion see Gramlich (1985) and Fisher (1996).
2. See Shapiro and Petchey (1994) for an economic analysis of Section 90 and the High Court's interpretation.
3. Walsh (1993) concentrates on the efficiency costs of the fiscal gap itself. He also argues that, because of these costs, there is a case for reducing the fiscal gap in Australia, principally, through a reduction in specific purposes transfers and the introduction of income tax sharing.
4. A residence-based tax is a tax for which liability is determined according to region or state of residence. These taxes are usually assumed to include state imposed income taxes, payroll taxes, property taxes, sales taxes and excise duties.
5. A source-based tax is a tax for which liability is determined regardless of residence. These include taxes on rents from natural resources.
6. By similar reasoning, business location decisions also can be affected by fiscal factors.

REFERENCES

Albon, R. P. "The Efficiency Implications of Locational-Based Factors in Commonwealth Grants Commission Determinations", Appendix to the Victorian Submission to the *Inquiry into Issues of Methodology*, Victoria's Response to the Discussion Papers, Inquiry into Grants Commission Methodology, 1990.

Boadway, R. W., and F. Flatters. "Equalization in a Federal State: An Economic Analysis." *Economic Council of Canada*. Ottawa: Canadian Government Publishing Center, 1982.

Boadway, R. W., and F. Flatters. "Efficiency and Equalization Payments in a Federal System of Government: A Synthesis and Extension of Recent Results." *Canadian Journal of Economics*, 15 (1982).

Boadway, R. W. "Federal-Provincial Transfers in Canada: A Critical Review of the Existing Arrangements." In *Federalism and the Economic Union, Vol. 65, Royal Commission on the Economic Union and Development Prospects for Canada*, edited by Krasnick, M., Norrie, K. and R. Simeon. Ottawa: Canadian Government Publishing Center, 1985.

Boadway, R.W., and M. Keen. "Efficiency and the Fiscal Gap in Federal Systems", Paper Presented at the International Seminar on Public Economics (ISPE) Conference on "Fiscal Policy in Emerging Federations," Nashville, Tennessee, USA, August 26-28, 1994.

Brennan, G., and J. Buchanan. *The Power to Tax: Analytic Foundations of a Fiscal Constitution*, Cambridge: Cambridge University Press, 1980.

Brennan, G., and J. Pincus. "A Minimalist Model of Federal Grants." Mimeo, 1994.

Breton, A. "Supplementary Statement". *Report of The Royal Commission on the Economic Union and Development Prospects for Canada, Ministry of Supply and Services*. Ottawa: 1985. (Reprinted as "Towards a Theory of Competitive Federalism", *European Journal of Political Economy*, Vol. 3+4: 1, (1987).

Breton, A. "The Existence and Stability of Interjurisdictional Competition." In *Competition among State and Local Governments*, edited by D. Kenyon and J. Kincaid. Washington: Urban Institute Press, 1991.

Brosio, G. "The Balance Sheet of the Australian Federation: Some Tentative Estimates." *Working Paper*, Federalism Research Center, Research School of Social Sciences, Australian National University, Canberra, 1992.

Buchanan, J.M. "Europe's Constitutional Opportunity." In *Europe's Constitutional Future*. Institute of Economic Affairs, 1990.

Buchanan, J. M., and C. J. Goetz. "Efficiency Limits and Fiscal Mobility: An Assessment of the Tiebout Model." *Journal of Public Economics*, 1, (1972).

Burbidge, J.B., and G. M. Myers. "Federation as Coalition Formation", Paper Presented at the International Seminar on Public Economics (ISPE) Conference on "Fiscal Policy in Emerging Federations," Nashville, Tennessee, USA, August 26-28, 1994.

Burbidge, J.B., and G.M. Myers. "Redistribution Within and Across the Regions of a Federation" *Canadian Journal of Economics* 27(3) (August, 1994): 620-36.

Clark, D.H. "Fiscal Needs and Revenue Equalization Grants". Canadian Tax Foundation, 1969.

Commonwealth Grants Commission. "Equality in Diversity: Fifty Years of the Commonwealth Grants Commission". Canberra: Australian Government Publishing Service, 1983.

Commonwealth Grants Commission. *Report on General Revenue Grant Relativities*, 1989 Update. Canberra: Australian Government Publishing Service, 1989.

Commonwealth Grants Commission. *Report on Issues in Fiscal Equalization*, Vols I and II. Canberra: Australian Government Publishing Service, 1990.

Cornes, R. C., and T. Sandler. *"The Theory of Externalities, Public Goods, and Club Goods."* New York: Cambridge University Press, 1986.

Courchene, T. "Interprovincial Migration and Economic Adjustment". *Canadian Journal of Economics* 3 (1971).

Courchene, T. "Equalization Payments; Past, Present and Future." Toronto: Ontario Economic Council, 1984.

"Stable Money, Sound Finances: Community Public Finances in the Perspective of Economic and Monetary Union." Report of an Expert Group, Brussels: Commission of the European Community, 1993.

Fisher, R.C. *State and Local Public Finance*. Chicago: Richard D. Irwin, Inc., 1996.

Flatters, F., V. Henderson and P. Mieszkowski. "Public Goods, Efficiency, and Regional Fiscal Equalization". *Journal of Public Economics* 1 (1974).

Gordon, R.H. "An Optimal Taxation Approach to Fiscal Federalism". *Quarterly Journal of Economics* (November, 1983): 567-586.

Gramlich, E.M. "Intergovernmental Grants: A Review of the Empirical Literature." In *The Political Economy of Fiscal Federalism*, edited by W. Oates. Lexington: Heath-Lexington, 1977.

Gramlich, E.M. "Reforming US Federal Fiscal Arrangements." In *American Domestic Priorities: An Economic Appraisal*, edited by J. Quigley and D. Rubinfeld. Berkeley: University of California Press, 1985.

Hartwick, J. M. "The Henry George Rule, Optimal Population, and Interregional Equity". *Canadian Journal of Economics* xiii No. 4 (1980).

Hercowitz, C., and D. Pines. "Migration with Fiscal Externalities". *Journal of Public Economics* 46 (1994).

King, D. *"Fiscal Tiers: The Economics of Multi-Level Government."* London: George Allen and Unwin, in Association with the Center for Research on Federal Financial Relations, ANU, 1984.

MacDougall Report. *Report of the Study Group on the Role of Public Finance in European Integration.* Brussells: (1977) Commission of the European Communities (Vol 1, General Report), 1977.

Mansoorian, A., and G.M. Myers. "Attachment to Home and Efficient Purchases of Population in a Fiscal Externality Economy". *Journal of Public Economics* 52 (1993): 117-132.

Mathews, R. "Federalism in Retreat: The Abandonment of Tax Sharing and Fiscal Equalization". Center for Federal Financial Relations, Australian National University, Canberra, 1982.

Maxwell, J. and C. Pestieau. *"Economic Realities of Contemporary Confederation."* Montreal: C.D. Howe Research Institute, 1980.

May, R.J. *"Financing the Small States in Australian Federalism".* Melbourne: Oxford University Press, 1971.

Myers, G. "Optimality, Free Mobility and Regional Authority in a Federation". *Journal of Public Economics* 43 (1990).

Norrie, K.H. and M.B. Percy. "Province-building and Industrial Structure in a Small, Open Economy." In *Economic Adjustment and Public Policy in Canada*, edited by D.D. Purvis. Kingston: John Deutsch Memorial for the Study of Economic Policy, 1984.

Oates, W.E. *"Fiscal Federalism".* New York: Harcourt Brace and Jovanovich, 1972.

Oates, W.E. "Tax Effectiveness and Tax Equity in Federal Countries: Commentary." In Conference Volume of the International Seminar in Public Economics, edited by Charles McLure, 1984.

Oates, W.E. and R.M. Schwab. "Economic Competition Among Jurisdictions: Efficiency Enhancing or Distortion Inducing?" *Journal of Public Economics* 35 3 (1988).

Petchey, J.D. "Equalization in a Federal Economy With Inter-State Migration". *Australian Economic Papers*. (December, 1993): 336-354.

Petchey, J.D. "Inter-State Cost Differences, Resource Endowments and Equalizing Transfers". *The Economic Record* 71, No. 215. (December, 1995): 343-353.

Petchey, J.D., and P. Shapiro. "One People One Destiny: Centralization and Conflicts of Interest in Australian Federalism". Paper Presented at the International Seminar in Public Economics (ISPE) Conference on "Fiscal Policy in Emerging Federations," Nashville, Tennessee, USA, August 26-28, 1994.

Reece, B. F. "State Taxation Reform Reports: Retrospect and Prospect on Research Directions." In *Issues in State Taxation*, edited by Cliff Walsh. Canberra: Center for Research on Federal Financial Relations, Australian National University, 1990.

Scott, A. "The Economic Goals of Federal Finance". *Public Finance* 19 (1964).

Shapiro, P., and J.D. Petchey. "Shall Become Exclusive: An Economic Analysis of Section 90". *The Economic Record* Vol. 70 209 (June, 1994): 171-182.

Shapiro, P., Petchey, J.D. and B.T. Coram. "Federal Stability, Secession and Uniform Tax Sharing: An Application of the Theory of the Core." Federalism Research Center, Australian National University, Canberra, 1996.

Shapiro, P, and J.D. Petchey. "Confederation and Federation: The Assignment of Authority With Inter-State Population Mobility." Mimeo, 1996.

Stigler, G. "The Tenable Range of Functions of Local Government." In *Federal Expenditure Policy for Economic Growth and Stability*, Joint Economic Committee. Washington, DC: US Government Printing Office, 1957.

Tiebout, C. M. "A Pure Theory of Local Expenditures". *Journal of Political Economy* 64 (1956).

Walsh, C. and J.D. Petchey. "Fiscal Federalism: An Overview of Issues and a Discussion of Their Relevance to the European Community", Federalism Research Center, ANU, Canberra, *Discussion Paper No. 12*, 1992.

Walsh, C. "Vertical Fiscal Imbalance: The Issues." In *Vertical Fiscal Imbalance and the Allocation of Taxing Powers*, edited by D.J. Collins. Sydney: Australian Tax Research Foundation, 1993.

Wildasin, D. E. *"Urban Public Finance"*. Harwood Academic Publishers, 1986.

5 TOWARD INCREASED CENTRALIZATION IN PUBLIC SCHOOL FINANCE[1]

William N. Evans, Sheila E. Murray, and Robert M. Schwab

INTRODUCTION

Traditionally, public elementary and secondary education has been highly decentralized in the United States. There are more than 16,000 school districts, each of which has significant responsibility for raising education funds and deciding how those funds are to be spent; as late as the 1920s, local governments provided well over 80 percent of public school revenues. Although state governments have shared in the cost of providing education, historically their major role has been to monitor curriculum, evaluation and standards. Moreover, the federal role has been small. Federal spending is low and even a modest effort to involve the federal government in standards through Goals 2000 met an early demise.

However, in recent years state legislatures have, on their own initiative or at the behest of state courts, begun to assume a much larger role in public school finance. This move toward greater centralization has sparked some of the most heated debates in public policy about the tradeoffs in efficiency from a decentralized system and equity under a centralized system. While the debate on the increased state role is long and ongoing, the trend is clear. In the past twenty-five years, the states on average have become an equal partner with the localities in school finance.

Figure 1 illustrates these trends. In 1972, local governments provided 53 percent of all K-12 revenues, state governments 38 percent, and the federal government 9 percent. Over the next 20 years, state spending grew roughly twice as fast as local spending and federal spending (on a per student basis) was essentially flat. Consequently, the distribution of education revenues was very different in 1992; local and state shares were nearly equal and the federal share had fallen to 7 percent.

In this paper, we examine some of the causes and consequences of this move toward centralization. The next section begins the discussion of the states' role in education finance with a description of state redistribution programs and an evaluation of the ability of the funding plans to achieve equity goals. In the third section, we review the experiences of several states that have reformed their finance system. We present and evaluate the evidence on the impact of efforts to increase state responsibility in school spending in the fourth section. The federal role in public education is explored in the fifth section. The final section offers a summary and concluding remarks.

THE STATES' ROLE IN EDUCATION

In the modern structure of schools, the state has played an important and increasing role in public school finance. A large part of the motivation for an increased state role has been concerns about equity in financing public education. Critics of locally financed schools have long argued that such a system is inherently unfair. Because differences in the tax base across school districts are large, the emphasis on local funding often leads to significant inequality in school spending. Opponents of local funding have pressed their case in court and with state legislatures. By 1995, the constitutionality of the public school finance system had been challenged in 43 states with state supreme courts overturning the finance system in 16 states (Murray, Evans, and Schwab 1996).

Some states (Utah, for example) have adopted finance reforms on their own without judicial intervention. Some states, including Georgia and Oklahoma, adopted reforms even though state courts upheld their finance systems. In other states, the key issue driving reform has been voters' dissatisfaction with the property tax. The property tax is the major source of revenue for local governments. Property taxes represent more than three-quarters of all local tax revenues; school districts generate 98 percent of all of their tax revenues from the property tax. State property taxes, however, are very low, typically no more than 2 percent of total state tax revenues. Thus decisions about which level of government will finance schools are implicitly decisions about tax structure. If local governments fund education, the property tax burden will be high; if the states fund education, property taxes will be low but other taxes -- often the sales tax and the income tax -- will be high.

The property tax is widely regarded as the least fair of all taxes. From time to time, the Advisory Commission on Intergovernmental Relations has conducted surveys and asked: "Which do you think is the worst tax - that is, the least fair? federal income tax, state income tax, state sales taxes, or local property tax?" In the latest poll taken in 1989, 30 percent chose the local property tax as the least fair tax, 26 percent the federal income tax, 19 percent the state sales tax, and 12 percent the state income tax (U.S. Advisory Commission on Intergovernmental Relations, 1991).[2] Putting these two issues together, voters can escape the tax they particularly dislike if school finance is shifted to the state.

State Aid for Education

States use a wide range of programs to fund their share of the cost of education. Our goal in this section of this paper is to describe those programs and to summarize some of the broad literature in this area. It is helpful to divide state aid programs into three groups: flat grants, equalization grants, and full state funding.[3] Flat grants were the earliest type of state aid to education. Though they differ in detail, the size of a flat grant that any particular district would receive is independent of the district's ability to pay for education or the district's actual expenditures, i.e., they are lump sum payments to districts. Thus a flat grant is simply the product of the statewide student grant and the number of students in a district. In the early 1900's, flat grants were the major source of school aid in 38 states. They became less popular as states became more concerned with addressing spending inequality across districts, though as late as 1971 flat grants were still the primary funding mechanism in 10 states. As Table 5.1 shows, in 1991 only North Carolina relied on flat grants as the major form of school

Table 5.1. State Redistribution Programs

STATE	FORMULA
Alabama	Modified foundation
Alaska	Foundation
Arizona	Foundation
Arkansas	Foundation; two-tiered
California	Foundation with flat grant
Colorado	Modified foundation
Connecticut	Percentage equalization
Delaware	Flat grant with equalization
Florida	Foundation
Georgia	Foundation with GTB
Hawaii	Full state funding
Idaho	Modified foundation
Illinois	Modified foundation/GTB with flat grant
Indiana	Foundation with flat grant
Iowa	Foundation with flat grant
Kansas	Percentage equilization
Kentucky	Foundation with GTB
Louisiana	Foundation
Maine	Modified foundation
Maryland	Foundation with flat grant
Massachusetts	Percentage equilization
Michigan	GTB with flat grant
Minnesota	Foundation
Mississippi	Foundation
Missouri	Foundation with GTB and flat grant
Montana	Foundation with GTB
Nebraska	Foundation
Nevada	Foundation
New Hampshire	Foundation
New Jersey	Foundation
New Mexico	Foundation, near full funding
New York	Percentage equalization with flat grant
North Carolina	Flat grant
North Dakota	Foundation
Ohio	Foundation
Oklahoma	Foundation with equalization
Oregon	Foundation
Pennsylvania	Percentage equilization
Rhode Island	Percentage equilization
South Carolina	Foundation
South Dakota	Foundation
Tennessee	Foundation
Texas	Foundation with guaranteed yield
Utah	Foundation
Vermont	Foundation with flat grant

STATE	FORMULA
Virginia	Foundation
Washington	Full state funding
West Virginia	Foundation
Wisconsin	GTB, two-tiered
Wyoming	Foundation

Source: Thompson, Wood, and Honeyman (1994). GTB denote guaranteed tax base equalization.

financial aid, though many states offered categorical or supplemental aid (e.g., grants for textbooks and libraries or transportation) as flat grants.

There are two broad categories of equalization grants. Foundation grants are designed to guarantee that every student in a state receives at least a specified minimum level of funding. Table 5.1 shows that they are the most popular school finance plan; in 1991, 38 states relied in whole or in part on foundation grants. The amount that a district would receive under a foundation grant would depend on several factors. In its simplest form, states would set the foundation level F; conceptually, F would represent the cost of what the state viewed as the minimum acceptable education. The state would also establish a minimum uniform tax rate r. If district j had per student wealth of V_j, it would receive state aid per student of $A_j = F - rV_j$, if $F - rV_j$ is positive, and zero otherwise. Thus aid provided under a foundation plan can be interpreted as filling a gap between need measured by F and ability to fund education measured by rV_j (Downes and Pogue 1994). Of the 38 states that use foundation programs, 31 include adjustments in their formulas designed to reflect differences in costs. The most common adjustment is to assign different weights to different types of students, with larger weights given to students who are more expensive to educate (e.g., handicapped students, students in large school districts). Districts are typically given some latitude to set a discretionary millage rate, so that total spending in a district can exceed the minimum foundation level. In some states, districts are allowed to choose a tax rate that is less than r as long as its tax base is sufficiently large that it spends at least F.

Other equalization grants take a different approach and are designed so that state aid depends on local spending rather than ensuring a minimum amount of funding. For example, under a percentage equalization plan first proposed by Harlan Updegraff in the 1920's, if district j had wealth V_j and

144

spent a total of E_j on education (inclusive of state aid), then it would receive aid from the state A_j equal to $\theta(V_j)E_j$ where $\theta' < 0$. That is, these plans are matching grants where the matching rate is a decreasing function of wealth.

District power equalization programs (DPE) are modern variants of percentage equalization programs (Coons, Clune, and Sugarman 1970).[4] Under a DPE, the state would choose a tax base per student V^*. District j would then act "as if" if its tax base were V^* rather than V_j (assuming for the moment that V^* is greater than V_j). That is, if it sets a tax rate t_j it will raise $t_j V_j$ from local sources, receive state aid $A_j = t_j(V^*-V_j)$, and thus spend $E_j = t_j V^*$ on education. To put things slightly differently, if a district wishes to spend E_j it would choose $t_j = E_j / V^*$ and therefore receive $A_j = E_j(1 - V_j /V^*)$. Thus a guaranteed tax base grant is an open ended matching grant with a matching rate of $1 - (V_j /V^*)$.

What happens in wealthy districts where V^* is less than V_j? A pure DPE scheme includes "recapture." All districts would receive $A_j = t_j(V^*-V_j)$, which could be either positive or negative, i.e., school districts where the tax base is larger than the guaranteed base would be required to return to the state the excess tax revenue that it raised. Theoretically, DPE plans could therefore be self-financing; it is possible to set the guaranteed base so that the funds collected from the wealthy districts could be redistributed to poorer districts and therefore ΣA_j would equal 0. In practice, however, no states with DPE require recovery; in fact, in most states even the wealthiest districts receive at least some state aid (Reschovsky 1994).

If the goal of state aid is to equalize funding across districts, full state funding is the most straightforward approach. Only Hawaii[5] has gone this far explicitly. Several other states have school finance systems that for all practical purposes should be considered fully funded state systems. Under the *Serrano* decision, for example, the California courts required that differences in per pupil spending across nearly all districts be no greater than $100 in real 1971 dollars.[6] The Florida legislature sets a range of approved local property tax rates and also determines allowable costs per pupil, with the state funding the difference. Almost every district chooses the maximum allowable rate, and therefore Florida effectively has full state funding (Thompson, Wood and Honeyman 1994). Wisconsin and Michigan have recently adopted dramatic changes in education finance and are now best regarded as virtually state financed systems.

An Evaluation of State Funding Plans

State funding is sometimes justified on efficiency grounds. For example, if some of the benefits from education expenditures in district j spill over into district k, then the state might wish to offer district j a matching grant that would internalize this externality. Fernandez and Rogerson (1996) show that the state could improve efficiency by funding education in the poorest communities if education is funded through distortionary, local taxes. Clearly, however, equity is usually the overriding question, and we will focus on equity issues in the discussion that follows.

Most discussions of school finance reform concentrate on spending per student. Many would agree with Ladd and Yinger (1994) who argue that we should be concerned with the distribution of real education resources rather than dollars. The cost of providing education can vary substantially across districts within a state; central cities, for example, often must pay higher wages to its teachers and must spend more to reach a given level of education in order to offset the effects of poverty. This suggests that any state education finance plan should incorporate differences in costs in its aid formula.[7]

As Reschovsky (1994) argues persuasively, an evaluation of a particular school finance plan depends crucially on the objectives of that plan.[8] He offers four possible definitions of equity. First, we might want to guarantee wealth neutrality, i.e., that educational expenditures are independent of a district's taxable wealth. Advocates of DPE plans have often argued in favor of DPE on the grounds that it would achieve wealth neutrality. Feldstein (1975), however, shows that in general this is not the case. The Feldstein argument can be summarized as follows. Suppose that expenditures in district j are a function of wealth V_j and the price of a dollar of education. By price we mean the increase in local revenues that must follow an additional dollar of education spending. Suppose, for example, that a \$1 increase in school spending would be financed by \$.80 of additional local spending and an additional \$.20 of state aid. Then the district's price of a dollar of education would be \$.80 in that case. Because state aid is often a function of wealth, price will depend on wealth and therefore we can write $E_j = E(V_j, P(V_j))$. It then follows that the elasticity of expenditures with respect to wealth must be

$$(1) \qquad \frac{d \ln E}{d \ln v} = \frac{\partial \ln E}{\partial \ln V} + \frac{\partial \ln E}{\partial \ln P} \frac{\partial \ln P}{\partial \ln V}$$

We argued above that under a DPE scheme, the state pays a proportion of expenditures equal to $[1 - (V_j / V^*)]$. Therefore the local price of a dollar of education is V_j / V^* and thus the elasticity of price with respect to wealth under DPE must be 1. Equation (1) then implies that in this case the relationship between expenditures and wealth depends on the relative magnitude of the elasticity of expenditures with respect to wealth and price. DPE will lead to neutrality only if the wealth elasticity equals the absolute value of the price elasticity. Most studies, however, find that the wealth elasticity is significantly larger and therefore wealth and expenditures are likely to be positively correlated under a DPE plan.

Second, Reschovsky suggests that we might focus on "taxpayer equity." We will have achieved taxpayer equity if two districts that set the same tax rate are able to spend the same amount on education. DPE plans will accomplish this goal; under these plans, any district that chooses a tax rate t will be able to spend tV^*.

Third, we might argue that we have achieved equity if all students receive at least a minimum level of education. This view of equity would suggest that we choose a foundation grant to meet our objective.

Finally, we might believe that equity requires equal spending throughout the state. In general, neither foundation nor DPE grants would allow us to reach this goal and we would instead have to turn to much more direct state involvement. We could, for example, equalize spending by moving to a fully funded state system (as in Hawaii) or by severely limiting the ability of districts to set their own budgets (as in California).

CASE STUDIES IN STATE EDUCATION FINANCE REFORM

We now turn to several case studies of education finance reform. We argued above that in many cases, the courts have been the prime mover behind education finance reform. These cases have raised a variety of legal issues and have elicited a range of responses from the state governments. Because these court decisions have had such an important effect on inequality, the level of spending and the state role in education, we summarize the main components of the history of finance reform in

California, New Jersey and Texas. Furthermore, among the states where finance systems have been overturned, these three states have the most students.[9] We also argued that voters' concerns over the property tax has been a key factor in finance reform in some states. We focus on recent developments in Michigan and Wisconsin to illustrate this point.

California. The California State Supreme Court's landmark ruling, *Serrano v. Priest* (1971), was the first to declare that a state's public school finance system discriminated against children from poor districts. Prior to this ruling, California had a foundation system that prescribed a minimum property tax rate and guaranteed each district that taxed at this rate the difference between the foundation amount and its property tax revenues. In addition to local property taxes and foundation aid, districts received a per pupil basic aid from the state and categorical funds from the state and the federal government.

Table 5.2 presents summary statistics on per pupil spending in California, Texas and New Jersey during the reform period. As the California panel shows, in 1972, before the state put any reforms in place, the state provided 42.2 percent of the resources used to run California's public schools.[10] Even though the state had a redistribution scheme in place, at the time of *Serrano* California's finance system was one of the most unequal systems. For example, as shown in Table 5.2 the within-state Theil index, a common inequality measure in education, for California in 1972 was 29.1, while the average within-state Theil for the nation was only 13.7.[11]

The plaintiffs, a group of parents of children in a poor Los Angeles school district, sued the state because of the wide variation in resources. They argued that the foundation system favored districts with higher taxable wealth per pupil, as any increase in per pupil spending above the foundation level would require a smaller increase in the tax rate of a wealthier district. An initial dismissal of the parents' case was reversed by the California Supreme Court in 1971 (Downes, 1992). Agreeing with the plaintiffs, the court wrote that the finance system " . . . discriminates against the poor because it makes the quality of a child's education a function of the wealth of his parents and neighbors" (*Serrano v. Priest*, p. 1). The court remanded the case to a lower court for trial.

148

Table 5.2: **Summary Current Education Expenditures, 1972-1992; California, New Jersey and Texas, 1972-1992**

	1972	1977	1982	1987	1992
California (1971)					
Real per pupil expenditures[a]	2,984	3,889	3,805	4,750	4,106
State share of expenditures	42.2	51.3	66.7	78.1	72.4
Theil index (x1000)	29.1	9.7	6.8	5.2	8.4
New Jersey (1973)					
Real per pupil expenditures[a]	3,655	4,159	4,396	6,127	7,008
State share of expenditures	24.8	37.6	42.4	41.8	49.1
Theil index (x1000)	11.9	10.2	10.0	10.6	8.7
Texas (1989)					
Real per pupil expenditures[a]	2,419	2,606	2,947	3,428	3,948
State share of expenditures	51.9	52.2	53.5	44.2	46.0
Theil index (x1000)	11.6	14.9	17.5	11.5	8.0
National					
Real per pupil expenditures[a]	3,044	3,494	3,671	4,547	5,023
State share of expenditures	38.3	43.4	47.6	49.7	46.4
Average within state					
Theil index (x1000)	13.7	14.4	14.0	12.6	13.4

[a] Constant 1992 dollars.

Sources: State per pupil expenditures and Theil indices are authors' calculations from *Census of Government F-33* files (Murray, Evans and Schwab 1996). State share of expenditures is the ratio of state expenditures for education (direct and intergovernmental) from the Census Bureau's *State Government Finances* to total educational expenditures from the National Center for Education Statistics *Digest of Education Statistics, 1994.* National per pupil expenditures and state share of expenditures are from the NCES, *Digest of Education Statistics, 1994.*

In 1973 the state passed legislation to respond to the anticipated ruling from the lower court. The critical elements of this legislation were an increase in the foundation aid and the introduction of revenue limits. The revenue limits were a key feature of the state's attempts to reduce the disparity in spending between districts. The limits worked in the following way. If a district's assessed valuation grew at a faster rate that its revenue limit, the district had to reduce its tax rate. Slow growing districts, on the other hand, were allowed to tax more. However, because the limits could be removed by a voter override, they did not remove the ability of the local board to tax.[12]

The lower court responded in 1974 to the Supreme Court's remand. The key feature of the ruling was the introduction of disparity bands-- "wealth related revenue disparities among districts in spending for basic educational services were to be reduced to 'amounts considerably less than $100 per pupil,' regardless of the district's property wealth" (Picus 1991). In *Serrano II* (1977) the California Supreme Court ruled that the reformed system was unconstitutional. Downes (1992) argues that the court had effectively ruled any financing system that allowed for a positive correlation between a district's wealth and per pupil spending was unconstitutional.

The passage of Proposition 13 in 1978, however, made responses to the *Serrano II* ruling obsolete. A constitutional amendment, Proposition 13 limited increases in assessments for current property tax increases and prohibited new property taxes. Many authors argue that Proposition 13 and *Serrano II* together changed the finance system from a foundation plan that permitted substantial variation in per pupil spending to essentially a state system that left the amount of spending up to the state and virtually equalized per pupil spending across districts (Downes 1993, Picus 1991, Fischel 1989).

In the current system, revenue limits are still in place. The legislature has enacted several policies to replace the loss in property tax revenues from Proposition 13 and other tax limitation initiatives passed by California voters. Because education had to compete with other state obligations, in the late 1980s, California earmarked lottery and general revenues are for education (Picus, 1991).

Table 5.2 points to two key consequences of these events in California. First, the decisions seemed to have their intended effect on the disparity of resources. Inequality fell sharply; by 1992, the Theil index had fallen by more than 70 percent to 8.4. Second, the state's role in education finance increased substantially as its share of resources rose to nearly 80 percent by 1987. The state share fell back to 72.4 percent in 1992 as the state was struck particularly hard by the recession.

Texas. In 1984, a group of poor school districts filed suit in Texas state courts, alleging that the finance system violated the Texas constitution's guarantee of equal rights, due course, and efficiency. Plaintiffs argued that the state did not provide children in low income school districts with an efficient system of free public schools nor with programs and services that are substantially equal to those available to any similar student. Also, because Mexican-American residents were concentrated in poor school districts, the state discriminated against them on the basis of poverty and national origin, thereby violating equal protection. Shortly after the suit was filed, the state agreed to develop a new plan and the suit was (temporarily) dropped. Dissatisfied with the revisions to the finance system, a group of school districts refiled the suit in 1985, *Edgewood v. Kirby* (*Edgewood I*). The state supreme court in 1989 overturned the finance plan on the basis of the efficiency provision of the state's constitution.

In 1990 the legislature responded to *Edgewood* with a substantial change in their state funding formula. The traditional Texas plan was largely a foundation plan that did not encourage poorer districts to increase spending. Although there were matching components in the program, the rates were very low. In addition to significant changes in the structure of the funding formula that equalizes expenditures, legislation passed in 1991 encouraged local spending by raising the tax rate matched by the state in the guaranteed-yield program. These trends are reflected in Table 2. Inequality in Texas steadily declined after the *Edgewood* case was threatened in 1984. Moreover, although state spending grew over this time period, the rapid growth in local spending led to a decline in the state share by 1987.

Nonetheless, the *Edgewood* litigation continued through three more challenges. In *Edgewood II* (1991), the plaintiffs argued that fiscal neutrality had not been achieved. The court agreed and the legislature devised a system of regional taxing units called County Education Districts (CEDs) to redistribute tax revenues from wealthy districts to poorer districts. This system was challenged in *Edgewood* III; this time the case included a challenge of the constitutionality of the CEDs. An earlier interpretation of the Texas constitution prohibited the state from recapturing a district's excess revenues. Furthermore, in Texas ad valorem taxes for school districts required voter approval. Although the state supreme court in 1992 declared CED taxes to be an unconstitutional state tax because they did not have voter approval, the court allowed the state to collect the CED taxes for two years until the legislature developed a new plan in 1993. The new plan, incorporated in Senate Bill 7, introduced wealth limits. The limits equalized expenditures by forcing the 100 high wealth districts to lower their property wealth to $280,000 per pupil. The state gave districts five options for shedding wealth. Virtually all districts chose to either purchase attendance credits from the state or support the schooling of students in other districts. This system was upheld by the court in January 1995.

New Jersey. The state supreme court overturned the New Jersey school finance system in *Robinson v. Cahill* (1973) on the grounds that the spending disparities did not enable the poorest 28 school districts to provide the educational opportunities needed in today's society. The court required the legislature to make per pupil spending in these districts "substantially equal" to the spending in the wealthiest suburban districts through a state income tax.

In 1989, the State supreme court again overturned the state's system on the same grounds. The court ruled in *Abbott v. Burke*, and later in *Abbott II* (1990), that the disparities were worse than at the time of *Robinson v. Cahill*. The legislature responded with the *Quality of Education Act of 1990* (QEA). The act changed the redistribution formula from a guaranteed tax base to a foundation formula, eliminated the payment of minimum aid to wealthy districts and increased state aid for poor urban districts. Table 2 illustrates these trends. While inequality has steadily fallen, the state share of spending increased substantially after the 1989 decision.

Partly in response to the legislature's decisions, New Jersey taxpayers rebelled. In 1992, the New Jersey legislature responded with QEA II which lowered property taxes and decreased state aid, especially in support of urban schools. The plaintiffs again claimed that disparities between urban and suburban districts widened under the amended legislation and filed another suit, *Abbott III*. Overturning the finance system again, a frustrated New Jersey Supreme Court in 1994 clarified its opinion and ordered 100 percent parity between rich and poor districts (*Washington Post*, July 13, 1994, pg. 1).

Michigan. In the summer of 1993 the Michigan state legislature passed a bill that virtually abolished using local property taxes to operate public schools.[13] The bill, as Courant et al. (1994) suggest, was a radical statement against the local property tax rather than an attempt to reform school finance. In the two decades prior to 1993 there were ten property tax cut initiatives placed on statewide Michigan ballots. The legislation ended the major system of local school finance (fully two thirds of public school spending in Michigan came from local property taxes) but did not propose any method of raising public school revenues. In the following year, the

152

state increased the state sales and tobacco taxes and imposed a statewide property tax on all property, a local property tax on nonhomestead property, and a real estate transfer tax.[14]

The new system also redesigned the redistribution plan to reduce the disparity in spending by increasing the revenues of the poorer districts and slowing the spending of richer districts. Unlike many of the court-mandated reforms, in order to make this system politically palatable, within-state variation in school spending is permitted. In the first year of the program, Fisher and Wassmer (1995) report that local property support fell from 66 percent to 25 percent of public school revenues. They also predict, based on simulation results, that in the first year of the program inequality as measured by the coefficient of variation would decrease by 9 percent.

Wisconsin. Reschovsky and Wiseman (1994) note that although the disparity in per pupil spending in Wisconsin is relatively low, the Wisconsin system of school finance has been under continuous attack. As was the case in Michigan, the driving force behind the most recent finance reform in Wisconsin was property tax relief. Wisconsin, the authors report, ranked 11th highest among the states in terms of the ratio of property taxes to personal income. In the 1993-95 biennial budget, the state legislature placed an indirect cap on local school district property taxes. Under the cap, a district is allowed only to increase revenues per pupil by the greater of a fixed amount per pupil or the rate of increase in the CPI. At the same time, the state increased state aid to schools by committing to increase the state share of public school spending from 39 percent in the 1993-94 school year to 66 percent by 1995-96. Thus, the restriction in revenues coupled with increased state aid would indirectly force schools to decrease property taxes.

THE IMPACT OF THE MOVE TOWARD CENTRALIZATION

As Manwaring and Sheffrin (1995) explain, a move to centralize school finance could have an impact on spending for several reasons. First, state control might significantly reduce voters' willingness to support education. Fischel's (1989, 1994) analysis of the California experience is consistent with that view. He argues that the California Supreme Court's ruling in *Serrano* led to the passage of Proposition 13. Before *Serrano*, California was roughly in a Tiebout equilibrium where the property tax was essentially a benefit tax that reflected the cost of education. Given this price, families "voted with their feet," i.e., they sorted themselves according to their demands for public goods, particularly education. As a consequence, high income families resided in school districts with high spending per pupil.

Serrano ended this system by redistributing property tax revenue from high spending to low spending districts. Prior to *Serrano*, citizens were willing to pay high property taxes because those taxes were the cost of a better education for their children. After *Serrano*, taxpayers would have to increase funding to every district in the state in order to increase funding to local schools, and thus the marginal benefit of paying property taxes was significantly reduced. Fischel argues that this decreased willingness to pay property taxes contributed to the passage of Proposition 13 and the subsequent decline in the level of education expenditures.

Second, Silva and Sonstelie (1995) suggest that school finance decentralization might have an income effect. Suppose states had no role in education and that we had perfect Tiebout sorting. That is to say, consider a world where communities were perfectly homogeneous with respect to the demand for education and income (assuming that education demand and income are closely correlated). Spending in each community would be determined by income in each community assuming a median voter model and thus mean spending in a state would be determined by the mean income in the state. Now suppose the state assumes responsibility for providing primary and secondary education. Spending in this case would be determined by the state median income. In most cases, mean income is greater than median income. Thus, since education is a normal good, increased centralization would decrease aggregate spending.

Third, education spending might fall after centralization due to a greater dependence of education expenditures upon the state budget. Theobald and Picus (1991) emphasize the increased competition for funds as the funding decision moves from the district level to the state level. At the district level, education has little competition for funding since most property tax dollars are spent on education. When the funding decision moves to the state level, education must compete with other programs. Thus in their view, demands for additional state spending on Medicaid and corrections would decrease funding for education in states where education is highly centralized but would have little impact in states where it is decentralized.

154

Fourth, Manwaring and Sheffrin (1995) discuss a base effect that includes the other effects that could be associated with litigation. For example, it is possible that when litigation or reform occur, education suddenly plays a more important role in the political process.

What does the available evidence tell us about the actual effects of centralization on school expenditures? We can draw on three sources: case studies, broader empirical studies, and simulation models. Not surprisingly, many of the case studies have focused on California. The general consensus from the California work has been that the shift toward state financing of education has led to a significant decrease in spending on education. Rubinfeld (1995), for example, shows that in 1971-72 California spending per pupil was 98 percent of the national average and that California ranked 19th among the states; by 1991-92, California spending was only 86 percent of the national average and the state had fallen to 39th.

Silva and Sonstelie (1995) try to estimate what proportion of this decline should be attributed to *Serrano* and ensuing policy changes, and how much should be attributed to other factors such as changes in income and number of students. They begin by estimating the determinants of education spending using data from all of the states other than California. Using this equation, they show that prior to *Serrano* in 1969-70, spending in California was consistent with that of the other states during the same period. They found a very different story in 1989-1990. Spending was significantly lower in California than would have been predicted given the state's income, number of students and so on. They conclude that roughly one-half of the decline in spending in California can be attributed to *Serrano*.

The second source of information comes from broader econometric studies based on data from all of the states. Manwaring and Sheffrin (1995) use a panel data set from 1970-1990 to examine the role of equalization litigation and reform in determining the level of education funding in a dynamic model. They found that on average, successful litigation or education reform raises education spending significantly. The average effect across all states varies from an annual increase of $124 to $177 (in 1990 dollars) per student -- 2.2 to 3.5 percent of expenditures -- depending upon which set of years and which model are used. The predicted dynamic path depends on the movement of the overall state budget, income and other factors. They also examined the forecast experience of four particular states and showed that different states would be expected to follow very different paths following education finance reform.

The Downes and Shah (1994) analysis is similar in some ways to the Manwaring and Sheffrin (1995) model. They show that the stringency of constraints on local discretion determines the effects of reforms on the level and growth of spending. Further, for any particular type of reform, the characteristics of a state's population determine the direction and magnitude of the post-reform changes in spending.

We took a somewhat different approach in Murray, Evans and Schwab (forthcoming). In that paper, we looked at the impact of court ordered reform on the distribution of spending within states as well as the average level of spending across a state. Our study was based on data for more than 16,000 school districts over the 20-year period 1972-1992. We came to three main conclusions. First, court-mandated education finance reform can decrease within state inequality significantly. Depending on the way we measure inequality, our results imply that reform in the wake of a court decision reduces spending inequality within a state by anywhere from 16 to 38 percent. Second, our results suggest that court ordered reform reduces inequality by raising spending at the bottom of the distribution while leaving spending at the top unchanged. As a result of court ordered reform, we found that spending would rise by 11 percent in the poorest school districts, rise by 7 percent in the median district, and remain roughly constant in the wealthiest districts. At times, finance reform has been characterized as a zero sum game that takes education resources away from the wealthiest districts and gives them to the poorest. Our results offer little support for that argument. Third, finance reform leads states to increase spending for education and leave spending in other areas unchanged, and thus by implication states fund the additional spending on education through higher taxes. As a consequence, the state's share of total spending rises as a result of court ordered reform.

In Evans, Murray, and Schwab (forthcoming 1996) we focused specifically on the impact of court ordered reform on state policy. We found that after court-mandated reform, per pupil revenues from state sources increased by about $437 (in 1992 dollars) per student, while revenues from local governments were unchanged. As a result, the state share of revenues increased by over four percentage points. More importantly, we found evidence that the increased state role reflected an aggressive redistribution policy. After finance reform, per pupil revenues from state sources increased by over $700 in districts at the 5th percentile of the distribution of local revenues, by $600 in districts at the 25th percentile, and over $300 for districts with the median local revenues. In contrast, we find no evidence of an increase in spending for districts in the top quartile of local per pupil revenues. We also found that finance reform that was not initiated by court decisions was largely ineffective. Legislature-initiated education finance reform did not change within-state inequality in revenues, state share of revenues, or average spending per pupil.

The final source of evidence on the effects of school reforms comes from simulation models. Recently, Nechyba (1995), Fernandez and Rogerson (1995) and Epple and Romano (1995) have all developed computable general equilibrium models that allow them to explore the effects of education finance reform. The Nechyba and Epple and Romano models are similar in spirit. Both models look at a metropolitan area and include housing markets, mobility, and a public sector where policy is determined as in the median voter model. In both, educational output depends on education spending and peer group effects. The Fernandez and Rogerson model does not consider peer group effects, but does offer one important extension. It is a dynamic model, and education instead of being a consumption good is an investment good. The current old care about the current young's income which is determined in part by education investments. All three models look at a fundamental question: what happens in a general equilibrium setting when we move from decentralized to centralized school finance?[15]

The answers these three models offer are intriguing. Fernandez and Rogerson find that there is an important tradeoff between a centralized and decentralized finance system. The latter permits individuals, given their income, greater scope for sorting themselves into communities that more closely offer their preferred bundles than does a centralized system that imposes uniform spending (the Tiebout explanation for decentralization). The former system reduces heterogeneity in education spending and can change the income distribution and could raise the average income in society. In principle, the net outcome is ambiguous. Given their specification of the model and choice of parameter values, they find that centralized finance leads to higher average income in the steady state, higher average spending on education, and higher welfare. The welfare improvement from centralization is on the order of 3 percent of aggregate income. Nechyba (1995) finds that both foundation aid and district power equalization grants increase the attractiveness of lower income communities and thus decrease segregation by income. Centralized finance systems in his model caused peer effects to lead to increased income segregation as peer groups become the only way to improve local schools.

An Evaluation of the Evidence

Each of the three sources of evidence on the impact of centralization of school finance has clear strengths and weaknesses. Case studies allow a researcher to look carefully at the nature of the reform, the institutional setting, the political response and a whole range of other factors that are key determinants of increased centralization. The weakness of these case studies is that it is very difficult to know the extent to which the experience of any particular state can be generalized. The analyses of the California experience make this point clear. As we noted above, nearly all of the early evidence on the effects of school finance reforms came from several careful studies of California, a pattern that is not surprising given the importance of the *Serrano* decision. That work strongly suggested that the state's increased role led to lower spending. Subsequent work, however, found that California may be an important outlier; in general, reform seems more likely to be associated with higher rather than lower spending. There are a number of sensible explanations of these results (including the possibility that since California is different from the rest of the country along virtually any dimension we can think of, perhaps we should have expected it to respond to court ordered finance reform differently). In particular, the California courts set a particularly strict standard in their definition of equality, requiring that the differences in per pupil spending among nearly all districts be no greater than $100 in 1971 dollars. It would be sensible to conjecture that while this strict standard might have led voters to pass Proposition 13, milder reform that simply required higher state support for the poorest districts would have led to a very different reaction.

Broader empirical work can address many of the shortcomings of case studies. By looking at data from many states, these empirical studies allow us to look at more general responses to school finance reform efforts. Unfortunately, such studies often force us to sacrifice some of the advantages that case studies offer. It is extremely difficult in empirical work involving many states to fully capture the important details of reform and a full description of the background into which those reforms have been introduced. Instead, such studies must rely on very broad measures of reform. In our own work (Murray, Evans, and Schwab 1996), for example, our measure of reform is a dummy variable that equals 1 if the courts have overturned a state's system of school finance. Such a measure (which is similar to the measures used in most of the other work in this field) lumps together all court ordered reforms and treats them alike. Thus these econometric studies can give us some insights into the average effect of reform efforts but are less likely to give us much guidance on the impact of any specific reform proposal. It would be possible to try to draw distinctions among different types of efforts to centralize school finance, but if this research tried to capture all of the important details in the end it is likely to become the equivalent of a set of case studies.

Simulation models designed to study the impact of centralized school finance share many of the strengths and weaknesses of other general equilibrium models. Their attraction is obvious. In an ideal world from a researcher's perspective, we would like to watch a society function under a decentralized finance system, and then rerun history after we give states the responsibility for funding schools. General equilibrium simulation models allow us to do that (at least on a computer).

The problem of course is that they are based on some very strong assumptions. Unfortunately, sometimes we have limited knowledge about important relationships in the models and it is therefore difficult for us to evaluate those assumptions. In the Fernandez and Rogerson (1995) model, for example, a key relationship is the impact of education on income. As we explained above, they concluded that centralized school finance will decrease income inequality significantly. This result turns on an assumption that (i) current education expenditures is an important determinant of future income, (ii) there are decreasing marginal returns to education. Thus, for example, suppose that person i's income is $f(E_i)$, where E_i is the education expenditures for person i. The Fernandez and Rogerson argument requires that f' is positive and large and that f'' is negative.

While both of these assumptions seem plausible, the evidence to support them is weak. Most of the evidence on the effectiveness of education expenditures focuses on the relationship between spending and education outcomes typically measured in terms of scores on standardized tests. Coleman (1966) argued strongly that tests scores and spending are unrelated and that instead, family socioeconomic status and perhaps peer groups are the key determinants of success in school. Most of the subsequent literature on education production functions has come to the same conclusion. Hanushek (1986), in his often cited review of this literature, summarized more than 150 studies that followed Coleman and concluded that "there appears to be no strong or systematic relationship between school expenditures and student performance." Betts (1995) using data from the NLSY finds no evidence that increases in spending raise wages.

There have been several recent attacks on this "money doesn't matter argument." Murray (1995) argues that because the relationship between test scores and important labor market outcomes such as wages is weak, it is more sensible to focus on different measures of education outcomes that clearly do have important implications. Her work looks at the impact of spending on the probability of finishing high school and starting college on the grounds that the amount of education someone receives is clearly linked to wages. She finds that additional spending can substantially increase the probability that students will finish school; her results imply, for example, that a 12 percent increase in spending by the poorest 5 percent of school districts would result in an 6 percent decrease in the dropout rate. Card and Krueger (1992) provide some important direct evidence that increases in education spending raise the rate of return to education. In all, it seems fair to conclude that the impact of expenditures on incomes -- the magnitude of f' in the notation we used above -- is an unresolved and important issue. Given the uncertainty surrounding the size of the marginal benefits of education spending, the rate at which those benefits decline -- f'' above -- must certainly be regarded as an open question.

Peer group effects are a key element of the Nechyba (1995) and Epple and Romano (1995) papers. A number of studies, including Coleman (1966), Summers and Wolfe (1977) and Henderson, Mieszkowski and Sauvageau (1978), found that the quality of students in a school will have a strong impact on the performance of any individual student.[16] Evans, Oates and, Schwab (1992), however, argue that we should probably be at least somewhat skeptical about these results. Most studies on this issue try to explain output (measured perhaps as test scores) as a function of school inputs, family characteristics, and the characteristics of other students in the school. Typically, these studies treat peers as an exogenous variable and proceed by estimating an ordinary least squares or other single equation model.

But peers are endogenous; parents choose the characteristics of their child's peers when they choose their child's school. Evans, Oats and Schwab go on to argue that it is quite likely that ignoring simultaneity leads to over estimates of peer group effects. They offer the following example to illustrate their point. Consider a family that cares a great deal about their child's education. This child is likely to do well in school for at least two reasons. First, his parents will see that he attends a school where the peer group is "better" than expected given the family's observed characteristics. Second, he will do well as a result of factors that cannot be observed: his parents will spend more time with him, they will emphasize the importance of education, they will help him with his homework. A single equation model, however, would mistakenly attribute all of their child's success to his superior peer group. They then go on to estimate the impact of peer groups on the probability that a teen will become pregnant and the probability that a teen will drop out of high school. In both cases they find significant peer group effects in single equation models but no such effects in simultaneous equations models that treat the peer group as an endogenous variable.

Certainly, we should not interpret the Evans, Oates and Schwab results as evidence that peer group effects are unimportant. As they argue, the potential for this sort of bias is present in virtually all peer group studies. The practical importance of their argument is unclear and deserves further attention: in their particular study, the bias turned out to be very large. Until further work has looked at this question carefully, we need to be somewhat cautious about the conclusions in this literature.

THE FEDERAL ROLE IN ELEMENTARY AND SECONDARY EDUCATION

We have argued that over the last 25 years, growing concerns over inequality in school spending have led state courts and legislatures in the U.S. to shift the responsibility for funding public education from local governments to state governments. It would be reasonable to suspect that these concerns would also have led the federal government to assume a larger role in education. In Murray, Evans, and Schwab (1996) we showed that fully two thirds of the variation in per pupil spending is between states, and thus state level reform can address only the one-third of inequality that can be attributed to differences in spending within states.

This has not been the case, however, in part because of the U.S. Supreme Court's 1973 decision in *San Antonio Independent School District v. Rodriguez* that education is not a fundamental right (as defined in the U.S. Constitution) and that poorer districts do not constitute a suspect class. The federal role in elementary and secondary education, until the passage of Goals 2000, was limited to categorical grants that target money to schools with poor children. Most of the growth of these programs occurred between 1965 and 1975. Prior to 1965, there were fewer than 10 federal programs for elementary and secondary education. By 1970 there were 29 federal programs accounting for almost 3 percent of federal spending. In 1994 there were 36 separate programs in the federal budget.

Table 5.3 sets forth spending on the major federal education programs from 1965 to 1994. As shown in the last row of that table, real federal spending on elementary and secondary education grew steadily between 1965 and 1975, increased slightly between 1975 and 1980, fell sharply between 1980 and 1985, and began to increase steadily after 1985. Figure 5.1 shows that the proportion of the average district's budget from federal funds has remained roughly constant at 6 to 8 percent of total revenue.

Chapter 1, the revised version of the Elementary and Secondary Education Act of 1965 (ESEA), is the largest Federal program aiding elementary and secondary schools. Chapter 1 divides responsibilities among the Federal government, state educational agencies and local school districts. Local school districts make decisions about grade levels, subject areas, kinds of services, teaching methods, classroom settings, and types of staff that are funded by Chapter 1. States distribute funds to school districts and monitor local projects. The federal government allocates funds to states and enforces the requirements governing the use of Chapter 1 dollars. These requirements attempt to ensure that Chapter 1 reaches the neediest schools and students. In practice, however, Chapter 1 provides grants to almost every school district in the country. In 1994, 90 percent of all districts and 75 percent of all elementary schools received Chapter 1 funds.

162

Table 5.3: **Federal Spending for Major Elementary Secondary Education Programs (millions of 1994 dollars)**

	Fiscal	Year					
	1965	1970	1975	1980	1985	1990	1994
Department of Education							
Grants for the disadvantaged		5269	5086	5826	5746	5143	6900
Impact aid program	1701	2581	1677	1255	884	934	983
School Improvement Programs	356	1133	1900	1435	719	1361	1663
Indian Education			109	169	112	79	82
Bilingual Education		82	252	307	214	216	257
Education for the handicapped	68	310	410	1495	1391	1850	3604
Vocational and Adult Education	643	1318	1778	1566	899	1496	1317
Education Reform - Goals 2000							19
Department of Agriculture	3036	2994	5113	7390	5650	6328	7801
Total, All Programs	9469	22940	28816	29145	23091	25160	34318

Source: U.S. Department of Education, Office of Educational Research and Improvement, *Digest of Education Statistics, 1994*. Deflated by the federal fiscal year budget deflator.

Figure 5.1 Trends in Education Finance, 1960-1992

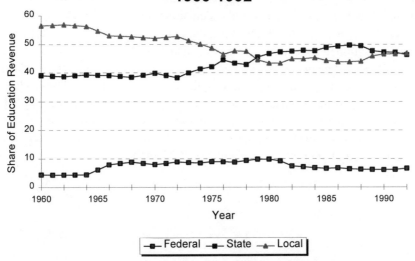

Education Reform and National Goals

At an education summit in 1989, President Bush and the nation's governors (including then Arkansas Governor Clinton) started the process of establishing national education goals. The point of setting goals was to focus attention on measurable results such as improving student achievement and increasing the high school graduation rate to 90 percent. In 1994, President Clinton signed into law "Goals 2000: Education America Act." The act was the federal government's first attempt to establish national academic goals and standards for schools *and* give money to meet them. The eight national goals that all schools and students should achieve by the year 2000 are described in Table 5.4. Participation in the goals program would be voluntary. No school or district would lose funds if they choose not to participate. States could apply for grants to help to meet the educational goals regardless of whether they participate in the program. Only three states -- Virginia, New Hampshire and Montana -- refused to participate.

The bill as it was passed on March 31, 1994 had wide spread bipartisan support. In addition many business leaders dissatisfied with the state of public schools backed the law. After the Republican victories in Congress in the November 1994 elections, however, Goals 2000 became a prime target of Newt Gingrich's Contract with America. The most contentious parts of Goals 2000 are the national boards that define standards and certify state programs to achieve the national goals. At one extreme are the Christian Coalition and a Republican presidential candidate who claim that " . . . Goals 2000 will lead the federal government too deeply into public schools, burden them with new regulations and bully them about how to teach everything from sex education to 'politically correct' history." The compromise reached in the Spring of 1996 is much weaker with respect to standards. Under this compromise, each state can vouch for the worthiness of its own plan, without reference to the national standards. If a state chooses, it may use its share of the $350 million appropriated for the program to buy computers for classrooms instead of participating in setting standards.

Table 5.4   The National Education Goals Declared by 103rd Congress

By the year 2000 ...
1.   All children in America will start school ready to learn.
2.   The high school graduation rate will increase to at least 90 percent.
3.   All students will leave grades 4,8 and 12 having demonstrated competency in English, mathematics, science, foreign languages, civics and government, economics, arts, history and geography.
4.   Teachers will have access to programs for the continued improvement of their professional skills and the opportunity to acquire the knowledge and skills needed to instruct and prepare all American students for the next century.
5.   United States' students will be first in the world in mathematics and science achievement.
6.   Every adult will be literate and will possess the knowledge and skills necessary to compete in a global economy.
7.   Every school in the United states will be free of drugs and violence.
8.   Every school will promote parental involvement in their children's education.

Source: "Goals 2000: Educate America Act."

International Comparisons

The role of the central government in education finance in other countries provides an interesting contrast to the U.S. experience.[17] In Australia, the federal government provides about 40 percent of public expenditure on education in 1991. Australia, as does many other countries, funds private schools with public resources. The states support the government schools, while the federal government finances private schools and provides additional resources to the states for government schools. In Germany, the federal government's only role in financing is to provide grants to students in secondary schools. The local communities provide the buildings, while the states cover personnel and operating costs. In France, education is principally financed by the national government, although the share derived from local resources is increasing. The French government also gives aid to families on the basis of family income and provides partial support to private schools. Closer to home, the intergovernmental relationships in Canada are very similar to the U.S. In 1994, half of the K-12 revenues were derived from provincial sources, 11 percent from federal sources and the remaining funding came from local property taxes.

SUMMARY AND CONCLUSIONS

Decentralized control of education is firmly rooted in the history of public schools in this country, as throughout the seventeenth and eighteenth centuries schools were virtually the sole responsibility of local governments. The trend over the last 30 years, however, has been toward greater state responsibility. In 1960, local governments' share of education expenditures was 57 percent and the states' share was 39 percent; by 1992, state and local shares were roughly equal. The federal government has always played only a small role in K-12 education.

What are the important implications of the growing centralization of public school finance? The evidence here is mixed. Much of the initial research on this issue focused on the California experience after the *Serrano* decision. It concluded that the shift toward state financing led to a sharp decrease in education spending. Subsequent research suggests that California may be an outlier. It now appears that, in general, court ordered reform is more likely to lead to an increase in expenditures, to encourage the states to assume more responsibility for funding schools and to reduce within-state inequality in education spending.

Many questions surrounding the trend toward increased centralization remain unanswered. We would argue future research should focus on at least three key issues. First, state government budgets have faced sharply higher demands for spending in several important areas, particularly corrections and Medicaid. These two categories now account for 22 percent of state spending, up from 7 percent in 1972. Thus public education is in a difficult position. It finds itself increasingly dependent on state governments for funding as states respond to school finance reform litigation. At the same time, states have been forced to devote more and more of their revenues to Medicaid and corrections. Thus demands for additional state spending on Medicaid and corrections could lead to sharp decreases in funding for education in states where education is highly centralized.

This issue has some important policy implications. In all likelihood, states in the near future will be asked to assume a much larger role on a range of issues that in the past were either the shared responsibility of state and federal governments or the sole responsibility of the federal government. For example, legislation that has passed both houses of Congress would replace the matching grants for Medicaid and many welfare programs with block grants to the states and then give virtually full responsibility for these programs to the states.

Second, many have argued that "money does not matter" in education, i.e., that the link between spending and education outcomes is very weak (see, for example, Hanushek 1986). One reason additional funds often fail to yield better outcomes is that increased spending sometimes does not actually flow through to the classroom. In 1990, instructional expenditures were only 60 percent of current education expenditures, down from 68 percent in 1970 (*Digest of Education Statistics, 1993*). It thus becomes important to study not only how increased centralization changes the level and distribution of education funds, but how those funds are actually used as well.

Third, increased centralization could lead more wealthy families to send their children to private schools. As Sonstelie (1982) shows, families will choose private schools when the deadweight loss from being forced to consume a suboptimal level of public education exceeds the cost of a private education. As spending falls in wealthy districts, this deadweight loss rises, possibly leading to a decline in public school enrollments. Downes and Schoeman (1993) and Husted and Kenny (1996) find some support for this argument, but Murray (1995) finds little evidence nationally. This is a topic that deserves further attention.

NOTES

1. This research was supported by the National Science Foundation under grant #SPR-9409499. We thank NSF for its support.
2. Cited in Fisher (1996).
3. This section draws heavily on Thompson, Wood, and Honeyman (1994) and Downes and Pogue (1994).
4. The school finance literature sometimes draws distinctions between guaranteed tax base, guaranteed yield and district power equalization programs. These differences are minor, and we therefore refer to all three as district power equalization programs.
5. Hawaii is the only state that does not use the property tax to support public schools. The Hawaiian system allocates resources centrally based on requests from individual schools. Despite the state tax source, there is some evidence of unequal resources. Hisht (1974) found a positive correlation between per pupil school spending and family income. More recently, Thompson (1986) notes that the recommendations of the central board are increasingly set aside in favor of pet projects of the legislature and the Governor.
6. In 1992 dollars, the range was $270.
7. See Oakland (1994) for a very different view on this issue.
8. This section of the paper draws heavily on Reschovsky (1994).
9. This section draws heavily on Picus (1991), Goertz (1993) and Picus and Hertert (1993).
10. The state share of expenses is the ratio of state expenditures for education (direct and intergovernmental) from the Census Bureau's *State Government Finances* to total educational expenditures from the *Digest of Education Statistics*. State and total expenditures include amounts for debt and capital outlays.
11. For state k the Theil index T_k equals

$$T_k = \frac{\sum_{j=1}^{J_k} P_{jk} X_{jk} \ln(X_{jk} / X_K)}{\sum_{j=1}^{J_k} P_{jk} X_{jk}}$$

where X_{jk} is per pupil expenditure in district j, J_k is the number of districts in state k, P_{jk} is the fall enrollment in district j in state k, and X_k is the pupil-weighted mean expenditure per pupil for the state. The Theil index rises whenever spending in a wealthy district falls by \$1 and spending in a poor district rises by \$1, and thus lower values of the index are associated with less inequality. It is not difficult to see that the Theil index reaches a minimum of 0 when spending is the same in all districts throughout a state, since in that case X_{jk} always equals X_k and the natural log of 1 is 0. The index reaches the natural log of the number of students in the state in the extreme case where one district accounts for all spending on education and the rest of the districts spend nothing.

12. These acts, incorporated in Senate Bill 90 (SB90, 1973), also included the introduction of several categorical programs. Subsequent legislation including Senate Bill 220 (1975) increased foundation aid, subjected the voter overrides of the revenue limits to power equalization, allowed the state to recapture local tax revenues (never exercised), and redistributed aid to urban schools.

13. Fisher and Wassmer (1995) point out that local property taxes were not completely abolished in the 1994-95 school year.

14. The Michigan reforms were not limited to school finance. The state increased standards and allowed provisions for charter schools and schools of choice.

15. Epple and Romer (1995) and Nechyba (1995) are also concerned with school choice issues.

16. See Jencks and Mayer (1990) for an excellent review of the literature on the effects of peer group on a broad range of social outcomes.

17. This section draws heavily on the *World Education Encyclopedia* (1988).

REFERENCES

Betts, Julian R. "Does School Quality Matter? Evidence from the National Longitudinal Survey of Youth." *Review of Economics and Statistics* 77, no. 2 (May, 1995): 231-50.

Card, David and Alan B. Krueger. "Does School Quality Matter? Returns to Education and the Characteristics of Public Schools in the United States." *Journal of Political Economy* 100 (February, 1992): 1-40.

Clark, Catherine. "Regional School Taxing Units: The Texas Experiment." *Journal of Education Finance* 21 (Summer, 1995): 87-102.

Coleman, James S., *et al. Equality of Educational Opportunity.* Washington: Government Printing Office, 1966.

Coons, John E., William M. Clune, and Stephen D. Sugarman. *Private Wealth and Public Education.* Cambridge: Harvard University Press, 1970.

Courant, Paul N., Edward M. Gramlich, and Susan Loeb. "Michigan's Recent School Finance Reforms - A Preliminary Report." In *Proceedings of the Eighty-Seventh Annual Conference on Taxation.* 29-36. Columbus: National Tax Association, 1994.

Downes, Thomas A. "Evaluating the Impact of School Finance Reform on the Provision of Education: The California Case." *National Tax Journal* 45 (December, 1992): 405-419.

Downes, Thomas A. and Thomas F. Pogue. "Accounting for Fiscal Capacity and Need in the Design of School Aid Formulas." In *Fiscal Equalization for State and Local Government Finance*, edited by John E. Anderson . Westport, Connecticut: Praeger, 1994.

Downes, Thomas A. and David Schoeman. "School Financing Reform and Private School Enrollment: Evidence from California." Unpublished working paper, 1993.

Downes, Thomas A. and Mona P. Shah. "The Effect of School Finance Reform on the Level and Growth of Per Pupil Expenditures." Unpublished working paper, October 1994.

Epple, Dennis and Richard E. Romano. "Public School Choice and Finance Policies, Neighborhood Formation, and the Distribution of Educational Benefits." Unpublished working paper, July 1995.

Evans, William N., Sheila E. Murray, and Robert M. Schwab. "School Houses, Court Houses, and State Houses after *Serrano.*" *Journal of Policy Analysis and Management*, forthcoming.

Evans, William N., Wallace E. Oates, and Robert M. Schwab. "Measuring Peer Group Effects: A Study of Teenage Behavior." *Journal of Political Economy* 100 (October, 1992): 966-991.

Feldstein, Martin S. "Wealth Neutrality and Local Choice in Public Education." *American Economic Review* 45 (March, 1975): 75-89.

Fernandez, Raquel and Richard Rogerson. "Income Distribution, Communities, and the Quality of Public Education." *Quarterly Journal of Economics* 111(February, 1996): 135-164.

Fernandez, Raquel and Richard Rogerson. "Public Education and Income Distribution: A Quantitative Evaluation of Education Finance Reform." Unpublished working paper, August 1994.

Fischel, William A. "Did *Serrano* Cause Proposition 13?" *National Tax Journal* 42 (December, 1989): 465-473.

Fischel, William A. "How *Serrano* Caused Proposition 13." Unpublished working paper, September 1994.

Fisher, Ronald C. *State and Local Public Finance* (2nd edition). Chicago: Richard D. Irwin, 1996.

Goertz, Margaret E. "School Finance Reform in New Jersey: The Saga Continues." *Journal of Education Finance* 18 (Spring, 1993): 346-365.

Husted, Thomas A. and Lawrence W. Kenny. "The Legacy of *Serrano*: The Impact of Mandated Equal Spending on Private School Enrollment." Unpublished working paper, March 1996.

Hanushek, Eric A. "The Economics of Schooling: Production and Efficiency in Public Schools." *Journal of Economic Literature* 24 (September, 1986): 1141-1177.

Hisht, Joseph C. "Full State Funding and the Distribution of Educational Resources in Hawaii." *National Tax Journal* 27 (March, 1974): 1-8.

Jencks, Christopher and Susan E. Mayer. "The Social Consequences of Growing Up in a Poor Neighborhood." In *Inner City Poverty in the United States*, edited by Laurence E. Lynn, Jr. and Michael G. H. McGeary. Washington: National Academy Press, 1990.

Ladd, Helen F. and John Yinger. "The Case for Equalizing Aid." *National Tax Journal* 47 (1994): 211-224.

Manwaring, Robert L. and Steven M. Sheffrin. "Litigation, School Finance Reform, and Aggregate Educational Spending." Unpublished paper, August 1995.

Murray, Sheila E. "Two Essays on the Distribution of Education Resources and Outcomes." Unpublished Ph.D. dissertation, 1995.

Murray, Sheila E., William N. Evans and Robert M. Schwab. "Education Finance Reform and the Distribution of Education Resources." Unpublished working paper, March 1996.

Nechyba, Thomas J. "Public School Finance in a General equilibrium Tiebout World: Equalization Programs, Peer Effects, and Competition." Unpublished working paper, July 1995.

Oakland, William H. "Fiscal Equalization: An Empty Box?" *National Tax Journal* 47 (1994): 199-210.

Picus, Lawrence O. "Cadillacs or Chevrolets?: The Evolution of State Control over School Finance in California." *Journal of Education Finance* 17 (Summer, 1991): 33-59.

Picus, Lawrence O. and Linda Hertert. "Three Strikes and You're Out: Texas School Finance After Edgewood III." *Journal of Education Finance* 18 (Spring, 1993): 366-89.

Reschovsky, Andrew. "Fiscal Equalization and School Finance." *National Tax Journal* 47 (1994): 185-197.

Rothstein, Paul. "The Demand for Education with 'Power Equalizing' Aid." *Journal of Public Economics* 49 (1992): 135-162.

Rubinfeld, Daniel L. "California Fiscal Federalism: A School Finance Perspective." Unpublished working paper, June 1995.

Silva, Fabio and Jon Sonstelie. "Did *Serrano* Cause a Decline in School Spending?" *National Tax Journal*, 47 (June, 1995): 199-216.

Sonstelie, Jon. "The Welfare Costs of Free Public Schools." *Journal of Political Economy* 90 (August, 1982): 794-808.

Theobald, Neil D. and Lawrence O. Picus. "Living with equal Amounts of Less: Experiences of States with Primarily State-Funded School Systems." *Journal of Education Finance* 17 (1991): 1-6.

Thomson, John A. "Funding and Spending in Paradixe: Notes on the Hawaii Model of Educational Finance." *Journal of Education Finance* 12 (Fall, 1986): 282-94.

Thompson, David G., R. Craig Wood, and David S. Honeyman. *Fiscal Leadership for Schools: Concepts and Practices.* New York: Longman, 1994.

U.S. Advisory Commission on Intergovernmental Relations. *Changing Public Attitudes on Governments and Taxes.* Washington: U.S. Government Printing Office, 1991.

U.S. Department of Education, National Center for Education Statistics. *Digest of Education Statistics, 1994* . Washington: U.S. Government Printing Office, 1995.

U.S. Congress. "Goals 2000 Education America Act." pub. l. 103-227.

Wells, Robert Marshall. "Goals 2000 Bill Clears Senate in Early-Morning Session." *Congressional Quarterly* (April 2, 1994): 804-5.

World Education Encyclopedia. New York: Facts on File Publications, 1988.

6 INTERGOVERNMENTAL FISCAL RELATIONS AND SOCIAL WELFARE POLICY

Therese J. McGuire[1]

INTRODUCTION

Several decades of experience with income redistribution policies have not eradicated the problem of poverty in the U.S. In fact, in the most recent decade there is evidence that the income distribution has become more disparate and that the number of poor has increased (Bradsher, 1995, Atkinson, 1995 and Atkinson, Rainwater, and Smeeding, 1995). These facts have led to a growing frustration with welfare policy among both conservatives and liberals. One possible (partial) source of the ineffectiveness of welfare policy in the U.S. is that responsibility for this government function has been placed at the wrong levels or units of government. In other words, the responsibility for financing and delivering welfare programs may be in the wrong governmental hands. The conventional wisdom has been that redistribution policies should be centralized because of the public good nature of redistribution and because of the potential for migration to undue any redistribution undertaken at the subnational level. Current political thinking in the U.S. and many other developed countries is that subnational levels of government may be more effective at designing and delivering welfare policy because they are closer to their voters and recipient populations and therefore have a better understanding of the needs and tastes of their residents. The issue explored in this chapter is whether the delivery of welfare policy would be improved by decentralization of governmental responsibility.

Many countries, in addition to the U.S., have recently debated or implemented decentralization of and decreased expenditures on social welfare programs. A rethinking of government's role in social policy is underway in Eastern Europe and the former Soviet Union, while Western European countries as dissimilar as Sweden and Great Britain have cut back on various social welfare policies. The sorting out of responsibility and coordination of social policies at three levels of government, including the supranational level, is currently being debated in the European Union. In the developed countries, severe budgetary problems at the national government level are forcing a rethinking of the government's role in alleviating poverty and a reexamination of which level of government is best equipped to deliver welfare programs.

The purpose of this chapter is to explore questions surrounding the choice of a fiscal federal arrangement for social welfare policy. By social welfare policy I refer to means-tested cash and in-kind transfer programs and not to social insurance programs that also transfer income. The chapter begins with an examination of actual intergovernmental arrangements for financing and providing welfare services in the U.S., currently and historically. Spending on welfare programs in other developed countries and intergovernmental arrangements for delivery of welfare programs in Canada are described in Section III. In Sections IV and V, I review the theoretical arguments and empirical evidence, respectively, for and against decentralization of responsibility for welfare policy. I turn in the final two sections to possible directions for future policy in the U.S. and with some thoughts on directions for future research.

PROVISION AND FINANCING OF WELFARE PROGRAMS IN THE U.S.

Responsibility for welfare policy in the U.S. has been shared between the federal government and subnational levels of government for several decades. Trends in the division of financing responsibility between the federal government and state and local governments are displayed in Table 6.1. The federal share of total U.S. spending on means-tested programs has increased steadily over time. In 1965, before the enactment of many of the welfare programs described below, the share was 50 percent, it had increased to 72 percent by 1980, and since then has been roughly 65-70 percent. Much of the increase in federal expenditures on public welfare has been through intergovernmental grants to state governments rather than through direct spending by the federal government. In 1965 federal direct spending was $105 million, while federal intergovernmental grants were $3,098 million. By 1992 the corresponding figures were $47,722 million of direct spending and $94,760 million of intergovernmental grants. These trends in financing provide a context for the current debate over the devolution of responsibility from the federal to the state governments.

Modern social welfare policy in the U.S. began with the passage in 1935 of the Social Security Act, which established the cash transfer program known as AFDC (Aid to Families with Dependent Children). The program largely serves single-headed families. AFDC is a joint federal-state program with benefit levels set by state governments, eligibility and other program design attributes either jointly set by the federal and state governments or solely by state governments, and the financing of the program nearly evenly split between the two levels of government, with the federal government providing a matching-rate grant to the states that is more generous to low-income states. There is a fair amount of variation across the states in AFDC benefit levels. In 1992, the average monthly payment per family ranged from $122 in Mississippi to $684 in Alaska, with an average of $374 (Fisher 1996). It is the AFDC program that most people have in mind when they consider the failure of welfare policy in the U.S. As a contributor to budgetary problems, it is illustrative to note that spending on AFDC represented in Fiscal Year 1993 less than three percent of total state own-source revenues (Advisory Commission on Intergovernmental Relations, 1995) and only about two percent of total federal spending on social welfare and insurance programs in 1992 (Bixby, 1995).

The current panoply of major welfare programs is briefly described in Table 6.2. In addition to AFDC, there are two other major cash programs: Supplemental Security Income (SSI), which is a federal program for low income individuals who are aged, blind or disabled, and the Earned Income Tax Credit (EITC). In addition to these three major cash programs, several states have general assistance cash programs that largely serve low-income individuals who do not qualify for the other cash programs. The two major in-kind programs are Food Stamps, which is a federal program of vouchers for food purchases for qualifying low-income individuals, and Medicaid. In addition, the federal government finances various public housing and

176

Table 6.1:   Federal and State-Local Government Shares of United States Public Welfare Expenditures, 1965-1992

	Federal Share	State-Local Share
1965	50	50
1970	59	41
1975	66	34
1980	72	28
1985	71	29
1990	65	35
1992	71	29

Notes: These shares were calculated by the author using data provided in Tables 25 and 28 of "Significant Features of Fiscal Federalism, Volume 2", U.S. Advisory Commission on Intergovernmental Relations, 1994.

Public Welfare is defined as expenditures on programs that support or provide assistance to needy persons contingent on their need.

housing subsidy programs, which are delivered by the states or local governments or local housing authorities. As can be seen in the table, SSI, EITC and Food Stamps are largely federal programs, general assistance programs are exclusively state programs, and the federal government shares with the states the financing, delivery, and administration of AFDC, Medicaid, and housing subsidies.

The largest of these programs is Medicaid, enacted in 1965 to provide health care for certain low income individuals who do not have private health insurance (AFDC and SSI recipients automatically qualify for Medicaid). Recently Medicaid coverage was expanded to include poor children. Medicaid is a joint federal-state program, with the federal government mandating certain aspects of the program and providing matching grants to the states (using a similar matching rate formula as for AFDC), and the states responsible for setting eligibility, administering the

Table 6.2: Major U.S. Federal and State Social Welfare Programs

	Year Established	Number of Recipients (Year)	Total Expenditures (Year)	Delivered by	Financed by
Cash Programs:					
AFDC	1935	4.8 million families (1992)	$25 billion (1992)	States	States and federal government
SSI	1972	5.6 million recipients (1992)	$22 billion (1992)	Federal government	Federal government
General Assistance	Varies	1.2 million recipients (1992)	n.a.	States	States
EITC	1976	13 million families (1991)	$11 billion (1991)[a]	Federal government	Federal government
In-kind Programs:					
Medicaid	1965	40 million enrolled (1993)	$126 billion (1993)	States	States and federal government
Food Stamps	1964	25 million recipients (1992)	$25 billion (1992)	Federal government	Federal government
Housing Subsidies	Varies	5 million recipients (1992)	n.a.	States and local governments	States and federal government

[a] Because of the expansions to the program in the early 1990s, expenditures on the EITC are expected to be between $20 and $25 billion by 1995.

Sources: "Green Book: Overview of Entitlement Programs", Committee on Ways and Means, U.S. Government Printing Office, 1994. <u>State and Local Public Finance</u> by Ronald Fisher, 1996.

program, and financing approximately 50 percent of total expenditures. In recent years Medicaid expenditures have grown at unsustainable rates, so that for many states, state spending on Medicaid has become the largest single category of expenditures. In 1992 Medicaid spending represented 15 percent of total state government expenditures in the U.S., and over 25 percent of state spending in New York (Fisher, 1996). Much of the recent growth in spending on Medicaid is attributed to the growth in the number of elderly and disabled recipients rather than families with children.

The most recent program is the EITC, which has been greatly expanded in recent years beginning with the 1986 Tax Reform Act and more importantly with the 1990 and 1993 Omnibus Budget Reconciliation Acts. The EITC provides refundable credits to low-income working families. The structure of the program has three components: for very low incomes it works as a wage subsidy, for a middle range of low incomes it provides a flat credit or grant, and for a higher range of incomes the credit phases out much like a negative income tax. The EITC has outstripped AFDC in terms of number of family recipients, and total spending by the federal and state governments is expected to be similar for the two programs by 1998. By 1998, the cost to the federal government of the EITC is expected to be over $24 billion, while the federal cost of AFDC is expected to be $16 billion (Dickert et al., 1995). Some states have enacted state-level EITCs that essentially mimic the federal program on a smaller scale by incorporating a refundable, wage-subsidy credit for low-income individuals as part of the state personal income tax.

The primary cash program delivered solely by the states (and their local governments) is general assistance. State general assistance programs vary substantially in terms of eligibility and benefit levels, and the benefit levels are relatively small compared to other state and federal welfare programs. These programs typically provide income support for portions of the population, such as single individuals, families without children, and the non-elderly, that do not qualify for AFDC and other federal-state cash programs. In recent years, several states have debated eliminating their general assistance programs altogether on budgetary grounds and on the controversial grounds that the populations served should be working rather than drawing welfare. As an example, Michigan eliminated its general assistance program in 1991, which, according to research by Danziger and Kossoudji (1995) as summarized in Danziger and Danziger (1995), may have caused an increase in the number of homeless persons seeking shelter (see Kilborn, 1995). According to a tabulation of number of recipients by the U.S. Department of Health and Human Services, 19 states effectively did not have general assistance programs in Fiscal Year 1992. Of the total number of general assistance recipients in the U.S. in 1992, fully 31 percent were in the state of New York (whose 1993 total population represented just seven percent of the total U.S. population). Many general assistance programs are both financed and administered by county governments.

It is clear from this description and Table 6.2 that the division of responsibility for welfare policy among levels of government in the U.S. is very much shared between the federal and state (and to a lesser degree local) governments. Even for programs that are largely federal operations, the states tend to have some administrative responsibility and also authority to add on to the federal programs as they see fit. Food Stamps, for example, is a program totally financed and designed by the federal government, but delivered by the states, while 26 states contribute voluntarily to the federal SSI program (Georges, 1995).

PROVISION AND FINANCING OF WELFARE PROGRAMS IN SELECTED OECD COUNTRIES

Welfare spending in other developed countries tends to be higher and more centralized than in the U.S. In Table 6.3, the U.S. is compared to selected OECD countries in terms of levels of social welfare spending as a share of GDP in 1980 and 1990. In these data, social protection spending is defined much more broadly than welfare spending to include virtually all income and transfer programs for the aged and social insurance such as unemployment insurance as well as programs targeted to low-income persons. By this broad measure, U.S. spending on social protection is relatively low, with only Australia and Japan among the ten comparison nations having lower spending. The highest spending country is, not surprisingly, Sweden, followed by France. Over the ten year period, Canada and Italy have witnessed increases of greater than 25 percent, while spending in Germany has fallen, and spending in Sweden and the United States has remained virtually constant as a share of GDP.

Obtaining information on intergovernmental arrangements for the financing and provision of welfare policies across countries is not a simple matter. A recent study by Blank and Hanratty (1993) does allow an examination of the arrangements in Canada. Canada, like the U.S., is a federal system, and the responsibility for welfare policy is shared between the federal and provincial governments. The primary cash assistance program for low income families and individuals in Canada is Social Assistance (SA). Like the AFDC program in the U.S., SA is jointly financed by the federal and provincial governments, but eligibility and benefit levels are largely the responsibility of the provinces, whereas both the states and federal governments have some say on eligibility in the U.S. While the benefit levels vary across provinces in Canada as they do in the U.S., the average maximum benefit under SA is substantially higher than under AFDC. Both countries have tax-credit programs administered by the federal governments for low-income households with children, but the EITC in the U.S. is only for working low-income families, while the Canadian program, the Child Tax Credit, is available to all qualifying low-income families with children. In summary, while the Canadian social welfare programs appear to be more generous in terms of benefit levels and eligibility rules than the U.S. programs, the division of responsibility among levels of government seems to be very similar with a joint federal-state (federal-province) partnership.

THEORIES OF THE DIVISION OF WELFARE POLICY AMONG LEVELS OF GOVERNMENT

The efficiency argument for national financing and provision of welfare policy is well articulated by Oates (1972, 1991). The argument has two parts. First, the amount of redistribution undertaken by a given local jurisdiction is limited by the potential in-migration of the poor and out-migration of the rich. The tax-price paid by the rich for redistribution to the poor will be higher in poorer communities, causing the rich to continue to move away from the poor until there is no longer an incentive to do so because the rich are segregated from the poor. This frustrates the ability of local governments to provide any redistribution. Second, if redistribution is a pure "national" public good so that nonresidents benefit from the redistribution provided in other localities, then the level of redistribution provided by independent local governments will be inefficiently low compared with the socially optimal level. These arguments are elaborated upon by Ladd and Doolittle (1982). They argue not only for a nationally determined level of welfare benefits, but also that welfare should be financed by the central government. Their argument is based on a presumption that preferences of residents throughout the country should be

Table 6.3: Total Expenditure on Social Protection as a Percentage of GDP

Selected OECD Countries

	1980	**1990**
Australia	10.98	12.96
Canada	14.37	18.79
France	23.85	27.26
Germany	25.40	22.94
Italy	19.75	24.96
Japan	10.48	11.57
Spain	16.76	19.95
Sweden	32.42	33.13
United Kingdom	21.30	24.03
United States	14.10	14.58

Source: Tables 1b and 1c, "New Orientations for Social Policy", OECD, 1994.

reflected in the welfare levels set in any particular jurisdiction, and that fair treatment of taxpayers requires tax burdens reflecting ability to pay, regardless of where taxpayers live.

Oakland (1983) challenges the empirical importance of mobility in the Oates framework, and he develops an alternative model of local redistribution in a federal system, where he assumes complete immobility. In his model, inefficiencies arise with local government provision of redistribution because of different local amenities and because of the externality of tax avoidance behavior induced by local efforts to redistribute income based on local income taxes.

In a slightly different context, Goodspeed (1989) contributes to our understanding of the importance of mobility in determining whether local government provision of welfare is efficient and feasible. Goodspeed examines the use of ability to pay taxes by local governments, which has a direct analogy to the provision of welfare or redistribution. In a realistic model of local governments that incorporates a housing market, he compares the efficiency and equity consequences of two forms of local taxation - a proportional income tax and a head tax. Focussing on the possibility for intercommunity inefficiency, i.e., that people will not be distributed across communities in an efficient manner as postulated by Oates (1972), he finds that the efficiency losses associated with using proportional income taxes rather than head taxes at the local level are small and that some amount of redistribution does take place. In his words: "These results suggest that the use of ability to pay taxes by local governments would result in some redistribution, relative to head taxes, without serious efficiency consequences resulting from migration." (p. 340). His model is general enough for his results to be relevant for explicit redistribution or welfare policies as well as for the choice of tax instrument. Epple and Romer (1991) develop a similar model and confirm that significant local redistribution is possible even with free mobility of heterogeneous agents among jurisdictions.

Pauly (1973) presents an efficiency argument for local provision of welfare policy. If tastes for welfare distribution differ and people have a stronger preference for redistributing to the local poor rather than poor people who are more distant, then it may be efficient for local jurisdictions to provide different amounts of redistribution. His efficiency argument rests on two assumptions: first, nonpoor individuals are assumed to care only about the poor in their own jurisdiction, and second, poor individuals are assumed not to move in response to differences in locally-set welfare levels. Interestingly, Pauly finds that even in the presence of mobility of the rich (or taxpayers), local governments are an efficient mechanism for redistribution.

Slemrod (1986), in an examination of the optimal progressivity for a state income tax, reviews much of this literature. He argues that the traditional view that state governments should not undertake redistribution (through ability-to-pay taxes in his case) can be challenged along two dimensions: first, many of the goods provided by state governments cannot be financed by benefit taxation, and second, differences in state residents' tastes for redistribution should be taken into account. He concludes that a state "should strike a balance between the desire of its citizens to allocate the burden of taxation "fairly" and the objective of minimizing the disincentive effects, including migration." (p. 137)

Clearly, mobility, both of low income and high income individuals, plays a large role in evaluating the validity of these competing theories. Brown and Oates (1987) explore the implications of mobility of the poor for the role of different levels of government in assisting the poor. They show that, because mobility of the poor results in an externality with increases in transfers in one jurisdiction affecting the utility and costs of transfers in another jurisdiction, mobility of the poor renders a totally decentralized system of relief for the poor inefficient. In their model the nonpoor care only about the poor in their own jurisdiction (as in Pauly (1973), there is no national public good), and the potential for poor people to move in response to benefit differentials can cause the nonpoor to choose an inefficiently low level of support for the poor. Brown and Oates briefly discuss a few additional arguments for a central government role in income redistribution, including the argument that relief for the poor is a national public good and the argument that considerations other than economic efficiency, such as social justice or decency, may matter. But their primary point is that mobility of the poor is a source of inefficiency in a decentralized system of income redistribution, and that some central government involvement is needed to internalize the externality.

A related difficulty with redistribution at the local level is that poor and rich populations may be segregated from one another by jurisdiction for reasons having little to do with welfare policy, thus rendering any redistribution infeasible. One of the implications of the Tiebout (1956) model is that people will sort themselves by tastes for public goods. If preferences for local public goods are strongly correlated with income, this sorting may result in local jurisdictions composed of individuals all of the same income level. In this scenario, even if high income individuals have a preference for income redistribution, their local government will not provide any redistribution because there would be no one to whom to redistribute income.

The theories of income redistribution in a federal system do give some guidance for thinking about the actual assignment to various levels of government of responsibility for welfare policy. The national public good argument and the limitations placed on decentralized provision by mobility suggest a major financing role for the central government. However,

184

varying tastes across individuals sorted into local jurisdictions suggest a role for state or local governments. The two seemingly divergent theories come together in a specific policy implication. Both theories suggest matching grants from the federal government to local jurisdictions in addition to a national minimum level of benefits with additional state or local supplements permitted. (See Wildasin, 1991 in which he derives a similar optimal policy in a model with perfect mobility and endogenous determination of wages.) This is roughly the arrangement for certain programs in the U.S. today. In particular, the two primary joint federal-state programs, AFDC and Medicaid, are characterized by matching rate grants. However, AFDC does not have a national minimal level of benefits.

EMPIRICAL EVIDENCE ON MOBILITY, DIFFERING TASTES, AND INCOME SEGREGATION

There are two primary issues raised by the theoretical literature that are amenable to empirical evidence. One is the question of whether tastes for welfare spending differ markedly across subnational levels of government, and whether any differences can be attributed to altruistic desires to relieve poverty locally versus nationally. The other is the question of whether differences in welfare benefits across subnational levels of government induce significant migration.

The fifty states in the U.S. provide a rich laboratory for exploring the evidence on differing tastes and incomes. In Table 6.4, mean household income, percentage of households above and below certain income levels (a crude measure of income dispersion), and percentage of population below the poverty line are displayed for all states for 1989. On average for the U.S., 13.1 percent of persons and 10.0 percent of families had incomes below the poverty level, 15 percent of households had incomes below $10,000, 4 percent of households had incomes above $100,000, and the mean household income was $38,453. Scanning the table for the fifty states and the District of Columbia reveals significant amounts of variation in all four variables, and strong, although not perfect, correlation among the measures. The southern states tended to have high rates of poverty, low mean household incomes, and small percentages of households with incomes above $100,000 (Arkansas, Louisiana, Mississippi, and New Mexico fit this description). We will also see below that many of the poorer states tended to have lower welfare benefit levels. This correlation may suggest that local altruism is not a strong factor in the determination of welfare policy.

Connecticut and New Jersey had below average poverty rates, high mean household incomes, and large percentages of households with incomes above $100,000. Michigan looked very much like the U.S. average on all of these measures in 1989. Nebraska and North Carolina demonstrated some compression of the income distribution in that these two states had average or slightly below average poverty rates and relatively small percentages of their households with incomes above $100,000. Both states also had below average mean household incomes. New Hampshire exhibited the lowest poverty rate among all the states, but had an average percentage of its households with incomes above $100,000. These characteristics combined to give New Hampshire an above average mean household income.

As an indicator of differences in tastes for welfare spending, we can examine the differences across the states in average benefit levels. An inspection of the five states with the lowest and the five states with the highest AFDC benefit levels does indeed reveal great differences. In 1992, with the U.S. average at $374, the lowest average monthly AFDC payments per family were $122 in Mississippi, $133 in Alabama, $157 in Texas, $171 in Louisiana, and $173 in Tennessee, all five southern states. The highest payments were $553 in Vermont, $556 in Connecticut, $591 in California, $592 in Hawaii, and $684 in Alaska, two northeastern states and three western states (Fisher, 1996, Table 21-4). These differences in welfare benefits reflect, at least in part, differences in tastes for providing welfare.

Clearly many factors are likely to be involved in determining these benefit levels, with political tastes for welfare being difficult to measure but potentially very important. In an analysis of state welfare spending, Craig (1991) estimates a model of the determinants of state spending on welfare, both AFDC spending and aggregate state welfare spending, using a panel data set of the 48 contiguous states from 1966 to 1985. He controls for various types of federal aid, and several economic and demographic variables including total population, percentage of population below the poverty line, income per capita, unemployment rate, and percentage of families headed by a female. He includes fixed state effects in the model and finds the state effects to be significant and to vary greatly. For example, the estimated fixed state effect in the total welfare equation is -$39 per

186

Table 6.4: Poverty, Income Distribution, and Mean Income by State, 1989

	Percentage of Families Below the Poverty Level	Percentage of Households With Incomes Less than $10,000	Percentage of Households With Incomes Greater than $100,000	Mean Household Income
Alabama	14.3	22	2	$30,484
Alaska	6.8	8	8	$49,587
Arizona	11.4	16	3	$35,426
Arkansas	14.8	24	2	$27,378
California	9.3	12	7	$46,247
Colorado	8.6	14	4	$37,504
Connecticut	5.0	10	9	$53,263
Delaware	6.1	11	5	$42,070
District of Columbia	13.3	17	8	$44,413
Florida	9.0	15	4	$36,517
Georgia	11.5	17	4	$36,810
Hawaii	6.0	9	7	$47,972
Idaho	9.7	16	2	$31,554
Illinois	9.0	14	5	$40,885
Indiana	7.9	15	2	$34,864
Iowa	8.4	16	2	$31,874
Kansas	8.3	16	3	$34,184
Kentucky	16.0	23	2	$29,354
Louisiana	19.4	25	2	$29,512
Maine	8.0	15	2	$33,605
Maryland	6.0	10	7	$47,905
Massachusetts	6.7	13	7	$45,472
Michigan	10.2	16	4	$38,064
Minnesota	7.3	14	4	$37,718
Mississippi	20.2	27	2	$26,880
Missouri	10.1	18	3	$33,441
Montana	12.0	20	2	$28,773
Nebraska	8.0	16	2	$32,147
Nevada	7.3	12	4	$38,611
New Hampshire	4.4	10	4	$42,502
New Jersey	5.6	10	9	$51,241
New Mexico	16.5	20	2	$31,006

New York	10.0	16	7	$44,121
North Carolina	9.9	17	1	$33,242
North Dakota	10.9	19	2	$28,614
Ohio	9.7	16	3	$35,333
Oklahoma	13.0	21	2	$30,539
Oregon	8.7	15	3	$34,062
Pennsylvania	8.2	16	4	$36,684
Rhode Island	6.8	15	4	$39,174
South Carolina	11.9	18	7	$36,810
South Dakota	11.6	20	2	$28,068
Tennessee	12.4	20	3	$31,864
Texas	14.1	18	4	$35,618
Utah	8.6	13	3	$35,071
Vermont	6.9	13	3	$35,493
Virginia	7.7	13	5	$41,663
Washington	7.8	13	4	$38,157
West Virginia	16.0	24	2	$27,115
Wisconsin	7.6	14	3	$35,180
Wyoming	9.3	16	2	$32,633
U.S. Average	10.0	15	4	$38,453

Source: U.S. Bureau of the Census, 1990 Census of Population, U.S. Summary of Social and Economic Characteristics, 1992.

capita for Arizona and $70 per capita for California. These fixed state effects may capture "taste" for welfare spending not captured by the other variables in the model.

In a study that explicitly examines political factors, Plotnick and Winters (1985) estimate a model of the determinants of the income guarantee levels set by the states. They examine AFDC benefit levels, and AFDC combined with Food Stamps and Medicaid benefits. They find both political and economic variables to be important in explaining income guarantee levels. Among the political variables that provide explanatory power are interest group strength, interparty competition, and local government cost share.

Orr (1976) provides another exploration of the factors behind the differences in AFDC benefit levels across the states. He finds that income per capita, racial composition of the recipient population, and regional effects are important determinants of benefit levels, along with variables reflecting the costs of providing welfare benefits such as the average and marginal federal shares. The Craig, Plotnick and Winters, and Orr studies provide evidence of taste differences for welfare provision, which may support the Pauly (1973) model of local provision of redistribution.

In the Pauly model, however, efficiency of welfare provision at the local level depends on immobility of the poor. Two studies in the mid-1980s, Blank (1988) and Gramlich and Laren (1984), find evidence that welfare recipients move in response to differences in welfare benefits across states. Gramlich and Laren employ two different methods, one based on state-level data and the other on micro data, to estimate both the effect of differences in AFDC benefits on migration of the poor and the effect of potential migration of the poor on the benefit levels set by states. They conclude that differences in AFDC benefit levels do result in migration of AFDC beneficiaries from low-benefit to high-benefit states, and while the effect appears to be small in the short run, the long run effect may be substantial. Gramlich and Laren draw strong fiscal federalism policy implications from their results: "state governments should be given less, not more, financial responsibility for determining income redistribution policies" (p. 492) and "it is an argument for altering the present AFDC financial arrangements ... and letting the national government set a benefit level" (p. 510).

Blank (1988) uses a micro data set drawn from the Current Population Survey to estimate the effect of wages and AFDC benefit levels on the location decisions of female-headed households. She specifies and estimates a model of the simultaneous choices of where to live and whether to participate in welfare, and the data allow her to examine the different behavior of welfare and nonwelfare participants. She finds that welfare payments, as well as other economic variables, have a significant effect on the migration decisions of female welfare recipients.

Moffitt (1992) reviews this early literature and concludes that the studies provide weak evidence for a positive effect of higher benefit levels on in-migration. However, he points to the econometric difficulties of the endogeneity of benefit levels and the use of cross-state variation to identify the models. This is potentially a serious problem with the Gramlich and Laren (1984) results.

The evidence presented by two recent studies, where the authors avoid these econometric problems, seems to contradict the earlier studies. Walker (1994) uses individual data from the County-to-County Migration Flow data base to compare the migration behavior of poor young women (a group potentially eligible for AFDC) to nonpoor young women and to poor young men (groups not likely to be eligible for AFDC). He limits his geographic focus to moves between contiguous counties in different states in order to control for other broad determinants of migration that might confound the estimated effects of welfare benefit levels, such as climate and proximity to friends and family. He concludes that there is no evidence to support the "welfare magnet" conjecture that people move in order to obtain higher benefit levels. Levine and Zimmerman (1995) employ a similar quasi-experimental design and use the National Longitudinal Survey of Youth data set to estimate probabilities of moving from one state to other states for welfare eligibles relative to different control groups. They define welfare eligibles to be low-income single women with children, and their control groups are poor single women without children, poor single men, poor married men, and poor married women. They find that individuals in their treatment group, who are eligible for AFDC, are no more likely to move from a low benefit state to a high benefit state than are individuals in their control groups, who are not eligible for AFDC. They conclude that there is little evidence that migration decisions are influenced by differences in welfare benefits.

In summary, the evidence seems to indicate that tastes for levels of welfare policy differ across the states, and that the economic situations and capacities to finance welfare policy also differ across the states. The more recent evidence on mobility indicates that recipients of welfare benefits are not sensitive to differences in welfare benefit levels in making location decisions. There is not good evidence on the crucial question of whether there is a local dimension to preferences for welfare, in other words, whether the rich care only about the local poor as opposed to caring about the poor wherever they reside. The fact that different states provide different levels of welfare only indicates that state governments, in setting welfare policy for their states, are reflecting the preferences of their residents only. It is highly unlikely that policy makers of a given state take into account the preferences of nonresidents for alleviating poverty in their state. The evidence on limited mobility of the poor across states, and varying tastes and economic conditions across the states, would seem to point to a joint federal-state role in providing welfare with significant financing and delivery roles for both levels of government.

FUTURE POLICY DIRECTIONS

The question of which level of government should be primarily responsible for providing welfare policy in the U.S. is being hotly debated in Washington and state capitols around the country. The impetus is for decentralization, but the tensions are strong between increasing the level of local autonomy and maintenance of national standards. The debate is not about principles of public finance, but is instead focussed on budgetary issues and administrative capabilities to carry out welfare policies. In particular, the primary arguments for devolution of responsibility to the states are that the states can act as laboratories to experiment with different, and hopefully more effective, approaches to welfare, and that the states have better knowledge than the federal government about what might work in their states. The argument is not the economic efficiency argument that states should be allowed to act on differing tastes for welfare (in fact, states have considerable leeway to do so under the present system), but rather that the federally driven policies have been such an unmitigated failure that allowing states to branch out on their own can only be an improvement. Allowing state experimentation in the short run need not imply a total devolution of responsibility to the states in the long run. Should some state hit on a magic formula for addressing poverty, there is no reason why the responsibility for delivering welfare services could not be re-centralized with the federal government mandating and financing the magic program for all states.

There are several directions that the devolution of responsibility for welfare programs could take. The most dramatic would be for the federal government to shed its responsibilities completely, no longer mandating nor partially financing welfare policy (as it currently does with Medicaid, AFDC and housing subsidies) nor carrying out the provision of welfare policy (as it presently does with SSI, EITC and Food Stamps). The least dramatic would be for the federal government to weaken various mandates and cut back on its matching rates for Medicaid and AFDC and to cut back on eligibility and benefit levels for SSI, EITC and Food Stamps. The most likely direction is somewhere in between these two extremes, but closer to the dramatic option.

As this chapter was being completed, Congress passed and the President signed major welfare reform legislation. The legislation eliminated entitlement to cash benefits under AFDC, converted the federal matching grant program for AFDC to a block grant, and gave the states greater leeway in terms of setting program design for cash benefits. Federal spending on welfare was expected to decline under the new proposals with the greater part of the savings coming about through cuts in the federal Food Stamp program and through elimination of federally-funded benefits for legal immigrants. The direction of the reform involved devolution of responsibility, both financing and policy setting, to the states. The change from matching to block grants is likely to exacerbate budgetary difficulties for states during economic downturns. Importantly, under the block grants, states will no longer be required to spend money in order to receive federal dollars.

While the rhetoric justifying the block grant proposals is that states should be allowed to experiment, it is clear that the primary motivation for these proposals is to cut federal spending on welfare programs. The implications for overall welfare spending, in other words, the implications for the spending responses of the states, are not clear, although block grants will provide less incentive for state spending than the present matching-rate grants. Certainly, the federal-state compact on welfare policy, which since 1935 has involved joint responsibility for the design, delivery, and financing of welfare policy, will be changed dramatically. These changes in the fiscal federal arrangement for welfare present several issues. One is that the states do appear to have differing preferences for welfare spending, which the devolution of responsibility purports to recognize. But, the current system for AFDC, which allows states to set benefit levels, appears to permit ample room for states to act upon their differing preferences. Additionally, the states can choose to supplement the federal SSI program, and they have complete control over general assistance programs. In fact, some observers have argued for a national minimum benefit level for AFDC because they view the levels chosen by some low-spending states under the current matching-rate grant system to be too low (Gramlich, 1985). Under a block grant system, the states will have even less incentive to raise benefit levels as they would be solely responsible for spending at the margin.

Another issue is recognizing and addressing the efficiency implications of the devolution of welfare policy from the federal government to the states. While the evidence on the lack of sensitivity to differences in welfare benefits in the migration behavior of poor people would appear to indicate considerable latitude for states in setting welfare policy, the evidence necessarily is based on current benefit levels. Under the block grant proposal, where entitlement is eliminated and states are no longer required to spend their own money in order to receive federal money, the differences in benefit levels could become much more pronounced, with unknown consequences for migration of the poor (and nonpoor). Another efficiency argument is that welfare (redistribution) is a national public good, with redistribution provided in any given state or locality benefiting the nonpoor throughout the country. In this situation, efficiency requires significant financing or provision responsibilities at the federal government, the opposite direction of current policy in the U.S.

A less central consideration is whether the states have the administrative and financial capacity to take over increased responsibility for welfare. In fact, it can be argued that the states are better suited to the task than the federal government. The states have greater knowledge of local conditions, and, because they have been delivering most of the welfare programs over the years under federal guidance and mandates, they have the bureaucracies in place to deliver the programs. On the other hand, Ladd and Doolittle (1982) note that there are likely to be economies of scale in welfare management, and that administrative capacity is likely to vary from state to state. Burtless (1990) has noted that the present multitude of overlapping welfare programs imposes a large administrative burden.

The differing tastes for welfare across the states, the potential for migration in response to big differences in benefit levels, and the differing capabilities of the states to deliver welfare programs, combine to raise the specter of a "race to the bottom" as welfare policy is devolved to the states. Given the public good nature of redistribution, it is theoretically possible for destructive competition among the states to lead to this outcome (McGuire, 1991). With no national minimum benefit level and no matching-rate grant to give states an incentive to spend on welfare, some predict that AFDC benefit levels and welfare spending in general will be competed down to unprecedented low levels (Zedlewski and Sawhill, 1995 and Georges, 1995). Some state governors and members of Congress refute this conclusion noting that states have historically taken care of their poor residents (Pear,

1995). But the very recent trend in areas of welfare policy where states already have great latitude is "inexorably downwards" (The Economist, August 12, 1995). One of the proposals before Congress addressed this concern by requiring states to continue to spend at least 80 percent of present levels (The Economist, October 28, 1995). Nonetheless, the broader issue of whether it is equitable and efficient to have 50 potentially very different welfare systems in the U.S. appears to be moot. Unless national minimum benefit levels are imposed, and such minimums are not currently on the table, this is the direction of future welfare policy in the U.S.

AN UNFINISHED RESEARCH AGENDA

The deficiencies in our knowledge of the fiscal federalism of welfare policy involve empirical rather than theoretical questions. The recent evidence on the mobility of low income individuals in response to differences in state welfare policies seems to indicate that welfare benefits have little effect on the migration of potential welfare recipients. But, we know very little about the response of high income individuals to differences in taxes imposed to finance different levels of welfare. It is likely to be very difficult to disentangle the effect of this one factor from other important factors on the location decisions of high income individuals. On the other hand, the quasi-natural-experiment techniques used in recent studies of the migration of potential welfare recipients in response to differences in welfare benefit levels might gainfully be applied to study the mobility response of high income taxpayers to differences in welfare policies and corresponding taxes levied to finance welfare. It is important to understand the migratory response of high income residents because mobility of either high income individuals or potential welfare beneficiaries would limit the ability of subnational levels of government to redistribute income.

One of the stronger theoretical arguments for national as opposed to local provision of welfare is the notion that redistribution is a national public good. However, we know very little about whether resident/voters consider this to be the case. There have been a few surveys of voter opinion (see Ladd and Doolittle (1982) for a brief discussion), but whether voters favor federal government provision because they desire to free ride or because they desire nationally determined welfare policy is very difficult to determine.

Finally, my review of the existing literature uncovered very little by way of international comparative studies of intergovernmental arrangements for the financing and provision of welfare policy. Is social welfare policy highly centralized in most developed countries? What are the conditions (fiscal, economic, demographic) that cause countries to decentralize provision of welfare policy? What can we learn about the division of responsibility for welfare among governments from the development of a supranational level of government for the European Union?

Income redistribution is one of few traditional functions of government that is not a serious candidate for extensive privatization. Solutions to the problematic state of welfare policy will involve government. Which levels of government are most appropriate for setting welfare policy remains a question for debate.

NOTES

1. I am very grateful to Becky Blank, Howard Chernick, Ron Fisher, Tim Goodspeed, and Hilary Hoynes for comments and conversations. Jessica Rio provided excellent research assistance.

REFERENCES

Advisory Commission on Intergovernmental Relations. "Medicaid, AFDC, and State Budgets." *ACIR Issue Brief* No. 1 (1995). Washington: 1-4.

Atkinson, A. B. *Incomes and the Welfare State: Essays on Britain and Europe.* Cambridge: Cambridge University Press, 1995.

Atkinson, Anthony B., Lee Rainwater and Timothy M. Smeeding. *Income Distribution in OECD Countries: Evidence from the Luxembourg Income Study.* Paris: Organization for Economic Co-operation and Development, 1995.

Bixby, Ann Kallman. "Public Social Welfare Expenditures, Fiscal Year 1992." *Social Security Bulletin 58* No. 2 (Summer 1995): 65-73.

Blank, Rebecca M. "The Effect of Welfare and Wage Levels on the Location Decisions of Female-Headed Households." *Journal of Urban Economics 24* No. 2 (September 1988): 186-211.

Blank, Rebecca M., and Maria J. Hanratty. "Responding to Need: A Comparison of Social Safety Nets in Canada and the United States." In *Small Differences that Matter*, edited by David Card and Richard B. Freeman. Chicago: University of Chicago Press, 1993.

Bradsher, Keith. "Widest Gap in Incomes? Research Points to U.S." *The New York Times* (October 27, 1995): D2.

Brown, Charles C., and Wallace E. Oates. "Assistance to the Poor in a Federal System." *Journal of Public Economics 23* No. 3 (April 1987): 307-30.

Burtless, Gary. "The Economist's Lament: Public Assistance in America." *The Journal of Economic Perspectives 4* No. 1 (Winter 1990): 57-78.

Craig, Steven G. "Welfare Policy: Spending and Program Structure." In *State and Local Finance for the 1990s: A Case Study of Arizona*, edited by Therese J. McGuire and Dana Wolfe Naimark. Tempe: Arizona State University, 1991.

Danziger, Sandra K., and Sheldon Danziger. "Will Welfare Recipients Find Work When Welfare Ends?" *Urban Institute Welfare Reform Briefs* No. 12 (June 1995): 1-4.

Danziger, Sandra K., and Sherrie A. Kossoudji. "When Welfare Ends: Subsistence Strategies of Former GA Recipients." Ann Arbor, MI: School of Social Work, University of Michigan, February, 1995.

Dickert, Stacy, Scott Houser, and John Karl Scholz. "The Earned Income Tax Credit and Transfer Programs: A Study of Labor Market and Program Participation." in *Tax Policy and the Economy 9*, edited by James M. Poterba, 1-50. Cambridge: National Bureau of Economic Research and MIT Press, 1995.

The Economist. "Pete Wilson's Horn of (Almost) Plenty." (August 12, 1995): 23.

The Economist. "Congress's Welfare Cheats." (October 28, 1995): 18.

Epple, Dennis, and Thomas Romer. "Mobility and Redistribution." *Journal of Political Economy 99* No. 4 (August 1991): 828-58.

Fisher, Ronald C. *State and Local Public Finance*. Chicago: Richard D. Irwin, Inc., 1996.

Georges, Christopher. "Depth of Welfare Cuts Under GOP Plan Depends As Much on the States as It Does on Washington." *The Wall Street Journal* (August 21, 1995): A10.

Goodspeed, Timothy J. "A Re-examination of the Use of Ability to Pay Taxes by Local Governments." *Journal of Public Economics 38* No. 3 (April 1989): 319-42.

Gramlich, Edward M. "Reforming U.S. Federal Fiscal Arrangements." In *American Domestic Priorities: An Economics Appraisal*, edited by John Quigley and Daniel Rubinfeld, 34-69. Berkeley: University of California Press, 1985.

Gramlich, Edward M., and Deborah S. Laren. "Migration and Income Redistribution Responsibilities." *The Journal of Human Resources XIX* No. 4 (1984): 489-511.

Kilborn, Peter T. "Michigan Puts Poor to Work But Gains Appear Precarious." *The New York Times* (October 24, 1995): A1.

Ladd, Helen F., and Fred C. Doolittle. "Which Level of Government Should Assist the Poor?" *National Tax Journal 35* No. 3 (September 1982): 323-36.

Levine, Philip B., and David J. Zimmerman. "An Empirical Analysis of the Welfare Magnet Debate Using the NLSY." NBER Working Paper No. 5264. Cambridge, MA: National Bureau of Economic Research, September, 1995.

McGuire, Therese J. "Federal Aid to States and Localities and the Appropriate Competitive Framework." In *Competition Among States and Local Governments: Efficiency and Equity in American Federalism*, edited by Daphne A. Kenyon and John Kincaid, 153-66. Washington: The Urban Institute Press, 1991.

Moffitt, Robert. "Incentive Effects of the U.S. Welfare System: A Review." *Journal of Economic Literature 30* No. 1 (March 1992): 1-61.

Oakland, William H. "Income Redistribution in a Federal System." In *Local Provision of Public Services: The Tiebout Model after Twenty-five Years*, edited by George Zodrow. City: Academic Press, 1983.

Oates, Wallace E. *Fiscal Federalism.* New York: Harcourt, Brace, and Jovanovich, 1972.

Oates, Wallace E. "Fiscal Federalism: An Overview." In *Public Finance with Several Levels of Government*, edited by Remy Prud'homme. City: Press, 1991.

Orr, Larry L. "Income Transfers as a Public Good: An Application to AFDC." *American Economic Review 66* No. 3 (June 1976): 359-71.

Pauly, Mark V. "Income Redistribution as a Local Public Good." *Journal of Public Economics 2* No. 1 (February 1973): 35-58.

Pear, Robert. "Senate Finance Panel Approves a Vast Restructuring of Welfare." *The New York Times* (May 27, 1995): 1.

Plotnick, Robert D., and Richard F. Winters. "A Politico-Economic Theory of Income Redistribution." *The American Political Science Review 79* (1985): 458-73.

Slemrod, Joel. "The Optimal Progressivity of the Minnesota Tax System." In *Final Report of the Minnesota Tax Study Commission, Volume 2, Staff Papers*, edited by Robert D. Ebel and Therese J. McGuire. St. Paul: Butterworths, 1986.

Tiebout, Charles, M. "A Pure Theory of Local Expenditures." *Journal of Political Economy 64* No. 5 (October 1956): 416-24.

Walker, James R. "Migration Among Low-income Households: Helping the Witch Doctors Reach Consensus." IRP Working Paper No. 1031-94. Madison, WI: Institute for Research on Poverty, April, 1994.

Wildasin, David E. "Income Redistribution in a Common Labor Market." *The American Economic Review 81* No. 4 (September 1991): 757-74.

Zedlewski, Sheila, and Isabel V. Sawhill. "Assessing the Personal Responsibility Act." *Urban Institute Welfare Reform Briefs* No. 5 (May 1995): 1-6.

7 METROPOLITAN-AREA FISCAL ISSUES

Dick Netzer

This chapter is concerned with fiscal issues characteristic of relatively large American metropolitan areas, say, the 75 largest with 1992 populations of more than 500,000, and even more the 40-odd with populations of over one million. While some of the nearly 200 smaller metropolitan areas (as officially defined) exhibit some of the structural properties of the larger areas that are associated with the fiscal issues--such as complicated or "fragmented" local government systems; income-segregated residential jurisdictions that, along with other variables, produce very large inter-jurisdictional disparities in tax bases and expenditure needs within the metropolitan areas; and awkward fiscal relations with their state governments--many of the smaller areas do not.

The chapter has seven sections. The first section describes the institutional arrangements concerning intergovernmental fiscal relations in metropolitan areas, that is, the relations between local governments and external levels of government and among the local governments in the area. The second section deals with tax and expenditure externalities in large urban areas; this, of course, is one of the two major reasons for intergovernmental intervention in the workings of individual local governments. The other reason is the subject of the third section: the distributional character of local public finance in urban areas, in terms of explicitly redistributive services, the implicit redistribution involved in other public services and the redistribution that may or may not be effected by local revenue systems.

The fourth section looks analytically at the institutional arrangements described earlier. Can we explain why the local government structures found in large urban areas have developed in the ways they have developed? Conversely, to what extent are the efficiency and equity properties (discussed in the second and third sections) a result of the governmental structures themselves? The fifth section is devoted to the two-way relationship between the fiscal arrangements and the location of households and firms in large metropolitan areas. This deals with two hoary questions: the locational effects of local tax and expenditure differentials, and the extent to which differences in land use patterns have fiscal consequences, notably the "costs of sprawl" issue. The sixth section addresses intergovernmental competition and cooperation within these large urban areas. The final section contains some brief concluding observations.

INSTITUTIONAL ARRANGEMENTS FOR INTERGOVERNMENTAL INTERACTION

Inter-level Fiscal Relations

Are the fiscal relations between local governments in large metropolitan areas and the state and federal governments systematically different from the comparable relations for other local governments? In many countries, there is a clear differentiation between the fiscal arrangements between the central government and the primate city and the fiscal arrangements among the central government and other subnational units of government. Often, there is less local autonomy for the local government of the primate city, but substantially more central government financing of public services in that city than elsewhere in the country.

There is no such pattern in the United States, and it would be unlikely simply because the most important intergovernmental fiscal relationship for cities is between the local governments and the states, and the states differ greatly in respect to fiscal arrangements. It is true that, in the past, the largest central cities and their affluent suburbs were viewed as places that had to "carry" the rest of their states in a fiscal sense: large shares of state taxes originated in the biggest cities and their suburbs, which paid for some state government services that were ubiquitous, some that were open to use by all people in the state, but were located far from the largest cities (with disproportionately low use by the big-city residents), like state parks, and some that were explicitly designed to disfavor the big cities, like equalizing school aid.

Perhaps the sharpest example of the latter was in highway finance. For decades before 1956, most state highway departments did little or no highway construction within the boundaries of cities and even less maintenance work, and state highway grants were heavily tilted toward non-urban parts of the state. Public assistance is another example. After the states enacted public assistance programs in the 1930s, cities and counties continued to be responsible for program operation and for significant portions of the costs in many states for some time. As late as the 1960s, local governments were responsible for a substantial part of the nonfederal share of the categorical programs--mainly AFDC--in ten states, and even larger shares for general assistance. The political assessment was that the rich big cities, where the welfare costs were concentrated, could afford to pay a large share of those costs on their own. There were analogous assessments, in some states, with regard to the costs of the court system, corrections (housing prisoners in local jails in the big cities, rather than in state prisons), health and welfare institutions and even higher education.[1]

However, all of this is much less true today. In each of the cases cited, there have been major shifts in responsibility to the state government level, with only a relatively few states in which the state government pays for services in the state at large but leaves the big cities and urban counties to fend for themselves, or makes them responsible for sharing costs of what in most states are state government responsibilities, like public assistance in New York (the system is locally administered and half of the non-federal share of the costs is provided by the counties and New York City). Indeed, some state governments now provide substantial state financing of some services that are of little or no concern outside large metropolitan areas, notably public transit.

Data on the differences in dependence on external grants for financing local government expenditure show relatively small variation associated with population size.[2] Local governments in the county areas (counties and independent cities not within county borders) with a population of 250,000 or more receive somewhat less state aid for all functions combined than do local governments in county areas with smaller populations. The larger areas receive more aid, relative to expenditure, for public welfare and health services, but less for education, highways and all other functions. Because school aid is two-thirds of the total, it determines the overall outcome. The school aid result is unsurprising: the measure of capacity in equalizing formulas is in money terms, property values and/or personal income, which are high in the largest metropolitan areas, so the state aid percentages tend to be low.

Federal aid direct to local governments is slightly more important in the larger metropolitan areas than elsewhere and even higher relatively for large central cities, but that aid finances only about 5 percent of total expenditure by all city governments (counting federal aid to states that passes through to local governments as state aid, as the Census data do). However, most of the aid to cities is explicitly redistributive in purpose and, as of the late 1980s, varied in importance among central cities directly with the poverty ratio (Netzer, 1993).

Intra-metropolitan Area Fiscal Relations

One commonly-held view of this is simple: within American metropolitan areas, there are poor central cities with terrible social problems and meager tax bases, surrounded by affluent suburbs whose fiscal problems seem to generate much heat, but for no apparent reason; the suburbs somehow manage to "exploit" the central city in fiscal terms. The simple view is of course correct in the sense that, on balance, the populations of the large central cities are poorer than the populations of their suburbs in nearly all cases, and major social ills always have tended to be concentrated in large central cities. Moreover, the near-monopoly on economic activity that the central city once had and that had provided a tax base that more than offset the relative poverty of the city's residents had been destroyed by the 1960s, if not earlier. Many large central cities have been "ailing" in fiscal terms at least since the 1970s, and their fiscal health has been getting worse, according to the work by Ladd and Yinger (1989).

However, there are other dimensions to intra-metropolitan fiscal relations than the question of how well or how badly the central cities fare vis-à-vis their suburbs. One difference among metropolitan areas is in the extent to which services are provided and financed by local government entities that cover a large part of the metropolitan area, a point that Ladd and Yinger take into account in their measures of central city fiscal health. States differ considerably in how numerous sub-county units are--if there are few if any sub-county units, one would expect most local public services to be financed at the county level.

Take the 22 states that are "most metropolitan" excluding New England, Alaska and Hawaii, in the sense that the metropolitan area population in 1990 was two-thirds or more of the state population.[3] At one extreme, metropolitan areas in Illinois, Indiana, Minnesota and Wisconsin had 25 or more sub-county units of government per 100,000 population (15 or more excluding special districts). At the other, Maryland and Virginia had fewer than 5 units per 100,000 population, with Florida, Georgia, North Carolina, Tennessee and Arizona having only slightly more.[4]

The states also differ in the extent to which powers are assigned to counties and special districts of county and larger size. Generally, county governments outside the Northeast have substantially more responsibility than those in that region, and therefore finance activities that are the province of small-unit finance in the Northeast. Another structural dimension is the extent of reliance on special districts that cut a wide geographic swath. For example, about 15 percent of the 2,000+ special districts in California metropolitan areas cover two or more counties. But only a handful of the 600+ special districts in New York metropolitan areas spill over a county's borders (but some of the few that do are major spenders).

There are only a few cases of truly consolidated metropolitan government in the United States, mostly cases in which relatively strong county governments were given substantial additional powers by their states. The most notable ones are in Florida and Tennessee. Indianapolis and Marion County were consolidated, surprisingly in that Indiana counties are not traditionally powerful units. A few area-wide special districts or authorities have broad powers, the most notable of which is in Seattle.

Finally, there is the issue of the fiscal relations among the large numbers of small units outside the central city in most of the large metropolitan areas. The aspect of this issue of most interest to economists clearly is the extent to which that real world represents a Tiebout (1956) world. Is the creation of a large number of small units a way of efficiently satisfying consumer preferences for public services in urban areas outside the large city? If so, what are the equity and other costs of the widely-lamented "fragmentation" of metropolitan government?

More broadly, what do these different structural arrangements imply with respect to externalities, redistribution, and the spatial distribution of households and economic activity across the urban region? To what extent is the structure endogenous, rather than a given that analysts must take as fixed? These are the subjects of the rest of this chapter.

EXTERNALITIES IN URBAN AREAS

It is inevitable that, if there are numerous local government units with substantial decision-making authority within a metropolitan area--defined as a geographic area within which there is substantial economic and social interaction--the tax and expenditure decisions of individual units will have effects, positive and negative, that spill over the boundaries of that unit and affect households, firms and governmental entities elsewhere in the metropolitan area. As in other cases, by no means all of the externalities will be relevant in efficiency terms. Some will be transfers and some will have no effect on anyone's decision-making, for example, because they are *de minimis*. But some externalities are relevant.

The classic statement of the externalities issue in local finance in metropolitan areas is in a 1962 paper by Harvey Brazer, which also is the source of the "tax-price" usage. Imagine a local public service that is entirely financed from locally-imposed taxes and that, when produced at the scale that is the minimum point in the average cost curve, generates significant benefits that cannot be appropriated by taxpayers. Suppose also that it is entirely possible to produce the service at a smaller scale and generate only trivial external benefits, but at higher unit costs. That lower scale of production has a lower total cost and satisfies internal demand. That is, the internal tax-price to voters is lower in the second case, and is chosen by them, since they place little value on the benefits to outsiders.

This resolution is of course inefficient in two senses. The output level chosen is not the least-cost level and even those local voters might (would?) have chosen a higher output level had the decision been made by a unit of government with wider geographic extension, thus permitting the benefits to be internalized--and all the beneficiaries taxed. Brazer's conclusion was that the existence of fiscal externalities will lend a bias toward what he called the "undernourishment" of public services in metropolitan areas and, presumably, lower local tax levels.

Real world cases are a lot messier than the one hypothesized. It is seldom possible to vary the scale of public output continuously, and it may be impossible to find a level of output that satisfies internal demand without generating substantial external benefits (or damages). There may not be increasing returns to scale, in which case resolution on the basis of internal demand alone is likely to be an efficient one. Nonetheless, there is clearly a lot to the point, even in the real world. For example, the existence of spillovers is the basis for the imposition by the federal and state governments of environmental requirements on local governments that require local governments to increase their expenditure for waste management.

Technological Spillovers

Expenditure externalities, positive and negative, that are essentially technological in origin, and usually dependent on the existence of increasing returns, have some obvious reality, if the services in question are produced by small-area local units and financed from local general taxes. That was the common case 40 years ago: waste (solid, liquid and gaseous) management and disposal were usually the responsibility of ordinary municipal governments, including very small ones, and financed by local property taxes; the state role in highway construction and maintenance ended at the municipal boundary in many states; there were few publicly-owned and operated transit systems and those few were (with only two notable exceptions, Chicago and Boston) the responsibility of central cities and some suburban municipalities; and even water supply usually the responsibility of individual municipalities.

But that is rarely the case today. There is much more provision of environmental and transportation services in urban areas by state government agencies and by various types of wide-area authorities and special districts. Moreover, there has been substantial federal financing of capital expenditure for these functions during the past thirty years. Also, the reliance on user charges for the financing of most such services has increased considerably (see Netzer, 1992). Thus, the extent of inefficiency associated with expenditure externalities of a technological nature is probably minor by now.

Migration-based Spillovers

In the 1960s, the Brazer argument was utilized mainly to add an efficiency strand to the equity case for shifting the financing of human resource expenditures from local to state and federal governments. The reasoning is that, given the high order of geographic mobility of the American population, the quality of education, health and social services will affect, in time, communities other than those in which people needing those services now live. But those other communities, as separate local governments, have no way to pay for the services to future residents, however much they might benefit from a healthier, better educated citizenry. The point is especially striking for elementary and secondary schools, which are operated in most large metropolitan areas outside the central city by small districts: the average product of the metropolitan area's public schools will spend the great majority of her post-school years living in a community other than the one in which she was educated.[5]

Redistribution can be treated as a public good, with choices in redistribution policy having efficiency consequences, in which case this externality argument has obvious validity. But that aside, whether there are consequential efficiency losses associated with differentials within metropolitan areas in local public spending for personal services depends on the extent to which the services are in fact public goods rather than private ones, and the relation between spending and service quality.

For example, there are substantial differences within metropolitan areas in the quality of emergency medical services (EMS), measured by response time. The main output of faster response times (and better equipped and trained emergency medical technicians) seems to be a considerable improvement in the heart attack survival rate, surely a private good, or if a public good, a very local one indeed. On the other hand, the more excess capacity each local EMS operation has, the better prepared the entire area is for major disasters, which is very much a public good.

The public goods aspect of local public school expenditure has been the main focus of concern about expenditure externalities, as indeed it should be, given that the public schools absorb about 50 percent of all local tax revenue and are the recipient of what is by far the largest component of intergovernmental grants. The general idea, of course, is that better schooling improves both the economic and political functioning of future residents, beyond the additional income and personal satisfaction that is captured by those who are so educated and their families. The skepticism of some economists on this point is not shared by anyone else in this, or indeed almost any other, society. But there is an efficacy issue, the relation between spending and the yield in terms of public goods.

In the 1950s and 1960s, the public goods case for more federal and state financing of the schools tended to be based on a picture of interregional migration that had some validity at that time: youngsters and young adults migrated, mostly to northern and western central cities, from rural areas that had terrible schools and spent very little for them. Grants that resulted in improvements in schools in the sending areas benefited the receiving areas, directly in the form of better-prepared pupils entering the northern big-city schools and indirectly in the usual ways. That picture is no longer valid in an important way: most large central cities are not experiencing significant in-migration of poor, minority people from other places in this country.

In fact, most children in poor big-city households are being educated in schools in which spending per pupil is quite high. This suggests that voters in central cities are not reluctant to spend money on schools because of the likelihood that the public-goods benefits cannot be fully appropriated within those cities. It also raises questions about the extent to which additional spending can in fact generate public-goods benefits, whether internally or externally realized. Rapid increases in real per-pupil expenditures for public schools over the past 25 years have been associated with declining, not improving, pupil performance as measured by test scores (Hanushek, 1986 and 1989; King and MacPhail-Wilcox, 1994). (Note, however, that skepticism about this conventional wisdom is expressed in the chapter by Evans, Murray and Schwab in this volume.)

Undoubtedly, the externalities problem can be demonstrated in the extreme cases, the cities that are so poor that they can raise very little indeed from local taxes for schools, pauper cities like East St. Louis, Missouri and Camden, New Jersey, and the occasional pauper suburban school districts in the largest metropolitan areas. Camden, for example, is a former manufacturing center that by 1980 had almost no functioning industrial plants; the mean market value of its privately-owned housing units in the early 1980s was a shockingly low $6,000, and its taxable property value per pupil was less than 14 percent of the statewide average in 1984-85.[6] However, suppose that the state has a reasonably equalizing school aid system and expenditures per pupil do not vary systematically with the local school tax base across the state in a state, except for a handful of pauper districts.[7] In these circumstances, we can be concerned about the potential losses from school spending externalities in that state's metropolitan areas only if we also believe that the external benefits are large relative to the internal benefits, and larger than the mean percentage of school expenditures financed from external funds.[8]

Discussion of externalities in local finance seldom deal with one of the largest objects of local government expenditure, public safety broadly defined. In part, this is because the externalities for some aspects of public safety are small. For example, fire protection is like emergency medical services: fires are extremely localized in the overwhelming majority of cases and often fire-fighting is close to a private good, but in large-scale disasters the fire-fighting capacity in place is an area-wide public good. Externalities may be more common in regard to police protection, because of both migration -- criminals moving among local jurisdictions -- and technology -- the highly specialized services that large-city police departments can afford. However, there are well-established co-operative and contractual arrangements among public safety agencies in different jurisdictions that are intended to resolve the externality issues.

Expenditure Externalities and the Level of Public Spending

If the "undernourishment" hypothesis is generally valid (and the theoretical literature since the Brazer article questions its validity), structural characteristics should make a real difference in the level of public spending. On balance, local public expenditure, standardized for population size and other control variables, should be higher when there are fewer and larger local government units within the metropolitan area. The empirical evidence generally is inconsistent with this supposition. For example, Burnell (1991) finds that the number of school districts within a county is associated with higher, not lower, spending for schools.[9] More generally, the level of local government expenditure is positively associated with personal income levels, and higher levels of personal income in a metropolitan area seem to be connected with more decentralization of suburban government (Fisher and Wassmer, 1994), a question discussed below.

Moreover, combined state-local public expenditure should be higher in states in which the state government finances a large share of total public spending than in those in which local governments are more self-sufficient. Time-series data do show that total state-local expenditure has risen most rapidly and consistently in periods in which the share of total expenditure financed by local revenue sources is declining most, but the cross-section data do not tell the same story. For example, school expenditure per pupil is negatively associated with the share of state government funding of the schools, not positively.[10] There is an obvious explanation: schools, like other local public services, have a large private goods content. The private goods aspect can be best served in a Tiebout world, where the expenditure decisions are made by small local units. State financing to supply the public goods--the externalties--has an income effect, but that effect is overwhelmed by the substitution effect, which is the local financing to provide the private good. However, in their chapter in this volume, Evans, Murray, and Schwab report their econometric work showing that increased centralization of school finance *resulting from court-ordered reforms* produces significant increases in total school spending.

Tax Externalities

Unless the only local taxes utilized are ones whose burden cannot be exported beyond the boundaries of the local jurisdiction that makes the decision to tax, the existence of autonomy in revenue decisions in metropolitan areas comprised of numerous local governments must generate tax externalities.[11] There are, of courses, significant differences in the exportability of the different revenue instruments. Among practicable local taxes (that is, excluding head taxes), land value taxes will be exported only to the extent that land is owned by nonresidents of the taxing jurisdiction, property taxes on owner-occupied housing generally will not be exported, and the same is likely to be true of local personal income taxes confined to residents.

The likelihood of net exporting is greater for local taxes on business receipts, profits, property and other inputs, and local income taxes on non-residents. This is, of course, a function of the highly uneven distribution of these tax bases across the taxing jurisdictions within a metropolitan area. If nearly all jurisdictions had approximately the same balance of resident workers and commuters, non-resident income taxes would be a pointless wash. If all types of retail establishments were ubiquitous, there would be no intra-regional sales tax exporting. But central cities still tend to have disproportionate numbers of commuters working in the city and house a variety of specialized business activities that are not found in all suburban areas. A relatively few suburban jurisdictions contain major retail complexes (and tend to be surrounded by jurisdictions with a paucity of "shopping-goods" retailers), major office centers and other important concentrations of economics activities. As Table 7.1 shows, although the suburbs in the 60 largest metropolitan areas grew much faster in every respect between 1970 and 1987 then the central cities, the central city growth rate for population was only about eight percent of the outside-central-city rate, while the ratio for employment growth was 44 percent.

In most states, the revenue powers of local governments do permit central cities and some suburban municipalities and school districts to do a great deal of exporting of tax burdens. How serious are the efficiency losses associated with this externalizing of local government costs? Clearly, the losses are small or non-existent to the extent that the ability to export tax burdens is the price that must be paid to induce a few communities to endure the environmental diseconomies associated with the physical presence of major business complexes--congestion, degraded air quality, visual ugliness, etc. American local governments do have the authority to control land uses: how many of them would tolerate shopping malls, Saturn plants, airport office complexes and the like if they could not make a fiscal "profit" from their presence, by exporting local tax burdens? On the other hand, those to whom the burden is exported, who usually have nothing at all to do with the environmental diseconomies, make economic choices in response to the changes in prices and income that reflect the exporting process.

Another argument along the lines that exporting is essential as a form of compensation for public costs otherwise borne by those jurisdictions that have relatively large concentrations of business activities is more direct: central cities in particular are alleged to be "exploited" by their suburbs, in that the central cities must provide costly services to the commuters, visitors and business establishments, without recouping from explicit user charges. Indeed, it has even been argued that the exported taxes are insufficient to pay for these additional costs. It should have been obvious that this must be nonsense, for at least 80 percent of central city government spending is for personal services to residents (like schools, health, social services, housing) and property services to residential property (like refuse collection, fire protection, water supply), while the bulk of city tax collections, in most central cities, comes from businesses, not residents and their housing. Few now argue in this vein (see Bradford and Oates, 1974),[12] although tax

Table 7.1: Employment and Population Growth in the 60 Largest Metropolitan Areas, 1970-1987 (Percent increase, 1970-87)

	Employment	Population
Entire metropolitan area	85.4	20.8
Central cities	58.0	2.8
Central business districts	25.7	-14.6[a]
Outside central cities	132.8	37.0

Source: Linneman and Summers, 1993.

Note: [a] Very few central business districts contained substantial populations, in 1970 or in 1987.

exporting is strongly urged by some on equity grounds (see Ladd and Yinger, 1989).

Logically, the clearest efficiency loss in tax exporting is the inducement it provides to those lucky places that are able to export large fractions of their tax burdens to spend far more than local voters would otherwise choose. These include resort communities with tiny year-round populations, whose school districts may spend far more per pupil than the richest suburban school district and, in some states, school districts that are the sites of major power plants and receive large fractions of the property taxes or gross receipts taxes paid by the utility.[13]

A different type of tax externality in metropolitan areas has arisen in recent years, in the form of competing for the location of economic activity by offering firms tailored tax reductions. This is dealt with in the sixth section of the chapter. It can be regarded as an externality in this sense: if a particular type of tax preference is offered by one jurisdiction in the metropolitan area, it is more likely to be matched by a similar type of preference than by a reduction in an entirely different tax. The result over time may be far less use of the particular revenue instrument throughout the area, and more use of other revenue instruments. This could have positive, or negative, effects on the economy of the entire area, surely an externality.

REDISTRIBUTION IN URBAN AREAS

Explicitly Redistributive Services

Before the Great Depression, explicitly redistributive expenditure--excluding the redistributive aspects of elementary and secondary education--comprised a trivial part (only about 5 percent of total expenditure) of a much smaller public sector, but that little was financed about half by state governments (in the form of state health and welfare institutions) and about half by local governments (much of that also in institutional care). By the mid-1960s, before spending for Medicare and Medicaid and other Great Society programs really expanded, the explicitly redistributive services accounted for close to 30 percent of total civilian public expenditure, with only about one-tenth of the financing for redistribution coming from local government sources.[14] It is true that most of that local government money was raised in the larger metropolitan areas but, with the exception of those in the few states in which local governments had significant financial obligations for public assistance, this form of redistributive expenditure was of small importance in the metropolitan fisc.

The relative importance of explicitly redistributive expenditure in the public sector as a whole has continued to rise during the past 30 years, under the impact of social security, Medicare and Medicaid. By 1979, the peak year for federal aid to state and local governments, the federal government was financing about 85 percent of the expenditure and local governments only about 3 percent. Excluding New York State, local financing was close to invisible.

Federal program changes since 1979 have increased the local share of total expenditure of this type somewhat. Equally important, health and social pressures that tend to be focused on large cities--AIDS, homelessness, drugs and the like-- have increased the absolute level of local expenditure in real terms considerably in major metropolitan areas. This is the case even though neither the states nor local governments have replaced many of the eliminated federal grants.

How much redistribution is entailed in the local government financing of these programs within metropolitan areas? It depends, first, on the specific distribution of responsibilities--the structure of local government. In many states, health and welfare services traditionally have been county rather than city services. If the county containing the central city is much larger in population than is the central city itself (the usual case for the larger metropolitan areas), if income and taxable wealth per capita is much higher outside the central city than within it, and if rather few affluent people still live within the central city, county responsibility will bring a good deal of spatial redistribution. There of course will be no such redistribution if the county and central city are co-extensive (or nearly so). The extent of both inter-jurisdictional and intra-jurisdictional redistribution also depends on the nature of the local government taxes employed to finance the redistributive services.

Implicitly Redistributive Services

In a sense, any public service financed by local government taxes will be redistributive among the people within the local jurisdiction, unless the consumption of that service has the same income-distribution characteristics as the taxes used to finance the service, which is highly unlikely. In unusual cases, services to property may involve a degree of redistribution from poor to rich, but the usual situation is redistribution in the other direction. Schools provide the most obvious case. Households with children under 18 generally have lower incomes than those without school-age children; those in the lowest income quintile are substantially more likely to have school-age children than those in the higher quintiles. It would take a severely regressive distribution of school tax incidence to overcome the redistribution implied by those demographic characteristics. However, the more homogeneous the taxing jurisdiction is with respect to income and taxable wealth, the less intra-jurisdictional redistribution--with respect to income status--is entailed in local school finance (there is, of course, redistribution with respect to household composition). Within larger school districts, there is likely to be a significant degree of redistribution with respect to income status, even in the large central cities with few remaining upper-income households.

The same point is true for many other services that are not explicitly redistributive in intent, like public safety and environmental services. But there will be spatial redistribution --across jurisdictional boundaries within the metropolitan area--associated with schools and these services only to the extent that these services are financed from federal and state grants, taxes levied by local units that encompass relatively large areas and include prosperous suburbs as well as poor central cities and poor suburbs, or central city taxes that can be exported to the rest of the metropolitan area.

Oakland (1979), in a discussion of appropriate federal assistance to large central cities, offers a good formulation of the redistribution issue with regard to ordinary local public services. He notes that, since the 1930s, it has been accepted that the federal and state governments should make cash payments to the indigent to assure a minimum standard of living in the form of privately-provided goods and services (including vendor payments for health care, housing and some other goods and services), but the provision of ordinary public services has been left to local governments. He argues that such services are as much part of a minimum standard of living of poor households as those provided through the welfare system. In the past, when central cities had dominant economic positions, this presented no real problems. But that now that numerous central cities are impoverished places, external aid is necessary for an appropriate redistributive solution.

Redistribution in the Metropolitan Tax System

The two principal variables are the extent to which the tax burden can be exported from the jurisdiction imposing the tax, a consideration that applies to all the local units within an area, and the extent to which there is redistribution of non-exported taxes, a consideration that applies mainly to the central city and the few other places that have populations with income heterogeneity. The question of intra-metropolitan tax exporting was discussed in the previous section.

Ladd and Yinger (1989) consider the local income tax as a good bet for central cities: the tax has real export possibilities and will be redistributive if exported, largely because high-paid commuters are thereby making a significant fiscal net transfer to poorer central city residents. The export possibilities exist, of course, only if the tax does apply to the income earned by non-residents within the city, which is by no means the case in all the states in which local governments use the tax. For example, in Maryland, New York and Pennsylvania (except for Philadelphia), the tax applies only to residents.[15] Even if the tax does reach non-residents, the redistributive effect may be only a short-term phenomenon: a high central city tax rate may reduce central city employment significantly and, like all tax-induced out-migration, the impact will be most severe for the least mobile, who are the least-skilled and therefore lowest-paid. Inman (1992) argues that this has been the case in Philadelphia, which has much the highest local income tax in the United States.

The typical local income tax, if confined to residents only, is likely to produce very little redistribution, perhaps even perverse redistribution, because the typical tax is a flat-rate tax on gross earnings, with no serious coverage of self-employment income.

Local sales taxes, which are by now very widespread, often are fairly uniform in rate across a state, so the extent of redistribution is little affected by migration in response to local tax differentials. Intra-metropolitan exporting, as from the small places with huge malls, is not inherently redistributive by income level. Large central cities that attract many visitors from other regions do export some of their sales tax burdens to people likely to be richer than the mean central city residents, but this is fairly small in magnitude. As for the distributive effects within the jurisdiction, the conventional American retail sales tax is now viewed as one that is mildly regressive in its application to consumption spending, and close to proportional if viewed on a life-cycle basis.

Large central cities have a good deal of rental housing and, after the waves of condominium conversions in the 1970s and 1980s, much of the rental housing is occupied by people who have incomes well below the metropolitan area averages. Property taxes on this housing usually are high (because of formal classification schemes, extra-legal but overt assessment discrimination, and failure to re-assess frequently enough to reflect deterioration in the marketability of lower-quality housing), and thus likely to be borne not by owners of capital in general, but partly by tenants in the long-term as the supply shrinks in response to the lower returns, and partly by the owners of the rental housing. Whether there is any positive redistribution will depend on who those owners are, and where they live: Are they working-class owner-occupants of two-four family houses, the case in some large cities? Are they richer people who live in the suburbs?

The redistribution, or lack thereof, involved in property taxes on business property--usually high in large cities--is similar to that for rental housing. A larger share of the tax burden probably is borne, at least in the short run, by owners of capital in general, which would make the taxes redistributive, even within metropolitan areas. However, the long-run migration effects are likely to be damaging to poorer people in central cities, except in those central cities that have below-average tax rates on business property. Two empirical studies of the incidence of property taxes on office buildings, one across jurisdictions in the Boston area (Wheaton, 1984) and one intra-jurisdictional for downtown Chicago (McDonald, 1993), support this view.

There is one opportunity for significant redistributive taxation, at least on a one-time basis, that will not be constrained by the potential for migration. Property taxes on land values are very low nearly every place in the United States, especially in large central cities, and tend to be lower the more valuable, relatively, the land is, because of systematic under-assessment. Poor city residents do not own land in central business districts or owner-occupied housing in prime residential districts. A shift toward heavier land value taxation surely would be redistributive in the usual sense.

The fundamental obstacle to intra-metropolitan redistribution through other measures is the existence of income-segregated jurisdictions with wide differentials in taxes and expenditures. Bradford and Oates (1974) characterize, tongue in cheek, the movement of the affluent from the central city to income-segregated dormitory jurisdictions as "suburban exploitation" of the central city: the affluent exploit the central city by moving away from redistributive taxation that is intended to exploit them. As long as such communities exist and new ones can be created easily, and small local government units provide and finance a considerable fraction of public services, redistribution through the metropolitan local finance system must be quite limited.

DEVELOPMENT OF LOCAL GOVERNMENT STRUCTURE

The preceding sections suggest the nature of the fiscal consequences of the structure of local government in urban areas in this country. It is worth considering the question of whether the structure of local government is exogenous with respect to the local fisc or is shaped in part by fiscal and economic considerations. Public finance economists know better, but sometimes write as if the local structure is entirely fixed and, therefore, *necessarily* exogenous.

Table 7.2 and the discussion later in the paper provides some empirical evidence of the lack of fixity in American local government structure over time: the dramatic shrinkage in the number of school districts, the sharp increase in the number of special districts, a modest rate of incorporation of new municipalities, a great deal of annexation activity by existing municipalities, and the occasional consolidation of municipalities and/or counties. These changes over time have not led to a perceptible convergence in the structure of local governments among metropolitan areas. As Fisher and Wassmer (1994) document, that structure remains highly varied, using measures like the mean area and population of the local government units in a metropolitan area.

Because the structure is heavily dependent on a state's legal framework and institutions, most of which are fairly old, it is tempting to seek an explanation of the differences in structure in the history and political cultures of the states, a common enough practice in trying to explain other differences in governmental practices and arrangements among the states. However, such attempts usually are frustrated by the large differences between adjacent states that presumably share histories and cultures.[16] Moreover, local government structure differs a good deal among the metropolitan areas *within* the larger states, notably the three largest.

Fisher and Wassmer have done an econometric analysis that demonstrates that there are plausible economic and fiscal explanations for the persistent structural differences, in addition to regional and other idiosyncracies. Their equations predict the number of general-purpose local governments and school districts within the 167 largest metropolitan areas, as of 1982, from variables reflecting size differences, political and institutional characteristics (notably, the relative importance of state, special district and county governments in that state and the ease or difficulty of annexation), economic characteristics (notably, characteristics of the central city vis-à-vis the rest of the metropolitan area), regional dummies, and a group of variables that have been found to affect the demand for government services.

The size and institutional variables are important and have the expected effects. Large differences between median incomes in the central city and in the suburbs are associated with more local government units, which would seem to confirm the proposition that voters really do see the existence of numerous small suburban jurisdictions as a way of avoiding redistribution within the metropolitan area, a proposition explicitly confirmed in at least one empirical study (Filer and Kenny, 1980). The public-service-demand or taste characteristics also are significant: the more

218

Table 7.2: Local Government Organization, 1972, 1982 and 1992: Number of Units of Government in the U.S.

	1972	1982	1992
Municipalities	18,517	19,076	19,279
Townships[a]	16,991	16,734	16,656
School districts	15,781	14,851	14,422
Special districts	23,885	28,588	31,565
Characteristics of special districts:			
Single-function	22,981	25,991	29,036
Multifunction	904	2,597	2,519
Percent distribution--			
Single-function	96.2%	90.9%	92.0%
Multifunction	3.8	9.1	8.0
Coterminous with other local government units	25.3%	23.6%	37.3%
Country	11.4	11.2	16.8[b]
City or township	13.9	12.4	20.5[b]
Non-coterminous	74.7%	76.4%	59.7%[b]
Special districts inside metropolitan areas, total number	8,054	11,725	NA

NA--Not available.

Source: Census of Governments, 1972, 1982 and 1992.

Notes: [a] Townships (called towns in some states) are treated as real units of government by the Census only in the minority of states, mostly in the Northeast, in which such units have significant governmental responsibilities, often indistinguishable from those of municipalities.
[b] A substantial number of special districts did not report on coterminality in the 1992 Census; the percentages are based on those that did report.

variation there is in such characteristics within a metropolitan area, the more numerous local governments are. Similar findings with respect to the link between income variation and the number of local governments are reported in Nelson (1990), who employs somewhat different institutional variables, and in Martinez-Vasquez, Rider and Walker (1994), whose main purpose is to examine the role of race in local government structure.

Earlier sections of this chapter conclude that "fragmentation" of the local fisc in American metropolitan areas probably does not impose serious problems of uncompensated externalities, except possibly in connection with schools, and does frustrate intra-metropolitan redistribution. The real gain that is conceivable is the Tiebout one: a metropolitan world of political jurisdictions within each of which tastes for public services are quite similar, so that there is something close to a market solution for the provision and financing of local public services, rather than the efficiency losses associated with majority decisions in communities housing consumers with diverse preferences. In that world, given appropriate land use controls exercised by the numerous local units, the local property tax is converted into a non-distorting benefit tax (Mieszkowski and Zodrow, 1989). This regime, however, requires that the number and size of local units are flexible, which seems to be the case.

In the real world of American metropolitan areas, do people vote with their feet a la Tiebout? Or do the simplifying assumptions of the Tiebout model that do not match reality prevent the Tiebout results from occurring? Empirical findings suggest that there is a considerable degree of heterogeneity in preferences for local public services among, but not within, small suburban jurisdictions (Gramlich and Rubinfeld, 1982). For example, there appears to be a high correlation between municipal tax rates and municipal expenditure levels, independent of the size of the tax base, but considerable variation in both tax rates and expenditures, in suburbs outside Chicago, in northeastern New Jersey and in the suburban counties north and east of New York City.

The real world of U.S. metropolitan areas does include the existence of the occasional small jurisdiction that is desperately poor, usually but not always a minority community. One may not see much of a case for the use of the local government system in metropolitan areas as an engine of redistribution, but still be concerned about the extent to which a splendidly efficient Tiebout solution brings with it the pauper suburb or small city.[17] Such units seem to be much more common in metropolitan areas, or parts of them, that are characterized by small jurisdictions than elsewhere, such as those in the Northeast and Midwest. Most were small freestanding towns, often quite old, with considerable economic activity but never much high-quality housing.

LOCATION DECISIONS OF HOUSEHOLDS AND FIRMS

For some years, urban economists have noted that most large metropolitan areas in the United States are substantially more decentralized, in both residential and firm location, than the conventional monocentric urban models predict. The key variables in those models are commuting costs (in time and money) and the price and income elasticities of demand for housing; the models do not include sophisticated measures of local government structure and finance, if indeed they say anything at all about government on the right-hand side. As we have seen, adding local government variables would increase predicted decentralization, for one or more of three reasons: people and firms establish and populate new communities to escape redistributive taxation in the existing ones (notably, the central city), to better exercise consumer choice in the Tiebout sense, or to indulge a taste for racial and ethnic segregation.

Substantial attention has been given to two empirical issues regarding the effect of local government finance on land use patterns in metropolitan areas. One is the effect of tax differentials as such, particularly in regard to the location of economic activity; business needs and preferences for public services are seldom issues in intra-metropolitan location choice. The other concerns the effect of fiscal zoning, that is, the use of land use controls to minimize spending demands and maximize revenue.

Tax Differentials and Industrial Location

There is every theoretical reason for expecting local tax differentials to affect location at the margin, at least for firms and activities that do not confront significant differentials in the costs of other inputs and when the tax differentials exceed the location rents available for the specific activity at a particular site, as Brazer elegantly explained in a 1961 article. Those conditions clearly are more likely to be met in connection with intra- than with inter-regional locational decisions. The real question of course is the empirical one: How big a difference in locational choices do what tax differentials make?

For years, most economists who addressed the issue found only limited effects. To a great extent, this was not because the effects were absent, but because the available data and technical tools were inadequate to discover the effects. These results were sometimes rationalized by the assertion that spatial tax differentials were small ones, an assertion that has been demonstrated to be false when the differentials are properly measured, for example, in comparison of after-tax rates of return at alternative locations.[18]

The view today is different:

> The most recent studies, employing more detailed data sets and more refined econometric techniques, have generated results which cast some doubt on the received conclusion that tax effects are generally negligible. In part, this conclusion arose from confounding the size of a coefficient with its statistical significance, which may be lowered by low-quality or inappropriate data or by inefficient estimating techniques. It is to be expected that an appropriately controlled specification will permit isolation of the marginal firms on which taxes do have an impact, ceteris paribus, so the debate can turn to the size of the relevant elasticities. These may, of course, be small but nevertheless statistically significant. (Newman and Sullivan, 1988, 232)

However, if the elasticities are small, then it makes little sense to give economic development the high priority in state and local tax policy that it seems to have in most parts of the United States today, or be exceedingly generous in granting tailored tax preferences to individual firms, the widespread practice that is discussed in the next section of this chapter.

Fiscal Zoning

Land use regulation by local governments for fiscal ends, generically known as fiscal zoning, is widely practiced by suburban jurisdictions in those large metropolitan areas characterized by relatively small units of government with major fiscal responsibilities. It is fairly obvious that the net fiscal impact of nonresidential development generally will be positive: firms receive few direct benefits from the services provided by the specific jurisdiction, like the school district, in which the plant is located, and pay substantial taxes. The net fiscal impact of residential development will not be favorable, unless it takes the form of expensive single-family houses or multi-family housing likely to be occupied by adults without school-age children. If the marginal public expenditures associated with new single-family houses are likely to exceed the marginal tax revenue from such houses, the fewer of them the better. That means low-density zoning, that is, minimum lot sizes larger than would occur without regulation. Ordinarily, municipalities rationalize such zoning on other grounds, because explicit fiscal zoning would be unlawful.

Fiscal zoning occurs mainly in the United States, because it requires that all of the following conditions exist, which is widely true only in this country:

1. Local governments are responsible for the provision of many public services and for a substantial share of the financing of those services.
2. Most local governments get a large portion of own-source revenues from a tax whose yield is directly linked to the land development that occurs over time within that jurisdiction, the property tax.
3. Those same local government units are the ones who exercise most land-use controls, notably zoning.
4. Local government units outside the central cities are, in many states, small in geographic size and population.

Given the existence of those conditions, fiscal zoning seems inevitable. In the absence of any one of the conditions, the reason for fiscal zoning is not clear. If local governments have very limited powers or revenue-raising responsibilities (as in, say, Australia), it would hardly seem worthwhile to control land-use for fiscal reasons. If the main sources of local revenue are tied only loosely to the nature and extent of land development or directly reflect the public service costs of each type of development (for example, marginal-cost-based user charges), the same is true. If the local government unit is large in area, the likelihood is that the development of the small fraction of the land area that occurs within a few years will not have much fiscal impact or that, over time, the jurisdiction will attract diverse types of development, including some that clearly "pay their way." And if zoning powers are not exercised by the conventional small local government at all, there is no reason to expect fiscal zoning to begin with.[19]

Some economists do not find efficiency problems in fiscal zoning, using club models or seeing fiscal zoning as a result of rational fiscal choice that maximizes the value of existing residential real estate. Fiscal zoning also is essential for the Tiebout model to work, and converts the local property tax in small suburban jurisdictions into a benefit tax, rather than a distorting excise tax. However, the extensive literature on the welfare effects of zoning is inconclusive, in that the theoretical models fail to include all the possible effects of zoning. Urban economists generally do agree that the equity effects of fiscal zoning are serious and objectionable: it tends to raise the price of housing in the lower half or two-thirds of the suburban housing market. It is expressly aimed at excluding poorer households from better-off suburban jurisdictions that provide high-quality services, notably education.

Fiscal Effects of Differences in Land Use Patterns

The practice of fiscal zoning--and the conviction on the part of most urban planners that the practice is a bad one--has been accompanied during most of the past 50 years by "fiscal impact" studies, which purport to show the impact of major zoning decisions on the local government fiscal position.

Most professional planners abhor the "urban sprawl" that is associated with low-density zoning, for various reasons--aesthetic, environmental, distributional and ideological. To counter the argument that large-lot zoning is necessary for fiscal reasons, they have produced a type of fiscal impact study that deals solely with the residential density question, almost always concluding that low residential densities result in relatively high per household costs for many types of locally-provided public services. However, the extensive literature is seriously flawed, in a number of respects.

For example, the most impressive empirical study of this subject, the Real Estate Research Corporation's 1974 study, *The Costs of Sprawl*, found that the per household cost of all services that are directly provided to housing units (rather than to persons) vary directly with residential lot sizes, over the range of densities that are conventional in the suburbs in large American metropolitan areas. In fact, the empirical relationship is amazingly uniform over densities and services. But, as Kain had noted a few years previously (Kain, 1967), this is largely a function of the fact that engineering standards and operating practices are essentially uniform over the conventional range of densities. If every residential street is of the same width and pavement thickness, then the per-housing-unit costs of street construction, maintenance, cleaning, snow removal, etc., *must* increase rapidly with lot size. It is convenient for local officials to post physical standards that do not vary with density. But this is not a matter of either physical or economic law.

Nearly all the writing about economies of scale with respect to population size or density in the production of local government services implicitly assumes that producers are in fact operating as efficiently as they can be expected to operate. Thus, actual data with respect to public spending per capita (or some other measure of unit costs) can be used to estimate true returns to scale. But this ignores entirely the question of X-inefficiency, in effect assuming that the barriers to achieving technical efficiency are invulnerable to change.

It is seems likely that unit costs with respect to density form the familiar U-shaped curve, with high costs at very low densities and high costs at very high density, the latter a function of (unpriced) congestion and possibly overcome with congestion pricing. If the bottom of the curve is a long flat section that encompasses most conventional suburban densities, then the fiscal "costs of sprawl" ought not to be major issue.

INTERGOVERNMENTAL COMPETITION AND COOPERATION

Fisher (1991, 262) has pointed out that *interjurisdictional* competition really is a misnomer: what is occurring is competition among people using governments as agents, and this competition is largely distributive. The implication is that one of the purposes of creating units of government is to assist in this interpersonal competition. The point should be kept in mind while reading this section on intergovernmental competition and cooperation in metropolitan areas.

Intergovernmental Competition

The most noted type of intergovernmental competition in the United States is tax competition, both among and within regions, to make the region or local jurisdiction more attractive as a place in which to do business and to live (for households that are relatively well-off and/or are likely to impose very low public-service costs). There is competition with respect to the overall level of tax burdens, heavily advertised by low-tax places. Obviously, it is difficult for high-tax places to do much to change their relative positions except over a very long period, short of a local boom unmatched elsewhere that permits tax reductions without much, if any, expenditure reduction, or a local revolution in attitudes toward government.[20] Moreover, this is something that is harder to accomplish within a metropolitan area, especially one largely confined to a single state: lowering state taxes, which can be the more important ones, may not give a competitive edge to one jurisdiction within that state over others in the same state.

More nearly ubiquitous is tax competition in the form of tailored tax preferences designed to attract new business investment, or to retain existing activities being lured by preferences in other jurisdictions. In a formal sense, such preferences were rare before 1960, but less formal--and extra-legal--local tax breaks in the form of underassessment of the property of major local manufacturing establishments in small jurisdictions was legendary and very widespread. Census of Government sales-assessment ratio study data from 1962 on showed relatively low levels of assessment for industrial real property in many states and counties in which uniformity was the legal standard. Improvement in assessment administration in many states in the past 30 years has made this form of tax preference less common, and probably contributed to the spread of state legislation authorizing formal economic development tax preferences.[21]

Among the first important such preferences were those adopted in the early 1960s in states in which effective property tax rates were extremely high in central cities, notably Massachusetts and New Jersey, in connection with large-scale urban renewal projects, where the new use was commercial. In Boston, for example, the prospect of an effective rate of ten percent on new office buildings and hotels had prevented any new construction at all after World War II. State legislation authorized specifically tailored property tax arrangements for such projects. Other states have followed suit, although in varied ways.

The types of tax preferences available on the state level are numerous, but that is less so for tax preferences that are differential among the local units within metropolitan areas (at least the part of the area that is within one state). In part, that is because the state government may resist differentiation in the provisions of state taxes for administrative reasons (or may be constitutionally restrained from so differentiating). Also, local governments can offer preferences only in connection with taxes that they impose. Consequently, property tax preferences are the most common ones. Many central cities impose gross receipts taxes on utilities, and a number offer reductions on utility sales to specific business customers. The exemption of major business purchases from local (and perhaps state) sales taxes to which such purchases are otherwise subject may apply to whole classes of businesses, or only as part of a package negotiated with one firm. Some central cities have specialized business taxes, like New York City's "commercial rent," which can be part of a package.

There also are frequent arrangements for substantial tax reductions and/or exemptions for business activities located within special zones, "free trade," "enterprise," "empowerment," and the like, in which all or most sales taxes on intermediate business purchases are eliminated, property taxes are drastically reduced, and significant reductions in corporate income taxes are provided.

The frequent form of property tax preference is a time-limited exemption of investment in a new building, with the exempt part of the value declining to zero over the ten or 20-year period of the tax preference. While this does not have as powerful an effect as a pure land value tax, or a property tax with permanently lower rates for the value of the building (as in Pittsburgh), it does work in the same direction. For example, if the usual effective rate on newly-built office buildings is three percent in a very large central city (which is high, but by no means rare in big cities), there is an exemption that declines to zero over 20 years and the assessed value of the building in the absence of the preference would rise on average by two percent annually, the net present value of the exemption is 22 percent of the investment, at a ten percent discount rate.

Tax competition of this type among the local governments within metropolitan areas usually is confined largely to those jurisdictions that already contain substantial nonresidential activities: central cities, smaller industrial cities, industrial suburbs, sites of major retail concentrations. Tax burdens often are higher in those places than elsewhere in the area, and other costs of doing business may be, or may be perceived to be, relatively high. The city sees no environmental externalities at the margin connected with the firm, so the issue is confined to the costs in foregone taxes of the jobs preserved or attracted. In contrast, other communities in the area are likely to view the taxes that new business investment brings with it as essential to overcome the environmental externalities.

Whether the tax preferences are necessary to secure the economic development advantages in the central city is of course open to question. The more places in the metropolitan area that offer the preferences, the more likely it is that the preferences are inefficient from the standpoint of the local government making the offer. But it is more likely that the tax preferences will not induce an inefficient pattern of location: if the tax deal is the same everywhere in the metropolitan area, presumably the firm will choose the economically optimal location.

One plausible test of whether a specific tax preference or program is efficacious from the standpoint of the local government unit granting the tax preference is to calculate the break-even point, that is, the proportion of the increase in investment or employment by the firms receiving the subsidy that must be induced by the subsidy, if the benefits are to equal the costs. If the break-even point is a very high percentage, it seems unlikely that the program will not be cost-effective, a not uncommon finding for state government investment credits against state corporate income taxes (see Netzer, 1991, 232).

Intergovernmental Cooperation

There are some very long-standing forms of intergovernmental cooperation in metropolitan areas, in many cases wholly involuntary. For example, in the great majority of states (38 according to the *1992 Census of Governments)*, county governments are the property tax assessors and collectors on behalf of all local units within the county.[22] In some states, there are similar arrangements with regard to some local nonproperty taxes, and in most states, local sales taxes are collected by the state tax collection agency. County governments may perform other supposedly ministerial functions as well, for example, in connection with the management of short-term investment funds, as local governments in Orange County, California, know, to their sorrow. In most states, the judicial system--to the extent it is not completely managed by the state government--is county-run, even in the case of courts labeled "municipal" or "town."

The creation of special districts and authorities historically often was done in order to overcome constitutional tax and debt limits (for example, most special districts in Illinois, "school building authorities" in a number of states, most authorities in New York, where ordinary governments may not issue revenue bonds), but such units mostly have boundaries co-extensive with general governments, even quite small ones. A good many of the 9,000 special districts created between 1972 and 1992 have boundaries that are *narrower* than those of conventional general governments ("tax-increment financing" districts, for example).[23] In contrast, the creation of special districts and authorities that extend beyond the boundaries of a single local jurisdiction is an important type of intergovernmental cooperation, albeit state-imposed, perhaps against the wishes of the local units who are superseded for that function. And more generally, the upward shifting of responsibility for any function, from intra-county units to counties and from local governments to the state, may be seen as a type of imposed intergovernmental cooperation.

Consolidation of separate units of local government into a single unit, sometimes covering a wider area, sometimes only a matter of simplification within the same boundaries, is another form of intergovernmental cooperation. This one is sometimes partly involuntary, decreed by the state legislature, and sometimes wholly voluntary, in that the approval of voters in each of the separate units is required. There was massive consolidation of school districts before 1972 (an 85 percent reduction in the number in 30 years), and continued slow consolidation since then, usually in metropolitan areas. In the states with very complex local government structures, consolidation of overlapping local units occurs with some frequency (for example, villages and townships in New York).

More important have been the few city-county consolidations, fewer than 20 since World War II.[24] However, a number of them have made notable differences in the structure of government in their metropolitan areas. For instance, Indianapolis/Marion County, Jacksonville/Duvall County and Nashville/Davidson County created what come very close to unitary metropolitan governments for the large central counties of those metropolitan areas. That of course is the ultimate in intergovernmental cooperation. It is, however, not clear that the fiscal effects of these consolidations have been great. One would not predict strong effects, because most successful consolidations, including these three, occurred in places in which there was not a great deal of government structure outside the central city -- few incorporated municipalities or school districts -- and very low levels of public services beyond the central cities before consolidation. These conditions were conducive to acceptance of consolidation by suburban residents (Harrigan, 1985).

There is little published work on either the reasons for success or failure in consolidation efforts or the results of consolidation.[25] Filer and Kenny (1980) find that the most powerful explanation for high pro-approval votes by central city residents is the extent to which consolidation might result in income transfers from suburbs to central cities, but their finding is open to alternative interpretations. Benton and Gamble (1984) discuss economies of scale in the Jacksonville consolidation.

Annexation, which is a form of consolidation, is very common in metropolitan areas (Fisher and Wassmer, 1994). The typical annexation is of a small area, previously in unincorporated territory, that was receiving minimal urban-type services. In a good many cases, annexation is an alternative to incorporation as a separate unit at some future date.

The other side of this coin is the creation of new units by incorporation: the Census of Governments reports a net addition of 762 municipalities between 1972 and 1992 (an increase of about four percent). And there is the steady and large increase in the number of special districts, mostly quite small, which complicates intergovernmental cooperation (see Table 7.2).

Non-structural voluntary cooperation also has a long history. In the 1940s, California authorized what was then known as the "Lakewood plan," under which any municipality in Los Angeles County may contract with the county, or with any other local government, for the provision of any service that the second unit is permitted to offer. The plan was extended to the entire state subsequently, and emulated in many other states. The obvious goal is the pursuit of economies of scale in capital-intensive services and in nearly all services in very small places, which are on the left-hand (downward sloping) arm of the U-shaped cost curve.

Paradoxically, the increasing popularity of privatizing the production of public services can actually increase the degree of intergovernmental cooperation that exploits scale economies. This occurs when a single firm makes winning bids in a number of communities in the metropolitan area, a common event in the waste management industry. Also, there are a few cases in which "privatization" means that the public agency providing the service in one community is permitted to bid, along with private firms, for contracts to offer the service in other places. The most dramatic example is bus service in Britain. Since 1986, the system has been completely competitive, with both private and public bus companies free to offer unsubsidized service anywhere and to bid to offer subsidized services. The result has been that former municipal bus enterprises in various cities are now operating bus services in other, widely scattered cities (Gómez-Ibáñez and Meyer, 1993, Ch. 4).

Finally, there is an important form of cooperation on the revenue side. For two decades, local governments in the Twin Cities metropolitan area in Minnesota have been sharing a percentage of the increase in the non-residential property tax base, on a formula basis. That is, all of the advantage to economic growth does not accrue to the specific municipality in which it occurs. The system was established under state law, but the initiative for the state law was agreement on the plan by most of the suburban municipalities, including those which had been growing most rapidly. This system clearly reduces the incentive for fiscal zoning and contributes to equity.

There is no great danger that intergovernmental competition will disappear but it needs to be reiterated that, from the efficiency side, there are no powerful arguments against this form of competition. Scale economies in the production of most local government services are exhausted at a fairly low point, the choice embodied in Tiebout-type competition is valuable, and tax competition is inherently self-limiting. There are more serious distributive consequences, of course but, as public finance economists traditionally have argued, those consequences call for appropriate inter-*level* fiscal arrangements.

CONCLUDING OBSERVATIONS

The conclusions in the preceding paragraph can be extended to characterize nearly all of the issues discussed in this chapter. Research by public finance economists and urban economists in the past quarter century shows that the fiscal structures, policies and practices that characterize government in large American metropolitan areas exhibit only modest degrees of inefficiency in general (although there can be no doubt that the extent of X-inefficiency is huge and pervasive). The welfare losses from intra-metropolitan expenditure-related spill-overs, locational decision distortion, competitive changes in tax regimes, and other matters discussed above, seem small relative to the welfare costs of dramatic changes that would produce much more centralization of decision-making on both the taxing and expenditure side. On the other hand, the equity problems remain severe ones.

The modest size of the losses in welfare should not foreclose further research, in a number of directions. On a number of issues, the research situation is similar to that concerning the locational effects of inter-jurisdictional tax differentials twenty years ago: the empirical research was inconclusive and sometimes unconvincing. A goodly number of first-rate economists attacked the problem and produced both conclusive and convincing results that showed that tax differentials do matter, and how much they matter. We are at a similar early stage in empirical research on questions about the determinants and consequences of differences in governmental structure and institutions. The recent work is promising, but just a beginning. For example, we know little about the fiscal consequences of consolidation and other changes in structure. There has been little empirical work on intra-metropolitan tax exporting that is based on the actual and complex local tax instruments that are used, rather than some stylized version of them that abstracts from the institutional reality (like the actual tax treatment of rental housing and business property or the actual utility taxes that are used, or the nature of the ownership of the taxed factor. This also is true of empirical work on intra-metropolitan redistribution through the local fisc. Both the technology and the supply of data surely must make it possible to go beyond the simplifications necessary in the past.

To a considerable extent, the equity issues in metropolitan area finance are inseparable from national redistribution policy: a withdrawal from serious redistribution at the national level makes any real change at the metropolitan level impossible. Nonetheless, it makes sense to do research on the intra-metropolitan aspects of conceivable national redistribution instruments of the future, such as the "local government as part of the standard of living" grant proposal of Oakland and proposals advanced in the 1980s, as the Federal retreat had begun, by Gramlich and other writers. It must help clarify discussion if economists can provide some empirical clothing--the predicted effects within large metropolitan areas--for what now seem wildly unlikely policies.

NOTES

1. Local government universities were not rare before the 1960s, notably in Ohio cities, New York and Wayne County, Michigan. Most two-year colleges were sponsored by local governments, which provided the bulk of their funding.

2. Author's calculations from Census Bureau data. There is little printed material on local government finances by county area that is more current than the 1987 Census of Governments.

3. New England is excluded from this comparison because the counties have quite limited (or no) functions. The geography of Alaska and Hawaii is quite different from that of the contiguous 48 states.

4. In Virginia, the municipalities are independent cities outside counties, but shown in the 1992 Census of Governments table as sub-county units.

5. Another source of inefficiency connected with differences in expenditure for these services would be migration in order to take advantage of the better services, leading to otherwise suboptimal location patterns. This point can be traced back to Buchanan (1950). However, it seems fanciful when applied to migration *within* metropolitan areas, and usually has been applied to interstate and interregional migration.

6. I prepared those estimates in connection with my testimony in the school finance constitutional challenge, Abbott v. Burke. The case was ultimately decided in favor of the plaintiffs, a group of very poor cities. In none of them was the taxable property value per pupil more than one-third the statewide average.

7. That was the situation in New Jersey at the time of the Abbott v. Burke filing, as the witnesses for the state pointed out.

8. Most state school aid is disbursed not as matching grants but as what amounts to lump-sum grants. However, independent school districts do not have the option of using the grants for non-school purposes. They can use some of the funds to reduce local taxes, and that likelihood appears to be taken into account in the political negotiations at the state capital about the annual or biennial school aid bill.

9. The paper addresses the simplistic public-choice hypothesis that bureaucratic empire-building within larger public organizations will

lead to higher expenditure. The results are inconsistent with this hypothesis, as well as with the "undernourishment" hypothesis.

10. Author's calculation, based on data in the 1994 *Statistical Abstract of the United States*. There is by now a literature that seems to show that a considerable fraction of the large relative decline in per pupil spending for schools in California since the mid-1970s can be attributed to the Serrano decisions and the passage of Proposition 13, together producing a massive shift to state financing of the schools (Silva and Sonstelie, 1995).

11. That is, unless all the jurisdictions choose to levy exactly the same taxes at the same rates, despite their authority not to do so.

12. The economists who, in the past, did make this argument seriously did so by asserting that the central city services consumed by commuters should be valued on the basis of the commuters' willingness-to-pay, not on the basis of the marginal costs of the additional service or capacity provided in order to accommodate the commuters. Thus, if the Sultan of Brunei visits the UN in New York, the services of the police motorcycle escort from the airport would be valued at, say, $5 million per hour, rather than the marginal cost to the city of perhaps $1,000 per hour. See Greene, Neenan and Scott (1974).

13. The extreme case is perhaps the school district in Suffolk County, New York, that was the site of the Shoreham nuclear power plant, a plant completed but never operated. Under New York's property tax treatment of utilities (they are treated as collections of discrete physical assets, each valued on the basis of the cost of reproducing the identical asset, regardless of its market value, in Shoreham's case a negative figure of $10 billion or more), the school district received vast amounts in property taxes for nearly 20 years, and spent accordingly.

14. The definitions of "civilian public expenditure" and the budget branches are those in Netzer (1974); the more recent experience is reported on the basis of comparable categories.

15. New York City levies a separate non-resident income tax at rates that are roughly one-tenth the rates applied to residents; there is essentially no effort to collect the tax except through withholding, which means that a considerable amount of self-employment income escapes the tax.

16. Washington and Oregon provide perhaps the best example of such a pairing. The two states differ substantially in many of their fiscal and government structure characteristics, including the mean population size of units of government within metropolitan areas.

17. Low levels of public services in such places are likely to coincide with consumer preferences. The evidence strongly suggests that most public services are not highly valued by low-income households, in the sense that they would spend any significant share of additional money income for these purposes. For example, there is virtually zero private spending among the non-aged near-poor for health care, the take-up rates for the lowest tuition sectors of public higher education are quite low, and private spending for low-cost safety devices like replacement batteries for smoke alarms and window guards are notoriously low in poor neighborhoods.

18. See Netzer, 1986, for a discussion of the nature of the evidence and argument during most of the 1960s and 1970s. It is likely that some economists were over-reacting, in their skepticism, to the very poor evidence and wild arguments presented by non-economists during these years.

19. I first made this point in Netzer, 1962.

20. An example of the former is the rapid economic growth of the Twin Cities area in the 1960s and 1970s, which permitted a significant reduction in the relative level of state taxes, previously among the country's highest; the obvious example of the latter is the passage of Proposition 13 in California in 1978, which quickly made California a low-tax, low-expenditure state.

21. The informal preferences have not disappeared, especially in connection with the taxation of business machinery and equipment in the majority of states that continue to subject such personal property to taxation. The absence of systematic sales data on used machinery and equipment permits both taxpayers and tax administrators a great deal of discretion in this largely self-administered form of property taxation. Estimates of the value of taxable machinery and equipment based on data in the Bureau of Economic Analysis series on national wealth suggest that massive discrimination in favor of major local employers is common.

22. In three of the 38 states, there are some non-urban counties in which there is primary assessment by smaller units within the counties, but supervised by a county agency.

23. See Table 7.2. Because of incomplete reporting of coterminality in the 1992 Census, the trend between 1972 and 1982 may be the better indicator: 4,000 of the newly-created 4,700 special districts were not coterminous with other units of government.

24. Major city-county consolidations were common in the 19th century, but there were none between 1907 and 1945. From then until 1976, there were nearly 70 efforts at such consolidations, of which 17 were successful. Since 1976, there have been few efforts. See Harrigan, 1985, 321-326.

25. I have been able to find only the two references noted in this paragraph in the Economic Literature Index.

REFERENCES

Benton, J. Edwin, and Darwin Gamble. "City/County Consolidation and Economies of Scale: Evidence from a Time-Series Analysis in Jacksonville, Florida." *Social Science Quarterly* 65 (1984):190-198.

Bradford, David F., and Wallace E. Oates. "Suburban Exploitation of Central Cities and Governmental Structure," In *Redistribution Through Public Choice*, edited by Harold Hochman and George Peterson. New York: Columbia University Press, 1974.

Brazer, Harvey R. "The Value of Industrial Property as a Subject for Taxation." *Canadian Public Administration* 4 (1961):137-147.

Brazer, Harvey E. "Some Fiscal Implications of Metropolitanism." In *Metropolitan Issues: Social, Governmental, Fiscal*. The Maxwell School, Syracuse University, 1962.

Buchanan, James M. "Federalism and Fiscal Equity." *American Economic Review* 40 (1950).

Buchanan, James M. 1974. "Who Should Distribute What in a Federal System?" In *Redistribution Through Public Choice*, edited by Harold Hochman and George Peterson. New York: Columbia University Press, 1974.

Burnell, Barbara S. "The Effect of School District Structure on Education Spending," *Public Choice* 69 (1991):253-264.

Evans, William N., Sheila E. Murray and Robert M. Schwab. "Toward Increased Centralization in Public School Finance." Chapter 5, this volume.

Filer, John E., and Lawrence W. Kenny. "Voter Reaction to City-County Referenda. *Journal of Law and Economics* 23 (1980):179-190.

Fisher, Ronald C. "Interjurisdictional Competition: A Summary Perspective and Agenda for Research." In *Competition Among States and Local Governments: Efficiency and Equity in American Federalism*, edited by Daphne Kenyon and John Kincaid. Washington: Urban Institute Press, 1991.

Fisher, Ronald C., and Robert W. Wassmer. 1994. "Economic Influences on the Structure of Local Governments in U.S. Metropolitan Areas." Mimeo.

Gómez-Ibáñez, José A., and John R. Meyer. *Going Private: The International Experience with Transport Privatization*. Washington: The Brookings Institution, 1993.

Gramlich, Edward M. "The Deductibility of State and Local Taxes." *National Tax Journal* 38 (1985):447-65.

Gramlich, Edward M., and Daniel L. Rubinfeld. "Micro Estimates of Public Spending Demand Functions and Tests of the Tiebout and Median-Voter Hypotheses." *Journal of Political Economy* 90 (1982):536-560.

Greene, Kenneth V., William B. Neenan and Claudia D. Scott. *Fiscal Interactions in a Metropolitan Area.* Lexington, MA: Lexington Books, 1974.

Hanushek, Eric A. "The Economics of Schooling: Production and Efficiency in Public Schools." *Journal of Economic Literature* 24 (1986):1141-1177.

Hanushek, Eric A. "The Impact of Differential Expenditures on School Performance. *Educational Researcher* 18 (1989):45-51.

Harrigan, John J. *Political Change in the Metropolis.* Boston: Little, Brown, 1985 (3rd edition).

Inman, Robert P. "Can Philadelphia Escape Its Fiscal Crisis with Another Tax Increase?" Federal Reserve Bank of Philadelphia *Business Review,* September-October 1992.

Kain, John. 1967. "Urban Form and the Costs of Urban Services." MIT-Harvard Joint Center for Urban Studies. Mimeo.

King, Richard A., and Bettye MacPhail-Wilcox. "Unraveling the Production Equation: The Continuing Quest for Resources that Make A Difference." *Journal of Education Finance* 20(1) (1994):47-65.

Ladd, Helen F., and John Yinger. *America's Ailing Cities: Fiscal Health and the Design of Urban Policy.* Baltimore: Johns Hopkins University Press, 1989.

Linneman, Peter D., and Anita A. Summers. "Patterns and Processes of Employment and Population Decentralization in the United States, 1970-87." In *Urban Change in the United States and Western Europe: Comparative Analysis and Policy*, edited by Anita A. Summers, Paul C. Cheshire, and Lanfranco Senn. Washington, DC: Urban Institute Press, 1993.

Martinez-Vasquez, Jorge, Mark Rider, and Mary Beth Walker. "Race and the Structure of Local Government." Research Paper No. 42, Policy Research Center, Georgia State University, May 1994.

McDonald, John F. "Incidence of the Property Tax on Commercial Real Estate: The Case of Downtown Chicago." *National Tax Journal* 46 (1993):109-120.

Mieszkowski, Peter, and George Zodrow. "Taxation and the Tiebout Model." *Journal of Economic Literature* 27 (1989):1099-1146.

Nelson, Michael A. "Decentralization of the Subnational Public Sector: An Empirical Analysis of the Determinants of Local Government Structure in Metropolitan Areas in the U.S." *Southern Economic Journal* 57 (1990):443-457.

Netzer, Dick. "The Property Tax and Alternatives in Regional Development." In *Papers and Proceedings of the Regional Science Association* 9 (1962):191-200.

Netzer, Dick. "State-Local Finance and Intergovernmental Fiscal Relations." In Blinder, Solow, Break, Steiner and Netzer, *The Economics of Public Finance*. Washington: The Brookings Institution, 1974.

Netzer, Dick. "State Tax Policy and Economic Development." *New York Affairs,* 9(4) (1986):19-36.

Netzer, Dick. "An Evaluation of Interjurisdictional Competition through Economic Development Incentives." In *Competition among States and Local Governments: Efficiency and Equity in American Federalism, edited by Daphne Kenyon and John Kincaid.* Washington: Urban Institute Press., 1991

Netzer, Dick. "Differences in Reliance on User Charges by American State and Local Governments." *Public Finance Quarterly* 20 (1992):499-511.

Netzer, Dick. "National Assistance to Urban Areas in the United States." In *Urban Changes in the United States and Western Europe--Comparative Analysis and Policy, edited by Anita A. Summers, Paul C. Cheshire and Lanfranco Senn.* Washington: Urban Institute Press, 1993.

Newman, Robert J., and Dennis H. Sullivan. "Econometric Analysis of Business Tax Impacts on Industrial Location: What Do We Know and How Do We Know It?" *Journal of Urban Economics* 23 (1988):215-234.

Oakland, William H. "Central Cities: Fiscal Plight and Prospects for Reform." In *Current Issues in Urban Economics,* edited by Peter Mieszkowski and Mahlon Straszheim. Baltimore: The Johns Hopkins University Press, 1979.

Oakland, William H. "Recognizing and Correcting for Fiscal Disparities: A Critical Analysis." In *Fiscal Equalization for State and Local Government Finance*, edited by John E. Anderson. Westport, CT: Praeger, 1994.

Real Estate Research Corporation. *The Costs of Sprawl.* Washington: U.S. Government Printing Office, 1974.

Regional Plan Association. *Spread City. Projections of Development Trends and the Issues They Pose: The Tri-State New York Metropolitan Region, 1960-1985.* New York: the author, 1962.

Silva, Fabio, and Jon Sonstelie. "Did *Serrano* Cause a Decline in School Spending?" *National Tax Journal* 48 (June 1995):199-215.

Tiebout, Charles M. "A Pure Theory of Local Expenditure." *Journal of Political Economy* 64 (1956):416-424.

Wheaton, William C. "The Incidence of Inter-Jurisdictional Differences in Commercial Property Taxes." *National Tax Journal* 37 (1984):515-527.

8 INTERGOVERNMENTAL ASPECTS OF GROWTH AND STABILIZATION POLICY

William F. Fox and Matthew N. Murray

INTRODUCTION

The stabilization function of subnational governments was a topic of considerable research prior to 1970.[1] Very rapid growth of state and local government expenditures in the years following World War II and lingering concerns about the causal role of state and local governments in the Great Depression are probable reasons for so much attention being focused on this issue.

Research on the stabilization function followed two threads. The first, which received most of the attention, sought to determine whether the aggregate effect of state and local governments was procyclical or countercyclical. The focus was on the overall stimulative effect of state and local expenditures and taxes. The analysis led to the so-called perversity hypothesis, which held that the aggregate effect of state and local governments is procyclical. The second thread was investigation of whether state and local governments should actively pursue countercyclical policies.[2]

Research on the stabilization function of subnational governments nearly died out after Musgrave (1959) and Oates (1972) convincingly argued that subnational governments have no appropriate stabilization role. But during the past several years the topic has arisen again, and this paper reconsiders the conventional wisdom on stabilization policies.

The efficacy of two types of stabilization policies is examined in this paper. First are policies intended to smooth out cycles in the growth trend. At the subnational level countercyclical policies are comprised mostly of properly timed tax and expenditure decisions. Some non-fiscal countercyclical policies may be pursued as well. For example, states may recruit businesses that are less cyclical, or at least states may seek to attract diverse economic activity in hopes that a more stable growth path will emerge. Second are policies to enhance trend economic growth. Traditionally, states have used policies such as business recruitment, tax abatement, expenditures on education and infrastructure, and other devices to achieve this objective.

Many activities undertaken to achieve stabilization goals also appropriately are pursued to achieve allocation or distribution goals. Following Breton and Scott (1978), in this chapter policies are presumed to fit in the stabilization branch if the policies' intents are stabilization, regardless of the fact that the same policies may be of importance for other functions. Similarly, allocation and distribution policies are not categorized as stabilization functions, even though they may have stabilization effects.

Given the current flux in macroeconomic thought, in many ways this paper is premature and should await further development of public economics. Dreze (1995, p. 123) said that ". . . public economics does not presently cover what had been an important concern of public finance, namely the macroeconomic stabilization function of government." His reasoning is that formation of microeconomic underpinnings for macroeconomics is well developed in a number of areas, but not in its interrelationship with public economics. He goes on to observe that neither the Keynesian nor the classical schools use methodologies that can be integrated easily with current approaches to public economics. He optimistically states that models combining macroeconomics and public economics will develop over the next several decades. One fruitful direction for this research would be to recognize the federalist structure of government in macroeconomic models. The ability to talk about states' roles in stabilization policy certainly can be expected to expand as understanding of the overall public sectors' role grows.

COUNTERCYCLICAL STABILIZATION POLICIES

Prior to the 1970s, at least some support can be found for regionally based stabilization policies. For example, Engerman argued that national stabilization policies would have widely different effects on subnational regions depending on the industry structure, economic diversity, and trend growth rate in the region. Thus, he concluded, "Since nationwide diffusion (of benefits from stabilization policies) is not to be expected, pinpointed policies could be more effective in reducing employment than comparable policies applied on a nationwide scale" (1965, p. 23).

Support for regional countercyclical policies virtually disappeared by the early 1970s. Wallace Oates (1968, 1972) summarized what had become the conventional wisdom on the viability of subnational countercyclical stabilization policies as, "A central government can best resolve the stabilization and distribution problems..." (1972, p. 14).

Six basic arguments have been articulated in support of the Oates' perspective. First, fiscal policy multipliers are small for subnational tax and expenditure programs because of the highly open structure of subnational economies. The national economy implicitly is presumed to be less open and, therefore, national multipliers are held to be relatively larger. Second, debt issued by subnational governments is argued to be largely external and debt held by national governments is internal. Therefore, repayment of principal and interest by subnational governments entails a transfer of real income from residents to non-residents, and repayment of principal and interest by national governments mostly requires transfers between residents. Also, debt limitations and balanced budget requirements constrain state and local governments in their use of debt. Third, cyclical economic shifts tend to be parallel in highly interdependent subnational areas, so cyclical movements become mostly national in scope. As a result, national countercyclical policies can meet the needs of most subnational areas. Next, local governments do not have access to monetary policy, an important tool for economic stabilization. Fifth, high labor and capital mobility can offset the benefits of state stabilization policies. Finally, Musgrave (1959) argued for central control of the stabilization function to ensure proper coordination of policies.

Recently, several authors have questioned the soundness of the six arguments that led to the conventional wisdom.[3] Re-examination of these arguments is refreshing as the current conventional wisdom frequently has been espoused without carefully examining whether the underlying assumptions are, or ever were, valid. For example, Oates' conclusion that subnational multipliers are small is derived from his analysis that demonstrated the multiplier for debt-financed activity falls as economies become more open. Similarly, Oates' statements about cycles being national in scope is predicated on subnational economies being highly interdependent. In both of these cases, Oates makes it clear that his result is derived from assumptions about regional economies. He does not empirically demonstrate that these conditions are present in regional economies. However, the importance of these assumptions to the policy conclusions has been lost in most subsequent discussions.

Can the Conventional Wisdom Be Supported?

Strong counter arguments can be made that four of the six justifications for limited subnational stabilization policies are a less significant constraint than has been presumed--the only exceptions being that U.S. states (and those in some other federations) are unable to use monetary policy and coordination is better with national policies. The counter arguments are either that the point being made is invalid or that the point is valid at both the national and the state levels.

Use of Debt. There are several reasons to question arguments that characteristics of state and local debt make it more difficult for subnational governments to engage in countercyclical policies than for national governments. First, it is true that states are constrained in their ability to operate under deficits, as 49 have balanced budget limitations. Nonetheless, states have a number of ways that they can and do participate in countercyclical expenditure policies, though their flexibility is more limited than the national government's. A case in point is the State of California, which ran recurrent deficits in the early 1990s in the midst of a serious recession. Second, the external character of the state debt burden creates a problem for subnational governments, but probably not a unique problem. Today's financial market for both national and subnational government securities is highly competitive. As a result, it is reasonable to think that much of both national and state government debt is external. This means repayment of principal and interest for debt-financed fiscal policy likely is a net burden to both. Further, debt-financed government expenditures will have no net effect on aggregate expenditures to the extent that the Ricardian equivalence theorem holds in practice. The Ricardian equivalence theorem leads to the conclusion that debt-financed fiscal policies have no stimulative effects, regardless the level of government.

Openness of State Economies. Fiscal policy multipliers are argued to be small because subnational economies are very open. Both Gramlich (1987) and Oates measure the degree of an economy's openness by the propensity to import and specifically the private propensity to import. Stated alternatively, openness is inversely related to the propensity to spend on domestically produced items. The smaller the propensity to import, the less open the economy, and the greater the expected domestic impact from state stabilization policies. Using input-output coefficients, Gramlich determines that at the margin the propensity to spend on intrastate-produced items in the United States ranges from 0.67 in California to 0.35 in Delaware. As a result, consumption of domestic production is sufficiently large so that multipliers are bigger than has been anticipated. Further, he concludes that services are nearly all domestically produced, so the openness of regional economies is declining as shifts occur away from consumption of goods and towards consumption of services. One illustration of this shift is that services rose from 15.5 percent of GNP in 1977 to 17.8 percent in 1992, while manufacturing declined from 21.3 percent to 18.5 percent of GNP during the same time period.

Linkages Between Regional Cycles. State responses to shocks may be less correlated than often has been presumed. One reason is that effects of certain shocks, such as oil price changes, may approach being zero sum with some states (like Texas or Oklahoma) winning and some (such as non-oil producing states) losing. Also, to the extent that state economies are less open and interrelated than usually thought, economic shocks affecting one state will have limited spillovers to other states. Further, downturns have disproportionate effects on durable goods manufacturing and construction, so regions where these industries are relatively more important will be more affected by cycles.

Two ways of empirically addressing whether states respond the same to shocks are provided here: the degree to which states move through cycles together and the magnitude of changes during cycles. Economic shifts during cycles are measured using employment growth rates, the same gauge adopted by Ziegler (1972) who used employment data to determine urban business cycles. Marston (1985) and Gramlich used unemployment rates to measure how business cycles affect states, so these data are reported as well. State employment growth rates and unemployment rates are illustrated in Table 8.1 for four recent time periods, during two of which the national economy was in recession (1982 and 1990) and two of which the national economy was in expansion (1982 to 1989 and 1990 to 1994).

The data suggest that cycles are somewhat, though not exclusively, nationwide in that most states are either in expansion or contraction at the same time. However, the range of growth rates differs widely between states. Thus, the case for regional rather than national countercyclical stabilization policies can be made mostly because the growth differentials are so large. This finding is similar to Ziegler's from two decades ago and to Engerman's from three decades ago.

A relatively small number of states failed to grow during the expansion time periods. Three states, Louisiana, Oklahoma, and Wyoming, lost employment during the expansion years between 1982 and 1989, likely because of demand shifts for energy and natural resources. Nine lost employment between 1990 and 1994, with California and northeastern states predominating. Regional differences also are easily discernable during recession years. Nearly all states, except energy producing states such as Alaska, Oklahoma, Colorado and several other states, experienced employment declines in 1982. Only northeastern states suffered employment losses during 1990.

Growth patterns in expansions and recessions clearly differ across states. Even casual observation of growth rates in Table 8.1 reveals that states have encountered widely different economic fortunes. Annual employment growth between 1982 and 1989 ranged from a low of -1.7 percent in Wyoming to a high of 5.1 percent in Arizona. The range was nearly as wide between 1990 and 1994 and was even wider during recession years. Standard deviations of annual employment growth rates are relatively high and exceed the mean growth rate during both recession years.

An alternative way to observe state variations in economic performance is by calculating the correlations between each state's annual employment growth and the nation's (see Table 8.2). Again, the differences often are large. For example, 12 states have correlation coefficients below 0.60 and 16 states have correlation coefficients above 0.85.

Together the data in Tables 8.1 and 8.2 provide evidence that some regional counter cyclical policies could be appropriate during both national expansions and recessions. For example, government spending could have been increased in California and the New England states during the first half of the 1990's expansion and decreased in other regions to smooth out differences. The problem is that consensus in Congress probably could not be reached that would effectively reduce spending in regions where growth is perceived as too high and increase spending in regions where growth is perceived as too low. The state's themselves could potentially take the lead, although there likely is an asymmetry in motivations. That is, while states may be willing to pursue policies to promote growth, few will be motivated to put on the brakes during periods of rapid growth.

Factor Flows. Even if cycles are regional in nature, both Gramlich and Marston observe that labor migration could offset the need for stabilization policy. However, they reach very different conclusions about the need for state stabilization policies. One key issue is whether migration of both employed and unemployed workers from high unemployment to low unemployment areas is expected. A second concern is whether the migration would be rapid enough to offset unemployment differentials before states could respond with countercyclical policies, given the lags in policy development and implementation.

Marston describes two models: an equilibrium model, where higher wages are paid to offset the propensity for an area to have higher unemployment, and a disequilibrium model, where workers move from high unemployment to low unemployment areas. He examines which model provides the best explanation of migration behavior and measures the persistent cyclical component to determine the duration of cycles. His empirical results indicate that the equilibrium model best explains behavior. This means migration to higher wage areas should not necessarily be expected because higher wages are intended as compensation to keep workers from migrating from the high unemployment that often characterizes these areas. Further, Marston concludes that persistent unemployment lasts less than one year, so state stabilization policies would be ineffective because of the recognition lag.

248

Table 8.1:   Job Growth and Unemployment Rates by State

Total Nonagricultural Jobs

	Percent Change				Unemployment Rate			
	1981-82	1989-90	1982-89	1990-94	1982	1989	1990	1994
Alabama	-2.60	2.15	2.88	1.74	14.4	7.0	6.8	6.0
Alaska	7.68	4.89	1.80	2.23	9.9	6.7	6.9	7.8
Arizona	-1.06	2.15	5.06	3.20	9.9	5.2	5.3	6.4
Arkansas	-2.70	3.37	3.13	2.90	9.8	7.2	6.9	5.3
California	-1.72	2.07	3.58	-1.38	9.9	5.1	5.6	8.6
Colorado	1.65	2.60	1.71	3.57	7.7	5.8	4.9	4.2
Connecticut	-0.62	-2.46	2.28	-1.42	6.9	3.7	5.1	5.6
Delaware	0.00	0.90	4.15	0.53	8.5	3.5	5.1	4.9
District of Columbia	-2.14	0.81	1.87	-1.07	10.6	5.0	6.6	8.2
Florida	0.67	2.40	4.91	1.85	8.2	5.6	5.9	6.6
Georgia	0.13	1.72	4.22	2.20	7.8	5.5	5.4	5.2
Hawaii	-1.33	4.53	3.42	0.36	6.7	2.6	2.8	6.1
Idaho	-4.76	5.22	2.29	4.73	9.8	5.1	5.8	5.6
Illinois	-2.94	1.43	1.83	0.82	11.3	6.0	6.2	5.7
Indiana	-4.09	1.72	2.91	1.83	11.9	4.7	5.3	4.9
Iowa	-4.29	2.18	2.04	1.84	8.5	4.3	4.2	3.7
Kansas	-2.98	2.28	2.08	1.74	6.3	4.0	4.4	5.3
Kentucky	-2.95	2.62	3.06	2.11	10.6	6.2	5.8	5.4
Louisiana	-1.44	3.34	-0.62	2.09	10.3	7.9	6.2	8.0
Maine	-0.88	-1.27	3.86	-0.17	8.6	4.1	5.1	7.4
Maryland	-2.33	0.74	3.66	-0.31	8.4	3.7	4.6	5.1
Massachusetts	-1.14	-4.01	2.35	-0.63	6.9	4.0	6.0	6.0
Michigan	-5.09	1.21	2.98	1.07	14.2	7.1	7.5	5.9
Minnesota	-3.09	2.05	2.91	2.07	8.2	4.3	4.8	4.0
Mississippi	-3.44	1.88	2.17	2.98	12.6	7.8	7.5	6.6
Missouri	-1.73	1.30	2.69	1.34	9.9	5.5	5.7	4.9
Montana	-2.87	2.16	0.88	3.45	8.8	5.9	5.8	5.1
Nebraska	-2.15	3.12	2.16	2.17	5.7	3.1	2.2	2.9

Table 8.1: Job Growth and Unemployment Rates by State (Continued)

Total Nonagricultural Jobs

	Percent Change				Unemployment Rate			
	1981-82	1989-90	1982-89	1990-94	1982	1989	1990	1994
Nevada	-2.46	6.83	5.44	4.37	9.8	5.0	4.9	6.2
New Hampshire	-0.05	-3.99	4.29	0.70	5.4	3.5	5.6	4.6
New Jersey	-0.25	-1.29	2.56	-0.64	7.8	4.1	5.0	6.8
New Mexico	-0.40	3.24	2.48	3.19	10.1	6.7	6.3	6.3
New York	-0.45	-0.41	1.85	-1.28	8.6	5.1	5.2	6.9
North Carolina	-1.86	1.42	3.93	1.90	9.0	3.5	4.1	4.4
North Dakota	0.12	2.11	0.60	2.60	5.9	4.3	3.9	3.9
Ohio	-4.48	1.35	2.24	0.98	12.5	5.5	5.7	5.5
Oklahoma	1.26	2.53	-0.63	1.74	5.7	5.6	5.6	5.8
Oregon	-5.63	3.51	3.34	2.17	11.5	5.7	5.5	5.4
Pennsylvania	-3.15	0.61	1.66	0.09	10.9	4.5	5.4	6.2
Rhode Island	-2.72	-2.32	2.43	-0.97	10.2	4.1	6.7	7.1
South Carolina	-2.86	3.02	3.71	0.99	10.8	4.7	4.7	6.3
South Dakota	-2.46	4.60	2.63	3.63	5.5	4.2	3.7	3.3
Tennessee	-2.92	1.15	3.48	2.51	11.8	5.1	5.2	4.8
Texas	1.35	3.81	1.27	2.18	6.9	6.7	6.2	6.4
Utah	0.52	4.70	3.03	4.44	7.8	4.6	4.3	3.7
Vermont	-0.69	-1.64	3.71	0.61	6.9	3.7	5.0	4.7
Virginia	-0.67	1.20	4.20	0.93	7.7	3.9	4.3	4.9
Washington	-2.68	4.86	3.91	1.77	12.1	6.2	4.9	6.4
West Virginia	-3.29	2.51	0.16	1.73	13.9	8.6	8.3	8.9
Wisconsin	-2.94	2.46	2.61	2.02	10.7	4.4	4.4	4.7
Wyoming	-2.60	2.96	-1.72	2.24	5.8	6.3	5.4	5.3
Mean	-1.72	1.85	2.62	1.56				
Standard Deviation	2.14	2.20	1.42	1.51				

Table 8.2: Correlation between State Employment Growth and U.S. Employment Growth, 1974 - 1993

State	Correlation Coefficient	State	Correlation Coefficient
Alabama	0.879	Nebraska	0.775
Alaska	-0.391	Nevada	0.773
Arizona	0.843	New Hampshire	0.818
Arkansas	0.760	New Jersey	0.833
California	0.883	New Mexico	0.681
Colorado	0.603	New York	0.797
Connecticut	0.870	North Carolina	0.900
Delaware	0.707	North Dakota	0.284
District of Columbia	0.589	Ohio	0.921
Florida	0.811	Oklahoma	0.234
Georgia	0.892	Oregon	0.795
Hawaii	0.342	Pennsylvania	0.934
Idaho	0.410	Rhode Island	0.809
Illinois	0.892	South Carolina	0.902
Indiana	0.858	South Dakota	0.524
Iowa	0.633	Tennessee	0.881
Kansas	0.766	Texas	0.524
Kentucky	0.827	Utah	0.782
Louisiana	0.322	Vermont	0.880
Maine	0.819	Virginia	0.898
Maryland	0.847	Washington	0.714
Massachusetts	0.822	West Virginia	0.511
Michigan	0.847	Wisconsin	0.856
Minnesota	0.894	Wyoming	0.245
Mississippi	0.721		
Missouri	0.932	**Mean**	0.708
Montana	0.434	**Standard deviation**	0.248

Source: U.S. Department of Commerce, Bureau of Economic Analysis, May 1995.

Gramlich accepts a disequilibrium model and concludes that both states and cities have cycles that are independent of the nation, that the cycles are not permanent, and that regional cycles are sufficiently long to allow regional stabilization policies to have an impact. He finds that cycles are long because the migration of unemployed workers from high unemployment rate areas to low unemployment rate areas operates very slowly.

A much broader literature exists on the extent to which labor migration responds to unemployment. At a minimum, it seems the literature cannot be interpreted as providing support for the contention that migration is too rapid to allow regional stabilization policies to be effective. In a recent survey of the literature, Herzog, Schlottmann and Boehm (1993) show that both the human capital and job-search models are consistent with the disequilibrium view of labor responses, where unemployed workers are more likely to migrate for job opportunities. Both personal and area unemployment potentially can encourage migration decisions. Eleven microdata-based empirical studies come to a nearly unanimous finding that unemployed workers are significantly more likely to migrate than are other workers. They find that the literature is less robust with regard to the effect of high area unemployment on migration, but conclude that out-migration is positively linked to high area (as opposed to personal) unemployment.[4] Still, only half of the studies find that high area unemployment leads to greater out-migration, and a study of the Netherlands found that a significant reduction in out-migration is associated with high area unemployment.

Marston argues there is no role for regional stabilization policy because wage premia are provided to workers in areas of high unemployment and migration is such an effective means of narrowing short-term unemployment rate differentials. Gramlich counters that migration is sufficiently slow so that stabilization policy is an appropriate strategy. An obvious assumption in both Marston's and Gramlich's work is that a primary policy target either is or should be the unemployment rate. While it is true that state and local governments may be concerned about their unemployment rate, more likely targets, even in the short run, are employment and population growth rates. To the extent this is true, job creation and labor force-providing migration in many ways are the targets rather than the means to achieve a target. Policymakers in high unemployment rate states probably are not comforted to learn that the unemployment rate will fall because unemployed workers will leave, since such a result will be viewed as failure. The more important issue to policymakers may be whether stabilization policies can increase job creation and in-migration. Thus, the possibility of out-migration may enhance, rather than retard, the likelihood that states will want to engage in stabilization policies. In this sense, a cornerstone of Marston's and Gramlich's conclusions, whether migration is rapid, is important, but for a very different reason. The greater the propensity for out-migration, the more likely that states will want to engage in fiscal policy to offset or reduce the migration. However, the basis for this motivation of state stabilization policies is altering the economic trend rather than the cycle.

Coordination of Fiscal Policy. Coordination obviously is easier if fiscal policy is conducted at the national level, regardless of whether the national stabilization policy treats the entire country as a single entity or involves differential policies depending on the needs of particular regions. The U.S. government is constitutionally precluded from using differential tax policies across regions, but can engage in differential expenditure policies to stimulate regional economies. A variety of programs with differential effects already exist, though these grant and expenditure programs normally are not designed as countercyclical measures. Funding of the Tennessee Valley Authority is one example. Also, grants to state and local governments often have a strong regional character, either by virtue of the grant's automatic structure, as with AFDC payments, or by discretion.

An advantage of designing countercyclical policies at the national level is the potential to engage in regional stabilization policies for whatever region is the appropriate size, whether multistate, single state, or substate. Another advantage of national stabilization is that policies can be chosen to maximize national well-being. Finally, the national government focuses on a broader set of policy targets, including price stability, international flows, and growth, and the best policy alternatives can be chosen to meet the range of goals. On the other hand, the political economy in which the national government operates precludes adopting a set of regionally appropriate policies that maximizes national well-being, so the ability to take a national perspective may be of little practical value.

Subnational governments normally focus on growth-oriented targets such as employment or population growth, and pay little attention to targets over which they can exert little control, such as price stability and international capital flows. Regional governments probably perceive that they receive little credit for achieving non-growth-oriented targets, and any benefits from achieving these targets must be shared with all other regions. Also, subnational governments may want to engage in a different stabilization policy from what is nationally optimal, because their intent is to maximize the wellbeing of the local rather than national populations. Thus, regional governments operating independently to achieve a narrower set of targets, and looking only at internal benefits from stabilization policies are not likely to select a nationally optimizing stabilization policy.

Regional Monetary Policy Effects. Additional evidence of the efficacy of regional stabilization policy can be found in research on the regional effects of monetary policy. Carlino and DeFina (1996) give three reasons why monetary policy can be expected to have a differential effect across regions. First, the mix of interest-sensitive industries, most notably manufacturing and construction, differs widely across regions. Second, small banks find it more difficult to obtain alternative sources of funding during periods of tight monetary policy, so regions with relatively more small banks are expected to be affected more by the policies. The Plains, Rocky Mountains and Southwest Regions have more small banks. Third, small borrowers are more likely to use banks as their lending source, meaning areas with many small borrowers are likely to be affected more by monetary policy actions. The authors conclude that manufacturing-intensive regions and regions with more small businesses are affected more by monetary policy. However, they determine that regions become less sensitive to monetary policy when they have higher percentages of small banks.

Should States Use Countercyclical Policies?

The conventional wisdom has been that states should not engage in countercyclical stabilization policies because the policies would be so ineffective that it would not be in the state's best interest to undertake them. Generally, the above arguments dispute the conventional wisdom and conclude that the policies may be effective and indicate that some degree of countercyclical policies may be appropriate from the state's perspectives. Gramlich uses a simple Keynesian and life cycle model and reasonable parameter values to calculate appropriate government responses to a demand shock. He finds that each state would improve welfare by reacting to a demand shock, though the appropriate degree of response varies by state.

Even some local governments could find it in their best interest to engage in countercyclical policies.

Subnational policies could be discretionary, such as building and then depleting rainy-day funds across cycles. Alternatively, the policies could be automatic, such as occurs with unemployment insurance funds. However, with infrequent exceptions, states do not explicitly engage in policies with the intent of slowing down growth,[5] even during expansions, because states are not directly concerned with fighting inflation. Still, buildup of rainy-day funds in expansions may have the same effect, even though the intent is to provide budget flexibility during recessions.

If states are to be discouraged from engaging in countercyclical policies, the case must be based on negative consequences for the nation as a whole, rather than on the individual states. State policies may be inappropriate from a national perspective because the national government maximizes welfare across a broader set of targets than do states, and state actions may hinder achieving the range of goals. Also, each state is likely to ignore spillover effects of its actions on other states.

Alternatively, states might be discouraged from engaging in countercyclical policies for the same reasons that national countercyclical policies have been questioned. For example, the recognition lag may be too long for states to react with effective policies. Also, the long-run efficacy of countercyclical policies has been questioned, because flexible prices and factor mobility will offset any gains. However, this argument may be less valid because attraction of mobile factors may be consistent with state goals, even if relative prices are unaffected in the long run.

We discourage adjustment of tax rates as a form of countercyclical policy, given the political and economic ramifications. Should states choose to use stabilization policies, the creation of automatic stabilizers (such as a more stable tax structure) or the discretionary use of substantial rainy day fund programs are preferred mechanisms. Either approach can smooth economic swings and at the same time lessen variations in budget policy.

The long-run effects of subnational tax and expenditure policies is effectively captured by the balanced-budget multiplier. Yet short-term boosts in the economy may be achieved through debt issuance or use of rainy day funds, and the affect could be greater than that implied by the balanced-budget multiplier. Moreover, and balanced-budget multiplier summarizes impacts of a state's actions across all jurisdictions, but impacts on the individual state could be larger or smaller than the multiplier implies.

Stabilizing Influences of Fiscal Structure and Discretionary Policy

The countercyclical or procyclical influence of subnational stabilization policy depends on automatic responses embedded in the revenue and expenditure structures, as well as on discretionary budget changes.[6] Consider, for example, an economic expansion where automatic influences tend to raise revenues. This revenue growth--coupled with reductions in spending on welfare and assistance programs--can then accommodate spending on existing activities or new initiatives. But the same expansionary environment that yields natural revenue growth may give rise to political pressure to enact discretionary tax cuts. While the policy objective for discretionary policies in this case may be to reduce tax burdens, an important potential impact is a procyclical impetus to growth. During economic downturns the automatic influence on revenue coffers is negative. On the expenditure side of the budget, new initiatives may be shelved, pay raises may be set aside and public assistance spending will rise. In some instances, broader spending cuts may be required. In the case of a downturn, however, discretionary responses take place in the face of the harsh realities of balanced-budget restrictions that may preclude discretionary tax cuts intended to promote growth. The ultimate policy response may be a tax increase that further dampens economic growth.

Discretionary Policy. Policymakers have both short-term and long-term options at their disposal for dealing with variations in revenues and expenditures over the course of the business cycle. Because of asymmetries in the costs and benefits associated with periods of rapid growth versus periods of decline, there is likely a bias in favor of dealing more aggressively with cyclical downturns. In the short run, policymakers can confront an economic downturn by deferring spending, accelerating collections or making accounting changes (such as changing pension reserves or shifting revenues from a cash to an accrual basis). Available reserves and cash balances can also be drawn down. These mechanisms can soften the need to reduce current expenditures, raise taxes or expand the tax base.

In the longer term subnational governments can alter their fiscal structure or fiscal institutions to better respond to cyclical and structural economic and fiscal problems. For example, states and local governments might choose a tax structure--inclusive of rates, tax bases and the mix of taxes--to promote fiscal and hence economic stability. While there is a substantial literature on tax stability, there is little if any evidence that state's purposely pursue such a strategy.[7] Moreover, revenue stability is the opposite of a countercyclical revenue structure as countercyclicality would require revenues to grow (decline) relatively faster during economic expansions (contractions) rather than the reverse. In addition, tax structure stability may be at odds with other policy objectives, including revenue adequacy and elasticity.

The procyclical nature of discretionary state policy is illustrated in Table 8.3 for 1994. The net tax reduction across all states was $1.6 billion during this year of strong economic growth, with tax increases of only $0.1 billion being more than offset by tax decreases of $1.7 billion. Gold (1995) argues this pattern of tax reductions during periods of economic strength is not a new trend, but is consistent with the longer term behavior of state governments. Table 8.4 provides corroborating descriptive evidence, illustrating discretionary changes in taxes for state governments for the period 1970-1993. In general, states have a propensity to raise taxes during periods of economic hardship, in turn reducing taxes when revenue growth rates are faster. As can be seen from Table 8.4, discretionary tax increases spiked upward noticeably during the years of national economic decline 1971, 1975, 1983 and 1991.[8] Adams (1988) has identified a similar pattern of discretionary tax increases for cities during periods of rising unemployment in the 1970s, although the analysis is confined to a small number of places.

Despite the casual evidence, the literature on the national stabilizing influence of discretionary subnational policies remains mixed. Rafuse (1965) seemed to reverse the pessimistic conclusions of Hansen and Perloff (1944) and others regarding the "perversity" (or procyclicality) of state and local budget policies with respect to national growth, concluding that subnational government behavior was mildly and increasingly stabilizing over time. Yet Ziegler (1972), who examined the behavior of urban governments, concluded such behavior was procyclical during expansions and countercyclical during contractions. More recently, Blackley and DeBoer (1993) found that state revenue policy was procyclical during the

Table 8.3:   State Tax Reductions and Increases in 1994

	Reductions			Increases	
State	Amount (Millions of $)	Percent of Total Revenue	State	Amount (Millions of $)	Percent of Total Revenue
Arizona	$46	1.0%	Alaska	2	0.1
Connecticut	3	*	Hawaii	3	0.1
Delaware	6	0.4	Idaho	6	0.4
Florida	1	*	Kentucky	22	0.4
Georgia	100	1.4	Louisiana	18	0.4
Indiana	1	*	Maine	2	0.1
Kansas	13	0.5	Missouri	34	0.7
Maryland	62	1.0	Oklahoma	18	0.5
Massachusetts	21	0.2	Rhode Island	7	0.5
Minnesota	16	0.2	South Dakota	2	0.4
Mississippi	4	0.2			
Nebraska	5	0.3			
New Jersey	649	5.1			
New Mexico	50	2.2			
New York	469	1.6			
Ohio	46	0.4			
Pennsylvania	166	1.0			
South Carolina	9	0.2			
Utah	19	1.0			
Washington	11	0.1			
Total	**$1697**		**Total**	**$114**	
Net decreases	**$1583**	**0.5**			

Source: *State Fiscal Brief,* January, 1995, Center for the Study of the States, Nelson A. Rockefeller Institute of Government, State University of New York, Albany, New York.

Note: *Less than 0.1% of total tax revenue. Michigan's net tax reduction was $1.022 billion, consisting of a local property tax cut of $4.808 billion and offsetting state increases of $3.786 billion.

Table 8.4: **Net State Tax Changes by Year of Enactment**

	Net Change in State Tax Revenues	
Calendar Year	Billions of Dollars	Percent of Annual Collections
1970	$0.8	1.7
1971	5.0	9.7
1972	0.9	1.5
1973	0.5	0.7
1974	0.4	0.5
1975	1.6	2.0
1976	1.0	0.9
1977	0.2	0.5
1978	-2.3	-2.0
1979	-2.0	-1.6
1980	0.4	0.3
1981	3.8	2.5
1982	2.9	1.8
1983	8.3	4.8
1984	2.3	1.2
1985	-1.3	-0.6
1986	1.1	0.5
1987	4.5	1.9
1988	0.6	0.2
1989	3.5	1.3
1990	9.2	3.5
1991	14.4	4.8
1992	1.4	0.4
1993	1.2	0.4

Source: *State Fiscal Brief.* January 1, 1995. Center for the Study of the States, Nelson A. Rockefeller Institute of Government, State University of New York, Albany, New York.

recession of the early 1990s, while Mattoon and Testa (1992) argue that state and local behavior has been countercyclical in every post World War II contraction. Poterba (1994) has shown that state fiscal institutions and political factors are important determinants of a state's policy response during periods of fiscal crisis. For example, states with more binding constraints on deficit finance and states with single-party dominance tend to respond quicker to fiscal crises by cutting expenditures and/or raising taxes, in turn imparting a destabilizing influence on the economy. Together the literature suggests that the influence of discretionary policy hinges on the unit of government, the way in which cycles and policy responses are measured, the time period examined, political conditions, and constraints on the discretionary behavior of policymakers.

Ongoing State Activities. States could conceivably make use of debt policy to promote economic stabilization. One option would be to choose debt (taxes) over tax (debt) financing in the face of an economic downturn (upswing). A second option would be to time capital spending and debt issuance to dampen cyclical swings, though considerable prior planning and information on recent economic activity would be necessary for such a policy to be effective.[9]

An examination of short-term and long-term debt behavior by state governments was undertaken for historical periods of economic expansion and contraction to determine whether debt policy was countercyclical or procyclical. Elasticities for debt retirement and debt issuance with respect to personal income were estimated for individual states using regression analysis. The regression approach was complemented by a descriptive analysis of debt policy for each of the historical time periods. This analysis failed to reveal any systematic responses on the part of state governments during periods of growth versus periods of decline.

Unemployment insurance (UI) programs offer a second mechanism whereby states can impart a stabilizing influence on the economy. As an illustration, in the 1982 recession year, UI benefit payments were .77 percent of personal income, while in the subsequent expansion years, the ratio of benefits paid to personal income declined steadily (with the exception of a slight upward blip in 1986) until 1988. As the economy then slowed, benefits as a share of personal income climbed, reaching .53 in 1991. A recent Department of Labor study (1991) finds UI benefits positively correlated with the unemployment rate and the GNP gap (with correlation coefficients of .90 and .77, respectively), and negatively correlated with GNP (-.67).

Despite the small size of UI programs, estimates of their potential expansionary influence are surprisingly large. One study (Department of Labor, 1991) used the DRI U.S. econometric model to simulate the way in which lower UI taxes and higher benefits could stimulate the economy during an economic downturn. It was estimated that state UI systems potentially could offset 2.9 percent of the loss in GNP during the trough of a monetary induced recession. However, concerns have arisen regarding the possible decline in the stabilizing influence of state UI systems due to a number of factors, including reduction in the insured unemployment rate relative to the total unemployment rate, and a decline in benefits paid relative to total wages over time.

Rainy day (or budget stabilization) funds represent a third mechanism that state's employ with potential countercyclical influences.[10] While rainy day funds could be used as a discretionary instrument to stabilize the economy, in practice they are intended to ease budgetary pressures. However, the budgetary pressures and use of rainy day funds are not always tied to cyclical imbalances in revenues and expenditures (Navin and Navin, 1994). Minnesota, for example, has a Budget Reserve Account that could be used to meet any of a number of state spending needs. Even in states with formal countercyclical programs, monies have been used for other purposes, as with Michigan's diversion of resources to support corrections spending in the late 1980s. To the extent that the accumulation of rainy day funds occurs during periods of growth and the expenditure of these funds takes place during recessions, such programs are countercyclical in nature.

States accumulate rainy day funds through the formal budget process, effectively appropriating fund balances as expenditures. In most states, discretion is exercised annually regarding increments to the rainy day funds. Navin and Navin (1994) have expressed the concern that legislators will not be adequately motivated to place monies in stabilization funds as they confront competing uses for state resources in a given year. Other states have formula-based schemes to build up rainy day funds while still others earmark the proceeds of specific taxes.[11] Concerns have been raised that the formula-based plans have potentially destablizing influences on state budgets (Pollock and Suyderhound, 1986). One explanation is that increments to and withdrawals from the rainy day fund may be tied to personal income growth rather than to the revenue and expenditure structure. The important lesson here is that for such funds to promote *fiscal* stability, they must be more closely tied to cyclical variations in revenues and expenditures. However, if the goal of the rainy day fund is to promote *economic* stability, linkages to personal income growth would be preferred.

To place the rainy day funds in perspective, state-level historical data are presented in Table 8.5. For most states the fund balances are quite modest and are expected to average only 2.5 percent of state general fund expenditures in 1996. But recognition of the importance of these funds has grown over time. As shown in Table 8.5, in 1984 only 13 states maintained nonzero balances in their rainy day funds; by 1996, only 11 states had yet to maintain nonzero stabilization fund balances. A National Conference of State Legislatures (1996) report indicates that the only jurisdictions without rainy day funds in 1995 were Arkansas, the District of Columbia, Hawaii, Illinois, Montana and Oregon.

While there is insufficient history to draw precise inferences, the rainy day fund balances appear to be countercyclical. During the 1980s expansion, rainy day fund balances generally grew. As the economy slipped at the turn of the decade, stabilization fund balances slipped as well. Even netting out the unique experience of California in 1991 and 1992 (where debt was issued to finance ongoing activities, resulting in negative balances), rainy day funds were 1.2 percent of general fund expenditures in these years, showing deterioration from prior years. With a rebound in economic activity after the recession of the early 1990s, rainy day fund balances rebounded as well.

Substate governments also make use of rainy day funds, although Wolkoff's (1987) survey of 50 large municipalities in 1985 suggests their use is not extensive. Of the 27 responses to his survey, only 7 municipalities noted their use of stabilization funds. The City of Milwaukee was the first to establish a rainy day fund; the objective was to avoid large annual swings in property tax rates rather than to affect economic performance. As the state-level use of rainy day funds has expanded since the mid 1980s, one would expect similar growth for substate governments.

Gross Impacts: Fiscal Structure and Policy. Together the influences of discretionary policy and automatic stabilizers determine whether subnational budgets are procyclical or countercyclical. Bahl and Duncombe (1988) have explored this issue by examining variations in the surplus of state and local governments (as measured in the National Income Accounts), to variations in real GNP. They find the surplus to be positively correlated with GNP, indicating a countercyclical stance on the part of combined state and local governments.

An alternative approach pursued here is estimation of state tax and expenditure buoyancies with respect to personal income. Similar to an elasticity, buoyancies capture the percentage change in revenues (expenditures) that result from a one percent change in personal income. As Fox and Campbell (1984) note, however, the proper focus for measuring pro or countercyclical behavior is short-term buoyancies over the ups and downs of the business cycle (respectively) rather than long-term (or average) buoyancies. Accordingly, subperiods of historical data for 1965-1992 were used to estimate revenue-personal income buoyancies, and data for 1978-1992 were used to estimate expenditure-personal income buoyancies. Buoyancies were estimated using ordinary least squares applied to pooled state data for each subperiod, controlling for state fixed effects.

The revenue-personal income buoyancy estimates are presented in Table 8.6 for several periods of economic growth and decline. A comparison of adjacent periods of expansion and contraction shows some tendency for total and general revenues to grow relatively more strongly in periods of economic decline, although there are exceptions. General sales and gross receipts taxes, as well as charges and miscellaneous revenues, also tend to have higher growth in periods of contraction. For these measures of state revenue, there is a procyclical influence.

The response of expenditures to variations in personal income are shown in Table 8.7. While the revenue side of state budgets impart a procyclical influence, state expenditures tend to have countercyclical effects. For most expenditure categories--including total and general expenditures-- the buoyancy estimates are higher during periods of economic contraction than during periods of expansion.

Together the buoyancy estimates reveal that both revenues and expenditures tend to grow more rapidly during economic downturns than in periods of expansion. However, there are exceptions over time and for

Table 8.5:   State Rainy Day Fund Balances (Millions of dollars)

Region/State	1984	1985	1986	1987	1988	1989	1990	1991	1992	1993	1994	1995	1996
Alabama	0	0	0	0	21	21	33	0	0	0	0	0	0
Alaska	282	298	436	0	0	0	0	802	1,007	1,633	614	1,584	1,477
Arizona	0	0	0	0	0	0	0	0	0	0	42	111	111
Arkansas	0	0	0	0	0	0	0	0	0	0	0	0	0
California	0	0	0	591	4	857	41	-1,643	-2962	118	-281	285	92
Colorado	0	0	0	0	0	92	99	16	113	229	405	545	398
Connecticut	165	200	198	320	320	130	102	0	0	0	0	0	3
Delaware	39	0	0	0	53	56	63	65	88	68	72	79	85
Florida	25	120	131	103	110	157	255	3	62	162	296	327	334
Georgia	38	138	151	151	163	194	0	0	0	123	267	267	267
Hawaii	0	0	0	0	0	0	0	0	0	0	0	0	0
Idaho	6	6	0	0	0	12	35	35	30	30	33	33	33
Illinois	0	0	0	0	0	0	0	0	0	0	0	0	0
Indiana	0	145	145	165	220	265	318	323	329	301	370	388	406
Iowa	8	0	8	68	0	0	0	0	2	2	35	76	195
Kansas	0	0	0	0	0	0	0	0	0	75	75	8	0
Kentucky	0	0	0	21	0	0	0	20	24	29	90	100	100
Louisiana	0	0	0	0	0	0	0	0	0	0	0	0	0
Maine	0	1	10	25	25	25	4	0	1	12	17	0	0
Maryland	0	0	0	50	65	92	118	0	0	51	162	286	512
Massachusetts	0	0	0	70	112	0	0	59	230	310	383	398	419
Michigan	4	372	358	352	381	419	385	182	20	303	779	1,069	1,133
Minnesota	0	0	0	250	265	550	550	400	400	360	500	500	350

Table 8.5: State Rainy Day Fund Balances (Millions of dollars) (Continued)

Region/State	1984	1985	1986	1987	1988	1989	1990	1991	1992	1993	1994	1995	1996
Mississippi	0	32	38	6	24	24	17	43	47	160	195	195	195
Missouri	0	0	0	0	0	0	0	0	17	25	37	21	25
Montana	0	0	0	0	0	0	0	0	0	0	0	0	0
Nebraska	36	36	22	24	18	50	40	32	27	17	28	33	33
Nevada	0	0	0	40	40	40	40	40	0	0	18	100	100
New Hampshire	0	0	0	27	27	29	28	0	0	20	119	123	123
New Jersey	0	0	0	0	246	0	0	0	0	65	159	289	289
New Mexico	0	0	0	63	155	113	108	63	0	215	0	0	0
New York	0	0	0	0	0	0	0	0	0	67	134	157	172
North Carolina	0	0	0	0	0	0	141	0	42	176	211	359	359
North Dakota	0	0	0	0	0	25	21	22	23	0	0	0	0
Ohio	0	125	141	263	284	340	364	300	0	21	281	893	893
Oklahoma	0	0	0	0	78	152	151	202	135	91	46	41	41
Oregon	0	0	0	0	0	0	0	0	0	0	25	0	38
Pennsylvania	0	0	25	51	80	112	127	2	2	5	30	66	129
Rhode Island	0	4	10	18	28	37	6	0	8	23	43	46	47
South Carolina	98	89	52	75	86	88	88	33	0	69	100	110	152
South Dakota	34	0	0	0	0	0	0	0	20	21	22	11	17
Tennessee	50	0	0	75	75	100	100	7	76	150	101	101	101
Texas	0	0	0	0	0	0	19	0	163	52	29	9	9
Utah	0	0	0	20	43	48	52	57	58	33	43	60	62
Vermont	0	0	0	0	8	13	10	0	0	0	1	1	2
Virginia	0	55	0	10	0	0	0	0	0	80	80	80	80
Washington	0	0	0	0	0	60	260	260	100	100	125	125	25
West Virginia	0	0	0	0	0	0	0	0	0	0	21	56	71

Table 8.5: State Rainy Day Fund Balances (Millions of dollars) (Continued)

Region/State	1984	1985	1986	1987	1988	1989	1990	1991	1992	1993	1994	1995	1996
Wisconsin	0	0	0	0	0	0	0	0	0	69	74	79	83
Wyoming	42	110	105	117	55	58	2	35	25	43	18	0	0
Total	827	1,731	1,830	2,955	2,986	4,159	3,577	1,358	87	5,308	5,799	9,011	8,961
General Fund Expenditures	167,149	184,196	203,869	217,965	236,041	259,283	274,733	289,125	302,425	311,997	331,516	363,273	357,732
Percent of Expenditures	0.0	0.9	0.9	1.4	1.3	1.6	1.3	0.0	0.0	1.7	1.7	2.5	2.5

Source: Fiscal Survey of the States, National Governors Association and National Association of State Budget Officers, various years.

266

Table 8.6: State Revenue/Personal Income Buoyancy Estimates

Buoyancy Estimates

Revenue Category	1969-1970 (Contraction)	1970-1973 (Expansion)	1973-1975 (Contraction)	1975-1980 (Expansion)
Total Revenue	1.0302* (0.0433)	0.8652* (0.0201)	0.8841* (0.0124)	0.8768* (0.0122)
Total General Revenue	2.0286* (0.3604)	1.0435* (0.6228)	0.9894* (0.0445)	0.9826* (0.0202)
Federal Inter-governmental Revenue	1.3410* (0.1277)	1.3286* (0.0611)	0.8292* (0.0769)	0.9066* (0.0198)
Local Inter-governmental Revenue	0.0934* (0.7187)	0.9266* (0.2244)	2.2459* (0.3671)	0.5940* (0.1352)
Total Taxes	1.6493* (0.1374)	1.0600* (0.0318)	1.0261* (0.0525)	0.9700* (0.0261)
General Sales & Gross Receipts	1.8386* (0.2773)	1.0604* (0.0448)	1.1902* (0.0747)	1.0090* (0.0186)
Selective Sales & Gross Receipts	1.3650* (0.1341)	0.8923* (0.0341)	0.3989* (0.0330)	0.5543* (0.0190)
Income	1.9158* (0.2479)	1.6213* (0.1238)	1.3266* (0.1190)	1.2946* (0.0457)
Charges & Miscellaneous	2.3917* (0.6726)	0.8602* (0.1025)	1.4304* (0.0912)	1.1616* (0.0391)
Insurance Trust Revenues	1.2555* (0.1158)	1.4091* (0.0501)	1.2110* (0.0803)	1.1821* (0.0584)

Table 8.6: **State Revenue/Personal Income Buoyancy Estimates (Continued)**

Buoyancy Estimates

Revenue Category	1981-1982 (Contraction)	1982-1990 (Expansion)	1990-1991 (Contraction)	1991-1992 (Expansion)
Total Revenue	1.0302* (0.1111)	1.1371* (.0137)	1.3189* (.1173)	1.6624* (.1409)
Total General Revenue	1.0077* (0.1202)	1.1371* (.0134)	1.4028* (.1065)	1.3665* (.1451)
Federal Inter-governmental Revenue	-0.7204* (0.1694)	1.0044* (.0227)	2.5642* (.1931)	2.4428* (.2075)
Local Inter-governmental Revenue	0.4329 (0.9535)	1.0538* (.1274)	2.2361 (1.4089)	3.0529* (.8971)
Total Taxes	1.4302* (0.1912)	1.1261* (.0196)	0.9036* (.1378)	0.8824* (.1581)
General Sales & Gross Receipts	1.5254* (0.1286)	1.2278* (.0254)	0.8726* (.1971)	0.8410* (.1609)
Selective Sales & Gross Receipts	1.2165* (0.1430)	.9857* (.0253)	0.6747* (.1931)	1.0524* (.2261)
Income	0.3223 (0.5379)	1.4040* (.0588)	1.2170* (.3254)	0.7027 (.3821)
Charges & Miscellaneous	2.0288* (0.2067)	1.3472* (.0260)	1.3886* (.1702)	1.2271* (.2254)
Insurance Trust Revenues	1.4275* (0.3086)	1.2161* (.0473)	0.7862 (.4231)	3.3927* (.3900)

The method of estimation is ordinary least squares applied to the 50 states for the time period indicated. Coefficients are reported with standard errors in parentheses.
*Significant at the 1% level.

Table 8.7: State Expenditure/Personal Income Buoyancy Estimates

Buoyancy Estimate

Expenditure Category	1975-1980 (Expansion)	1981-1982 (Contraction)	1982-1990 (Expansion)	1990-1991 (Contraction)	1991-1992 (Expansion)
Total Expenditures	1.0444* (0.0420)	1.1388* (0.1037)	1.0842* (.0113)	1.9521* (.1373)	1.5271* (.1288)
General Expenditures	1.0521* (0.0417)	1.0566* (0.1016)	1.1470* (.0127)	1.8353* (.1306)	1.4636* (.1464)
Intergovernmental Expenditures	0.9175* (0.0664)	1.4333* (0.2107)	1.0910* (.0230)	1.6210* (.1880)	0.9199* (.1636)
Direct Expenditures	1.0895* (0.0493)	0.8770* (0.1114)	1.4531* (.0225)	2.0807* (.1663)	1.7400* (.1308)
Educational Services	0.9684* (0.0415)	1.1661* (0.1250)	1.0615* (.0154)	1.6072* (.1766)	1.0426* (.1504)
Social Services & Income Maintenance	1.0235* (0.0470)	0.9482* (0.1280)	1.1559* (.0208)	2.9482* (.1910)	2.9439* (0.2651)
Transportation	1.2975* (0.0780)	-0.0832* (0.3467)	1.1748* (.0340)	1.2958* (.3441)	0.7339* (.2503)
Public Safety	1.1641* (0.0642)	1.6310* (0.1735)	1.4663* (.0275)	1.9314* (.2163)	0.6766* (.1740)
Environment & Housing	0.9863* (0.0892)	1.1629* (0.2390)	1.3322* (.0414)	1.1912* (.3121)	0.6909* (.2311)
Government Administration	0.9963* (0.0796)	1.7086* (0.2660)	1.3621* (.0278)	1.6595* (.2354)	0.9764* (.1917)

The method of estimation is ordinary least squares applied to the 50 states for the time period indicated. Coefficients are reported with standard errors in parentheses.
*Significant at the 1% level.

specific categories of revenue and expenditure. Changes in the structure of the economy, revenues and expenditures; the unevenness of expansion and contraction across regions; and differential policy responses are some of the explanations for variability in budgetary influences over time.

SUBNATIONAL GROWTH POLICIES[12]

The use of economic development incentives in the high stakes bidding war over new jobs and industry is perhaps the most visible subnational government policy directed towards promoting economic growth. The State of Utah, for example, recently won the bidding war over a new computer chip manufacturer that offered the promise of a $1.3 billion investment and the creation of up to 3,500 high-wage jobs. Utah's willingness to pay between $100-300 million--or as much as $86 thousand per job--to attract this facility suggests that state policymakers are convinced they can affect economic growth.[13]

Despite the visibility of incentives and their seemingly important role in influencing economic development, they are a small part of a much larger arsenal of policies designed, in whole or in part, to enhance the growth of state and local economies. From the broadest possible perspective, any policy that affects the size of the aggregate economy--as measured by total output, employment, capital investment, population and so on--might be construed as a growth policy. Examples range from the provision of basic education to amenities, from the design of broad tax structure to specific regulatory policies, and from road construction to library maintenance. While subnational governments likely have a bias in favor of economic expansion, there are instances where policies are used to rein in growth. For example, local governments frequently rely on general land use restrictions (such as zoning) to promote controlled growth. Impact fees are a specific mechanism that can be used to slow the otherwise rapid pace of growth, as well as provide financing for both ongoing services and infrastructure development.

The extensive application of growth policies by subnational governments seems to fly in the face of the conventional wisdom that states and localities can do little or nothing to affect their economic growth. But subnational policymakers are keenly aware of their ability--or the perception of their ability--to steal economic activity away from other jurisdictions, even if their is no improvement in national economic conditions and there are negative welfare consequences for the economy as a whole.[14] Moreover, the pursuit of certain growth strategies (such as providing education and training) suggests the possibility that subnational policy can improve both regional and national growth.

Subnational growth policies, as with subnational countercyclical policies, are highly interwoven with activities to achieve allocational or distributional objectives. For example, while targeted programs such as enterprise zones potentially improve trend growth, the primary intent is to address allocative efficiency problems (related to the long-term underutilization of resources) and distributional objectives (the transfer of resources to distressed regions). Similarly, policies intended to affect trend growth may at the same time have implications for other public sector objectives. An example is policies that cultivate growth of automobile assembly and parts manufacture that in turn heighten regional instability over the course of the business cycle. As with the treatment of countercyclical stabilization policies, the emphasis here is on those subnational policies whose primary intent is to affect trend performance of the economy rather than distributional or allocational objectives.

Growth Theory and Subnational Economic Growth

Neoclassical growth theory and regional economic modeling are two competing candidates that might be used as a conceptual basis for examining the nature and consequences of subnational growth policy. While the use of regional economic models has the most extensive tradition in the literature on subnational economic performance, the modern variants of growth theory are a superior framework.[15] One reason is that growth theory can accommodate exogenous and endogenous growth, whereas regional models rely on exogenous growth through exports and the infusion of new purchasing power.

A second and related reason is growth theory's emphasis on forward linkages on the supply side of the economy, including the ability to accommodate analysis of policies intended to promote input utilization, increase productivity and raise long-term growth. An illustration of the differing conclusions is provided by the traditional treatment of changes in investment in the competing frameworks. In regional economic models the emphasis lies on the change in regional demand resulting from the new investment, including attendant multiplier linkages. Note, however, the emphasis on backward linkages in the regional modeling framework. Using an input/output model, for example, one traces out the backward linkages of the change in investment to intermediate and primary products. But the input/output approach is not nearly as friendly in terms of its ability to explain forward linkages. If regional supply of a specific input commodity was increased, the input/output model cannot determine with much specificity the uses to which inputs would be placed. Moreover, there is little capacity to determine how new capital investments alter a region's productivity, its potential growth path and its potential rate of economic growth.

Growth theory, on the other hand, accommodates demand-side (i.e., spending) influences of new investment (including multiplier effects), but the primary focus is on how the investment influences output via affects on productivity and growth. While there is considerable practical interest in the short-term demand shocks emanating from new investments, knowledge of forward linkages is critical to the design, implementation and evaluation of subnational growth policies that are intended to foster long-term growth. In general, growth theory and its formal modeling structure offer the greatest promise for resolving open conceptual and empirical questions related to subnational growth policies and their effectiveness.

Early formulations of growth theory had limited applicability to subnational governments, and, accordingly, were seldom if ever used to examine subnational economic growth. The stylized neoclassical growth framework typically included--in addition to the usual assumptions regarding perfect competition--constant returns to scale production technology that allowed input substitution, an exogenous rate of growth in the labor force, a savings rate tied to some measure of aggregate economic activity and a closed economy. Net change in the capital stock was defined to equal savings (minus depreciation). The height of the economy's potential growth path was determined by the accumulated stock of capital per worker and the savings rate; the potential growth rate was itself a function of the growth rates of the labor force and productivity.

The closed economy assumption of early growth models is clearly inconsistent with the openness of subnational economies. In addition, early growth models ignored or postulated naive formulations of technical progress despite the fact that technology development transfer and assimilation are important paths to improved growth. Moreover, the earliest models--including Solow's classic formulation--were largely positive in nature and were not intended to address the role of policy on growth. As a result, the policy handles that might be employed to affect subnational growth were seriously circumscribed by the theory itself. Given the assumptions of the model, the rate of economic growth was driven by fertility rates and savings, leaving subnational governments largely impotent in their ability to improve growth.

As growth theory has matured there have been numerous efforts to remedy its limitations, in turn making the modern formulations much more amenable to analysis of subnational economic performance.[16] This is not to say that growth theory has resolved all of the issues related to growth. For example, considerable controversy exists over the proper specification of technical change and the convergence hypothesis. Nonetheless, the more recent models that accommodate trade, technology transfers and spillovers, and policy have added important elements of realism and have enhanced understanding of the causes and consequences of growth.

The implications of these extensions can be illustrated by example. In static, closed economy models that ignore technology development and transfer, production adheres to the comparative advantage dictated by initial endowments. In more general models that accommodate trade and innovation, dynamic comparative advantages can emerge over time. In some special cases (Grossman and Helpman, 1991) the dynamic comparative advantage may have little or nothing to do with initial endowments, in sharp contrast with static models. Hence the economic fate of subnational economies is not written in stone, but is instead malleable and potentially subject to policy influence.

As growth theory has broadened our understanding of the potential importance of input accumulation, productivity growth, technical change and trade to a nation's growth, the same set of factors has surfaced as the primary determinants of the pace of subnational economic progress. Thus, if subnational governments can affect the level of inputs or their productivity, or influence trade and technical progress, they may in turn realize higher levels of economic performance and/or higher rates of growth.

It is important to distinguish between two different types of policy that subnational governments might pursue. First are actions that can move the economy from the actual to the potential growth path. For example, if resources are not fully employed, subnational governments may prime the pump to move the economy closer to its frontier. However, such actions are more appropriately categorized as countercyclical policies (discussed above) as opposed to growth policies. The second are actions that change the potential growth path, including its height and/or slope. These are the policies that affect trend growth.

Subnational policymakers are likely more concerned about new trade opportunities, research and development activities and input and output growth rates than they are the levels of aggregate input employment or production. For example, few political kudos accrue to the governors of large states simply because they have high levels of capital investment and employment, and a large gross state product. The level of economic activity can always be attributed to a host of historical and other forces, whereas current trends and growth rates will better capture the attention of the public, press and other policymakers. As a result, there is likely a policy bias toward the input side of the production function. For example, state governments aggressively promote new capital investment and job creation. However, this preoccupation with inputs and their utilization may obscure implications for the economy in terms of factor returns, factor substitution, regional production and efficiency effects.

Actual Practice

Following the growth theory framework, actual growth policies are categorized to include activities that seek to expand regional output by increasing trade, the quantity of inputs, and savings or by raising productivity or the pace of technical progress. The discussion is intended to provide numerous examples rather be a comprehensive listing of subnational growth policies.

Trade Policy. Through trade and sales promotion activities, subnational governments can move the economy closer to its potential growth path (a stabilization policy) or can generate excess demand for its output with the hope of attracting more inputs through regional migration of mobile factors (a trend growth policy). At the same time, subnational governments have limited means at their disposal to affect regional trade and sales directly as market forces heavily dictate trading patterns. Further, states' use of explicit trade restrictions is severely limited by the Interstate Commerce Clause of the U.S. Constitution. Some states have pursued

274

import substitution schemes whereby preferential treatment is afforded to "domestic" producers of state-procured goods and services while local governments and chambers of commerce often sponsor "Buy Hometown" campaigns.

Subnational governments make use of advertising and targeted investments in sporting, recreation, historical and other facilities to promote tourism, offering another vehicle for exporting goods and services.[17] States also have staff dedicated to promoting domestic and foreign trade (as well as attracting foreign capital). As shown in Table 8.8, most states had at least one overseas trade office in 1990. These facilities effectively provide marketing support for state and local governments.

Inputs. Many targeted state and local policies are intended to increase the quantity of inputs, in turn raising the output of the subnational economy. Examples include tax credits for job creation and capital investment, sales tax exemptions for manufacturing equipment, financial incentives for investments in new plant and equipment and in-kind site development assistance.[18] But the reality is states can do little to grow their own resources and there is a resulting bias towards attracting mobile factors of production from other jurisdictions and countries. There are, however, important exceptions. For example, business incubators, small business assistance and entrepreneurship training are intended in part to promote grassroots growth. Another exception would be the use of policy to promote higher birth rates, in turn influencing long-term growth in the labor force. Wittington, Alm and Peters (1990) find that the personal exemption under the U.S. personal income tax induces higher birth rates while Zhang, Quan and Van Meerbergen (1994) show that the Canadian tax-transfer system has positive impacts on fertility. Admittedly the goal of policy in this context is primarily distributional. At the same time, the empirical evidence suggests another mechanism subnational governments might exploit to influence economic growth.

Savings. Subnational governments use their taxing power and borrowing authority to supplement the region's savings, in turn financing private sector investments in plant and equipment. States can, for example, use the expected revenue stream from overall economic activity to finance tax expenditure-based incentives targeted to new firms. Also, local governments frequently use industrial revenue bonds (coupled with reductions in property taxes) to finance private sector investments within

Table 8.8:   State Foreign Trade Programs, Fiscal Year 1990

State	Spending (Millions)	Staff	Overseas Offices
Alabama	$1.5	9	3
Alaska	3.5	15	3
Arkansas	0.5	15	3
Arizona	0.5	7	1
California	5.0	66	5
Colorado	1.5	13	3
Connecticut	0.5	10	2
Delaware	0.5	6	3
Florida	3.5	47	6
Georgia	3.5	19	5
Hawaii	5.0	11	2
Idaho	0.5	6	2
Illinois	n/a	64	11
Indiana	1.5	24	6
Iowa	1.5	14	3
Kansas	n/a	18	9
Kentucky	1.5	9	4
Louisiana	1.5	19	3
Maine	0.5	3	0
Maryland	5.0	19	6
Massachusetts	0.5	7	1
Michigan	5.0	53	5
Minnesota	n/a	35	8
Mississippi	1.5	15	3
Missouri	1.5	22	4
Montana	0.5	6	2
Nebraska	0.5	2	0
Nevada	0.5	8	3
New Hampshire	0.5	1	0
New Jersey	3.5	20	1
New Mexico	0.5	2	0
New York	5.0	40	6
North Carolina	n/a	18	4
North Dakota	0.5	3	1
Ohio	3.5	46	5
Oklahoma	1.5	19	4
Oregon	5.0	23	3

276

Table 8.8: State Foreign Trade Programs, Fiscal Year 1990 (Continued)

State	Spending (Millions)	Staff	Overseas Offices
Pennsylvania	1.5	16	3
Rhode Island	n/a	8	3
South Carolina	1.5	8	5
South Dakota	0.5	4	0
Tennessee	0.5	4	0
Texas	3.5	19	6
Utah	1.5	13	4
Vermont	0.5	2	0
Virginia	3.5	19	2
Washington	1.5	24	2
West Virginia	0.5	4	1
Wisconsin	3.5	31	4
Wyoming	0.5	7	1
AVERAGE	1.9	17.5	3.22

Source: *Governing*, August, 1992, pg. 59.

their jurisdiction, with in-lieu-of-tax or tax increment financing schemes used to retire the debt. While these actions do little to raise aggregate savings, they could lead to the reallocation of some economic activity, benefiting certain jurisdictions at the expense of others.

Productivity. A potpourri of other state policies seek to promote productivity improvements, including basic, higher and continuing education; research, development and technology transfer programs; and public infrastructure investments. Ohio's Thomas Alva Edison Partnership Program and Pennsylvania's Ben Franklin Partnership Program are two of the most aggressive state technology and research and development activities in the nation.[19] These programs are intended to support specific lines of research, with the hope of creating technological advances and capturing the prestige that follows. But most states are more circumspect in their policies towards research and development in recognition of substantial technology spillovers.

A more common state-level activity is support for small-scale technology development and technology transfer programs, which often are focused on improving manufacturing productivity by taking advantage of technology spillovers from other regions. Because many manufactured products are exported, such efforts may improve the region's competitiveness. Improved competitiveness can help attract mobile factors of production as well. Also common are incentives for the location (and sometimes expansion) of high technology firms. However, the intent of such incentives has more to do with prestige and increasing inputs than raising productivity.

Education usually is the largest category of state and local government spending. While elementary and secondary education prepares youth for gainful employment, the adequacy of funding, governance structure, curriculum and accountability have all been questioned as fears rise that America's entry level workers are not sufficiently skilled. Accordingly, numerous states have endeavored to reform their education systems to improve educational outcomes and to raise the odds of economic success. Adult education and industrial training programs, which may impart general or specific human capital skills to trainees, have expanded as states and local governments have tried to improve their competitiveness and stave off industrial decline. Workers with obsolete skills, such as displaced workers or workers in declining industries, have increased access to specific training to improve their employability and competitiveness.

State and local governments also have primary responsibility for providing and maintaining many forms of overhead capital (ranging from roads to sewer facilities) that are necessary to support economic growth.

Can and Do Subnational Growth Policies Work?

In light of the substantial resources expended by state and local governments on policies to promote economic growth, it is natural to ask whether policies such as those outlined in the previous section can and do achieve their objectives. Unfortunately, as will be shown, there is no unequivocal answer to this question.

The ever-expanding empirical literature is an important means of evaluating actual affects of state policies.[20] A considerable portion of this research has explored the linkage between public policy and net changes in economic activity, the latter measured by output (for example, gross state product or personal income) or input utilization (for example, employment or capital investment). In general, the results show that higher taxes have small negative impacts on economic activity, while the opposite holds true for higher expenditures. Impacts of fiscal policies tend to be larger for intraregional as opposed to interregional economic activity.

There is rather strong evidence that public policy directly influences the location of mobile labor and capital. Fox, Herzog and Schlottmann (1989) and Herzog and Schlottmann (1986) find that state and local tax and expenditure policies influence labor migration. For example, Fox, Herzog and Schlottmann (1989) show that high taxes encourage the decision to move from a community, while education, fire and police services help mitigate the repellant force of taxes. Amenities such as parks, which can be directly influenced by policy, are also shown to affect migration decisions.

The location of physical capital is also sensitive to public policies. For example, Bartik (1989) finds small business starts to be discouraged by higher taxes; Fox and Murray (1990) show firm entry rates to be affected by local tax and expenditure policies; and Charney (1983) illustrates the effect of policy on firm relocation decisions. While there are exceptions to these findings, the growing consensus of the empirical literature is that policies targeted to mobile capital do in fact matter.

Levels of educational attainment are highly correlated with both individual and area economic performance. For example, Wasylenko and McGuire (1985) find that higher education spending improves state employment growth and Helms (1985) finds local school expenditures raise state personal income. Others, including Quan and Beck (1987) and Mofidi and Stone (1990) find mixed effects of schooling on the economic growth of subnational economies. There is also evidence that support for higher education is correlated with state economic growth. Helms (1985) finds that spending on higher education improves state economic performance and Jaffe (1989) shows that university supported research and development may enhance private research and increase productivity. Little is known about the efficacy of training programs; however, the evidence for major training programs in the U.S. is not very positive (The Economist, 1996).

Research offers limited certainty regarding effects of other subnational policies on economic growth. For example, despite renewed interest in the role of public infrastructure on the growth process, fundamental questions of causality and substitutability/complementarity with private capital remain. While there are numerous instances of positive infrastructure impacts on growth (e.g., Fox and Murray, 1990 and Mofidi and Stone, 1990), doubts remain as to the exact transmission mechanism.

When subnational policies are placed in the context of growth theory and the empirical literature is surveyed, it seems clear that there is wide latitude for states and localities to influence their economic fortunes. There are, however, four important qualifications. First, at the margin the impact of state and local government policies on regional economic growth is likely to be quite modest. This conclusion is consistent with the extensive empirical literature on regional growth and economic development that reveals relatively small elasticities for traditional state and local taxes and expenditure programs. Moreover, there are compelling practical reasons to expect modest outcomes for policies even after affects on productivity and mobility of factors of production are considered. For example, states may provide amenities to attract mobile labor, yet such gains may be shortlived if other states react with similar strategies that in turn lead to labor's exodus.

A second qualification is that many subnational policies reflect a beggar-thy-neighbor strategy. This is especially true of those programs that seek to attract footloose "foreign" capital. The conventional wisdom (see Murray, 1990) is that many policies represent a zero-sum form of interjurisdictional competition, at least when there is no market failure. That is, the use of public policy does not create new economic activity, but only influences its geographic location. There are exceptions, including policies such as education that may affect productivity and increase the size of the national and subnational economic pie. It is no surprise that when markets fail there is greater latitude for gains from the use of public policy. For example, if taxes on mobile capital are set above the benefits received by mobile capital, locational distortions result. The use of public policy to compete for mobile capital may enhance efficiency and represent a positive sum game for the economy as a whole (Oates and Schwab, 1988).

A third issue is the recognition that the use of development policies is driven in part by political considerations and rent seeking behavior, and takes place in an environment of uncertainty (Wolkoff, 1992). The organizational structure of state and local governments, coupled with the self-interested behavior of the relevant economic agents, may lead to the design and use of development policies (including incentives) that yield inefficiencies and seemingly irrational outcomes. Hence, while economic development policy may make something happen, whatever happens need not be in the best interest of the subnational economy itself.

Finally, the traditional approach to estimating the influence of subnational growth policies has not been carefully targeted to the needs of policymakers. Greater attention should be focused on general equilibrium and dynamic responses to state and local growth policies (including attendant welfare effects) in order to determine the ultimate impact of policy on various dimensions of growth. For example, are subnational policy effects short-run, long-run or both? Is industrial recruitment a cost-effective growth strategy? If employment increases, who receives the jobs (i.e., existing residents versus inmigrants) and does regional output in fact expand? What, more generally, are the welfare consequences of economic development policy? What is the impact of capital subsidies on factor employment, factor substitution and factor shares? How rapidly does technology spill over subnational jurisdictional lines? These are just some of the open questions that have yet to be answered by the voluminous literature on subnational economic development policies.

NOTES

1. See Hansen and Perloff (1944) for a classic article in the area.
2. For example, see Engerman (1965).
3. For example, see Gramlich (1987) and Fisher (1993).
4. Neither Marston nor Gramlich investigates whether high personal unemployment affects migration.
5. One exception is Oregon, which has had a limited growth policy at times.
6. Note that subnational policy may be procyclical or countercyclical in its influence on the subnational economy or the national economy.
7. For examples, see Enomoto, Erickson and Ghosh (1992), Dye and McGuire (1991), Pollock and Suyderhound (1986), Fox and Campbell (1984), White (1983) and Williams, et al. (1973).
8. The trough of the early 1980s recession was November 1982, with fiscal woes carrying over into 1983.
9. The timing of debt issuance may be of less importance than the timing of the disbursement of bond proceeds. States typically encumber funds generated through bond issuances, dispensing these funds as capital projects are developed. These lags could be important in determining the underlying influence of debt policy.
10. National Association of State Budget Officers (1995) discusses state rainy day funds and other mechanisms states use to promote budget stabilization. For a more detailed treatment of stabilization funds, including their design, see National Association of State Budget Officers and National Governors' Association, Center for Policy Research (1985).
11. See Vasche and Williams (1987) and National Association of State Budget Officers and National Governors' Association, Center for Policy Research (1985).
12. This section draws primarily on the experience of the U.S., although subnational governments in other federal systems make use of similar policies. For discussions of economic development policy that pertain to the Canadian experience, see Wellar (1981) and Savoie (1986).
13. An alternative interpretation is that policymakers are in pursuit of economic rents as they play the incentives game. See Wolkoff (1992).
14. Courant (1994) suggests that subnational policymakers should avoid the use of distortionary incentives because of the inherent welfare losses that follow. But the benefits of distortionary policies (including

increased jobs and capital investment) may accrue to the subnational economy while the adverse welfare consequences are dispersed across the entire economy.

15. See Nijkamp (1987) for a review of regional economic models. Elementary introductions to growth theory are available in most advanced texts on macroeconomics; Rostow (1990) provides an historical survey. Examples of growth theory being applied to subnational economic performance include Smith (1975) and Holz-Eakin (1993).

16. Romer (1994), Lucas (1988) and Grossman and Helpman (1991) represent some of the more important recent contributions to growth theory.

17. Information on state export programs is available from Bureau of National Affairs (1987).

18. See National Association of State Development Agencies (1995) and Conway Data, Inc. (1995) for menus and descriptions of state and local development incentives.

19. National Association of Development Agencies (1995) provides some information on state-level technology initiatives. For additional descriptions see LFW Management, Inc. (1988) and Southern Growth Policies Board (1987).

20. See Fox and Murray (1993), Bartik (1991) and Wasylenko (1991) for reviews of the literature.

REFERENCES

Adams, Charles F. Jr. "Tax Base Composition and Long-Run Growth in City Taxes." *Urban Affairs Quarterly* 24 (1988): 315-326.

Bahl, Roy and William Duncombe. "State and Local Government Finances: Was There a Structural Break in the Reagan Years?" *Growth and Change* (Fall, 1988): 30-48.

Bartik, Timothy J. *Who Benefits from State and Local Development Policies?* Kalamazoo, MI: W.E. UpJohn Institute for Employment Research, 1991.

Bartik, Timothy J. "Small Business Start-ups in the United States: Estimates of the Effects of Characteristics of States." *Southern Economic Journal* 55 (1989): 1004-1018.

Blackley, Paul R. and Larry DeBoer. "Explaining State Government Discretionary Revenue Increases in Fiscal Years 1991 and 1992." *National Tax Journal* 46 (1993): 1-12.

Breton, Albert and Anthony Scott. *The Economic Constitution of Federal States*. Toronto: University of Toronto Press, 1978.

Bureau of National Affairs. *State Export Programs: A Resource Guide*. Bureau of National Affairs, 1987.

Carlino, Gerald A. and Robert H. DeFina. "Does Monetary Policy Have Differential Regional Effects?" *Business Review*: Federal Reserve Bank of Philadelphia, (March/April, 1996): 17-27.

Charney, Alberta H. "Intraurban Manufacturing Decisions and Local Tax Differentials." *Journal of Urban Economics* 14 (1983):184-205.

Conway Data Inc. *Industrial Development and Site Selection Handbook*, various issues.

Courant, Paul N. "How Would You Know a Good Economic Policy if You Tripped Over One? Hint: Don't Just Count Jobs." *National Tax Journal* 47 (1994): 863-881.

Dreze, Jacques H. "Forty Years of Public Economics: A Personal Perspective." *Journal of Economics Perspectives* (Spring, 1995): 111-130.

Dye, Richard F. and Therese McGuire. "Growth and Variability of State Individual and General Sales Taxes." *National Tax Journal* 44 (1991): 55-66.

The Economist. "Training and Jobs: What Works?" April 6, 1996, 19-21.

Enomoto, Carl E., Christopher A. Erickson and Soumendra N. Gosh. "Revenue-Stabilizing Tax Rates Over the Business Cycle." *Quarterly Journal of Business and Economics* 31 (1992): 84-97.

Fisher, Ronald C. "Macroeconomic Implications of Subnational Fiscal Policy: The Overseas Experience." In *Vertical Fiscal Imbalance and the Allocation of Taxing Powers*, edited by D.J. Collins. Sydney: Australian Tax Research Foundation, 1993.

Fox, William F., Henry W. Herzog, Jr., and Alan M. Schlottmann. "Metropolitan Fiscal Structure and Migration." *Journal of Regional Science* 29 (1989): 523-536.

Fox, William F. and Charles Campbell. "Stability of the State Sales Tax Income Elasticity." *National Tax Journal* 37 (1984): 201-212.

Fox, William F. and Matthew N. Murray. "State and Local Government Policy." In *Economic Adaptation: Alternatives for Rural America*, edited by David Barkley. Boulder, CO: Westview Press, Inc., 1993.

Fox, William F. and Matthew N. Murray. "The Effects of Local Government Public Policies on the Location of Business Activity." In *Industry Location and Public Policy*, edited by Henry W. Herzog, Jr. and Alan M. Schlottmann. Knoxville, TN: The University of Tennessee Press, 1991.

Fox, William F. and Matthew N. Murray. "Local Public Policy and Interregional Business Development." *Southern Economic Journal* 57 (1990): 413-427.

Gold, Steven D. "State Tax Cuts: 1994 As Prelude To 1995." *State Fiscal Brief* No. 24 (1995).

Gramlich, Edward M. "Subnational Fiscal Policy." *Perspectives on Local Public Finance and Public Policy*, Vol. 3 (1987) 3-27.

Grossman, Gene M. and Elhanan Helpman. *Innovation and Growth in the Global Economy.* Cambridge, MA: The MIT Press, 1991.

Hansen, Alvin H. and Harvey S. Perloff. *State and Local Finance in the National Economy.* New York: W. W. Norton, 1944.

Helms, L. Jay. "The Effect of State and Local Taxes on Economic Growth." *The Review of Economics and Statistics* 67 (1985): 574-82.

Herzog, Henry W. Jr. and Alan M. Schlottmann. "State and Local Tax Deductibility and Metropolitan Migration." *National Tax Journal* 39 (1986): 189-200.

Herzog, Henry, Alan Schlottmann and Thomas Boehm. "Migration as Spatial Job-search: A Survey of Empirical Findings." *Regional Studies* 27, No. 4: 327-340.

Holz-Eakin, Douglas. "Solow and the States: Capital Accumulation, Productivity and Economic Growth." *National Tax Journal* 46 (1993): 425-439.

Jaffe, Adam B. "Real Effects of Academic Research." *American Economic Review* 79 (1989): 957-970.

LFW Management Associates, Inc. *Centers of Excellence: A Catalogue.* Alexandria, VA: LFW Management Associates, Inc, 1988.

Lucas, Robert E., Jr. "On the Mechanics of Economic Development." *Journal of Monetary Economics* 22 (1988): 3-42.

Marston, Stephen T. "Two Views of the Geographic Distribution of Unemployment." *Quarterly Journal of Economics* (February, 1985): 57-79.

Mattoon, Richard K. and William A. Testa. "State and Local Governments' Reaction to Recession." *Economic Perspectives* (March/April, 1992): 19-27.

Mofidi, Alaeddin and Joe A. Stone. "Do State and Local Taxes Affect Economic Growth?" *The Review of Economics and Statistics* 72 (1990): 686-691.

Murray, Matthew N. "The Incentives Game: Win, Lose or Draw?" *Proceedings of the Eighty-Second Annual Conference.* Columbus: National Tax Association, 1990.

Musgrave, Richard A. *The Theory of Public Finance.* New York: McGraw-Hill, 1959.

National Association of State Budget Officers. *Budget Stability: A Policy Framework for States.* Washington, DC: National Association of State Budget Officers, 1995.

National Association of State Budget Officers and National Governors' Association, Center for Policy Research. *Budgeting and Fiscal Uncertainty: Stabilization Funds and Other Strategies.* Washington, DC: National Association of State Budget Officers and National Governors' Association, Center for Policy Research, 1985.

National Association of State Development Agencies. *Directory of Incentives for Business Investment and Development in the United States.* Washington, DC: National Association of State Development Agencies, 1995.

National Conference of State Legislatures. "States Broaden Scope of Rainy Day Funds." Washington, DC: National Conference of State Legislatures, 1996.

Navin, John C. and Leo J. Navin. "An Evaluation of State Budget Stabilization Funds Among Midwestern States." *Growth and Change* 25 (1994): 445-466.

Nijkamp, P. (ed). *Handbook of Regional and Urban Economics: Volume I Regional Economics* Amsterdam: North-Holland, 1987.

Oates, Wallace E. "The Theory of Public Finance in A Federal System." *Canadian Journal of Economics* (February 1968): 37-54.

Oates, Wallace E. *Fiscal Federalism.* New York: Harcourt Brace Jovanovich, 1972.

Oates, Wallace E. and Robert Schwab. "Economic Competition Among Jurisdictions: Efficiency Enhancing or Distortion Inducing?" *Journal of Public Economics* 35 (1988): 333-354.

Quan, Nguyen T. and John H. Beck. "Public Education Expenditures and Economic Growth: Northeast and Sunbelt Regions." *Southern Economic Journal* 54 (1987): 361-376.

Pollock, Richard and Jack P. Suyderhoud. "The Role of Rainy Day Funds in Achieving Fiscal Stability." *National Tax Journal* 39 (1986): 485-497.

Poterba, James M. "State Responses to Fiscal Crises: The Effects of Budgetary Institutions and Politics." *Journal of Political Economy* 102 (1994): 799-821.

Rafuse, Robert W., Jr. "Cyclical Behavior of State-Local Finances." In *Essays in Fiscal Federalism*, edited by Richard A. Musgrave. Washington, DC: The Brookings Institution, 1965.

Romer, Paul M. "The Origins of Endogenous Growth." *Journal of Economic Perspectives* 8 (1994): 3-22.

Rostow, W.W. *Theorists of Economic Growth from David Hume to the Present.* New York: Oxford University Press, 1990.

Savoie, Donald J. *Regional Economic Development: Canada's Search for Solutions.* Toronto, University of Toronto Press, 1986.

Southern Growth Policies Board. "State Technology Development Programs in the South." Research Triangle Park, NC: Southern Growth Policies Board, 1987.

Smith, Donald Mitchell. "Neoclassical Growth Models and Regional Growth in the U.S." *Journal of Regional Science* 15 (1975): 165-181.

Vasche, Jon David and Brad Williams. "Optimal Governmental Budgeting Contingency Reserve Funds." *Public Budgeting and Finance* (Spring, 1987): 66-82.

Wasylenko, Michael. "Empirical Evidence on Interregional Business Location Decisions and the Role of Fiscal Incentives in Economic Development." In *Industry Location and Public Policy*, edited by Henry W. Herzog, Jr. and Alan M. Schlottmann. Knoxville, TN: The University of Tennessee Press, 1991.

Wasylenko, Michael and Therese McGuire. "Jobs and Taxes: The Effect of Business Climate on State's Employment Growth Rates." *National Tax Journal* 38 (1985): 497-512.

Wellar, Barry. *National and Regional Economic Development Strategies: Perspectives on Canada's Problems and Prospects.* Ottawa: University of Ottawa Press, 1981.

White, Fred C. "Tradeoff in Growth and Stability in State Taxes." *National Tax Journal* 36 (1983): 103-114.

Williams, William V., Robert M. Anderson, David O. Fruchle and Kaye L. Lamb. "The Stability, Growth and Stabilizing Influence of State Taxes." *National Ta Journal* 26 (1973): 267-274.

Wittington, Leslie A., James Alm and H. Elizabeth Peters. "Fertility and the Personal Exemption: Implicit Pronatalist Policy in the United States." *American Economic Review* 80 (1990): 545-556.

Wittington, Leslie A. "State Income Tax Policy and Family Size: Fertility and the Dependency Exemption." *Public Finance Quarterly* 21 (1993): 378-398.

Wolkoff, Michael J. "Is Economic Development Decision Making Rational?" *Urban Affairs Quarterly* 27 (1992): 340-355.

Wolkoff, Michael J. "An Evaluation of Municipal Rainy Day Funds." *Public Budgeting and Finance* (Summer, 1987): 52-63.

Zhang, Junsen, Jason Quan and Peter Van Meerbergen. "The Effect of Tax-Transfer Policies on Fertility in Canada, 1921-88." *Journal of Human Resources* 29 (1994): 181-201.

Ziegler, Joseph A. "Interurban Cycle Differentials and Fiscal Behavior." *National Tax Journal* (March 1972): 91-95.

INDEX